Free Speech and Ha
in the United States

MW00332271

Free Speech and Hate Speech in the United States explores the concept and treatment of hate speech in light of escalating social tensions in the global twenty-first century, proposing a shift in emphasis from the negative protection of individual rights toward a more positive support of social equality.

Drawing on Axel Honneth's theory of recognition, the author develops a two-tiered framework for free speech analysis that will promote a strategy for combating hate speech. To illustrate how this framework might impact speech rights in the United States, she looks specifically at hate speech in the context of symbolic speech, disparaging speech, Internet speech, and speech on college campuses.

Entering into an ongoing debate about the role of speech in society, this book will be of key importance to First Amendment scholars, and to scholars and students of communication studies, media studies, media law, political science, feminist studies, American studies, and history.

Chris Demaske is an Associate Professor in the School of Interdisciplinary Arts and Sciences at the University of Washington Tacoma.

Routledge Research in Communication Studies

For more information about this series, please visit: https://www.routledge.com

Free Speech and Hate Speech in the United States

The Limits of Toleration

Chris Demaske

Routledge
Taylor & Francis Group

NEW YORK AND LONDON

First published 2021
by Routledge
52 Vanderbilt Avenue, New York, NY 10017

and by Routledge
2 Park Square, Milton Park, Abingdon, Oxon, OX14 4RN

Routledge is an imprint of the Taylor & Francis Group, an informa business

© 2021 Taylor & Francis

Library of Congress Cataloging-in-Publication Data
A catalog record for this title has been requested

ISBN: 978-0-367-49609-8 (hbk)
ISBN: 978-1-003-04685-1 (ebk)

Typeset in Sabon
by codeMantra

Contents

Acknowledgments

Writing any book is not a solitary process. The completion of this book was no different. I am grateful for the massive amounts of support I received throughout the past several years. I would like to thank the University of Washington Tacoma for the year-long sabbatical that allowed me the time and intellectual space to bring this book to life. I also would like to thank the School of Interdisciplinary Arts and Sciences for funding that afforded me the opportunity to present my work at various stages of its development. Through conference presentations at the International Association for Media and Communication Research, Law and Society, and the Union for Democratic Communication, I received valuable critiques that helped to shape my ideas. Some of the text appeared previously in *Communication Law and Policy*, 24:3 (2019), and the editing process for that article further refined my thoughts. Also, I would like to thank the editors at Routledge. They were amazing throughout the entire process of getting this book to print.

The individuals, both professional and personal, who played a role in the creation of this book are numerous. While I can't thank everyone, I would like to recognize a few people who were generous with their time, encouragement, and assistance. SIAS Dean Anne Bartlett offered constant confidence in me, reassuring me frequently of the importance of my work.

Many colleagues provided feedback at various stages of the process. Turan Kayaoglu offered crucial commentary on the book proposal. Several colleagues read material early in the process, including Bill Kunz, Randy Nichols, Sarah Hampson, Michael Forman, Cynthia Howson, and Kearston Wesner (Quinnipiac University). Caitlin Carlson at Seattle University supplied helpful suggestions regarding the first seven chapters. Special thanks to Sara Bannerman at McMaster University who went above and beyond by reviewing the entire manuscript. Her thorough read and insightful recommendations were invaluable.

Support when writing a book takes many forms. Throughout the past two years, colleagues Riki Thompson, Ed Chamberlain, Randy Nichols, Emma Rose, Andrea Modarres, and Heather White (University of Puget Sound) came to my house weekly for research and writing sessions. The camaraderie and accountability propelled me forward when I was discouraged, tired, or overwhelmed with other obligations. Khristine Wolfe, Susan Wolfe, Colleen Carmean, Sally Cook Stewart, and Raelin Musuraca allowed me to drone on and on about the book for several years. Special thanks to my dear friend Brenda Fetsko who always seemed to have just the right thing to say at exactly the moment I needed to hear it. And finally, my greatest appreciation of all is to my wife Adrienne Ione and our sweet dog Sasha for allowing me to turn our house into a research and writing center, showing unconditional support, and keeping me sane and grounded.

Introduction

On August 3, 2019, 21-year-old Patrick Crusius walked into a Walmart in El Paso, Texas, with a semi-automatic rifle and opened fire. In the deadliest shooting that year in the United States and the seventh deadliest in the country since 1949, he killed 22 people and injured two dozen others. Crusius, who would allegedly tell police that he went to the Walmart to "kill Mexicans," published shortly before the attack a white-nationalist manifesto on 8chan, an anonymous online forum linked to violent extremist.[1] On August 6, three days following the massacre, I was home writing this very book when I received an email from a business editor at the *Seattle Times*. Epik, a Seattle-area web hosting firm, had decided to discontinue hosting 8chan, a decision that appeared to be a reversal to its previous claims to unfettered freedom of speech under the First Amendment.[2] The writer for the *Times* was looking for my perspective on what I thought this might be saying about the evolution of Internet speech.

To be clear, this wasn't the beginning of the story about concerns over the relationship between Internet hate speech and hate crimes. Still, it was one of the first times I had encountered a major mainstream media outlet considering the possibility that perhaps we have reached a point in the United States where the price of protecting hate speech might be too high.[3] Even the *New York Times* published an article a few days after the attack discussing in somewhat nuanced ways how France and Germany both "prize freedom of expression" but also draw the line at speech that promotes racial hatred or justifies terrorism.[4]

As a long-time proponent of hate speech restriction, I welcome these discussions – however fleeting and far between they might be – but I also worry that they have yet to really interrogate the intensity or complexity of the problem of hate speech today. The United States is at a time of social crisis. There is simply no way to overstate or exaggerate the severity of the problems related to social inequality today. From Confederate flags being placed across the campus at American University to violent attacks on churches and synagogues to the continued public naming of sexual predators fueled by the #metoo movement, tensions are increasing and placing more people at risk. The intensity is escalating as evidenced by the FBI data showing a 17 percent increase in hate crimes between 2016 and 2017 in the United States.[5] Exacerbating this problem is that in comparison to the international community, the United States is significantly more lenient regarding hate speech on the Internet. As a result of this permissible position, the United States is increasingly becoming a virtual safe haven for hate groups. While there is no empirically proven cause and effect link of hate speech leading to hate crimes, there is a strong correlation between the two. Past attempts by states to regulate hate speech, as well as recent case law, substantiate the connection between certain crimes and hate bias motives. In addition to the possibility of hate speech leading to hate crimes, hate speech in and of itself can have devastating effects. For example, hate speech can silence those who are its targets. For this reason, hate speech is a separate injustice from physical hate crime acts.

Historically, the U.S. Supreme Court has supported the old axiom that the answer to speech that people don't like is simply more speech, not restriction of speech. Traditionally, First Amendment scholars have echoed this position, calling for an almost absolutist protection of free speech. Those jurists and scholars have and continue to exercise what Steve Shiffrin recently called "free speech idolatry." However, the current treatment of hate speech in the United States is problematic in light of a myriad of social tensions that are continuing to escalate. The well-established arguments that free speech serves as a societal pressure valve and that open speech leads to truth hold little sway when, 200 years later, hatred against groups based on their identity is still rampant and insidious. This hardline position on the protection of hate speech becomes even more problematic when the global medium of the Internet is brought into the conversation.

In this book, I maintain that as currently applied, the free speech clause of the First Amendment presupposes a level of equality among so-called autonomous individuals that does not actually exist. As a result, certain types of speech, including hate speech, are protected under the assumption that less government regulation of speech fosters greater speech rights for everyone. However, it is this very discourse about freedom of speech, equality, and autonomy that serves to further silence members of disempowered or marginalized groups. This book, *Free Speech and Hate Speech in the United States: The Limits of Toleration*, encompasses two main objectives. First, the heart of this book is interested in addressing the question: What can be done to curb the proliferation of hate speech and hate acts in the United States? My answer is that we need to restrict some hate speech using my construction of a framework for case analysis that can withstand First Amendment scrutiny. Adequately addressing this problem within the confines of the First Amendment, however, is impossible without a change in the fundamental way we think about the role of speech in society in regards to how and when we restrict it. As a result, the second objective of this book is to shift the discourse around free speech protection away from one based in a Kantian conception of individual autonomy toward a model grounded in social justice. Specifically, I ground my inquiry and the development of my legal analytical framework in recognition theory, a social and political position that proposes that interaction forms individual identity.[6] In other words, recognition theory forces the conversation away from the autonomous individual and places it instead within a human dignity framework. The ramifications of this shift in the fundamental underpinnings of free speech theory are radical, with implications extending far beyond hate speech regulation.

The concept of hate speech and the subsequent calls for possible restriction raise complicated issues. There is no easy fix. Without question, the First Amendment is an important guiding document in the United States, and freedom of speech a necessity for a well-functioning government. Many First Amendment scholars claim that even speech that is considered hateful must be protected lest we begin a slippery slide into the abyss of censorship. However, as legal experts and critical race theorists Richard Delgado and Jean Stefancic recently asked: "But is it really so hard to distinguish between the hateful kind [of speech] and that which we all wish to protect?"[7] Just as the courts have made choices about speech restrictions in terms of areas such as libel and obscenity, they could think in more nuanced ways about hate speech regulation as well. In other words, those in the legal system need to move past old ways of thinking about hate speech restriction and adopt a new strategy to deal with this issue within the constraints of the First Amendment commitment to freedom of expression. This move will require multiple steps, including revisiting 'why' speech is protected, what the level of commitment to social equality is (or should be), and how to create a better balance of free speech interests with concerns of social equality.

Inevitably the hate speech debate raises ideological questions concerning absolute freedom of speech, the nature of democracy, and the importance of other human rights. Studies indicate that hate acts based on group membership have been escalating exponentially in the United States since the election of Donald Trump. The advent and subsequent global growth of the Internet further magnifies this already volatile climate, allowing for an easy traverse of traditional communication boundaries. The legal restriction of some level of hate speech in the United States will require two actions. First, there must be a fundamental shift in thinking about the role of speech in society. This shift requires a willingness to question past conceptions of why, when, and how speech is protected, and to what ends. If the overall reason for speech protection is to promote and foster a free democratic society, then the protection that is legislated needs to be considered in relation to actual outcomes. Second, once a new way of thinking about the power of speech in modern society has been theorized, then the courts will need to craft a legal tool that simultaneously protects both speech by members of minority groups and the highest amount of free speech in general.

Free Speech and Hate Speech in the United States is entering into an ongoing debate about the role of speech in society and, as a result, will engage in a diverse body of scholarship. Both First Amendment doctrine and traditional First Amendment theory are grounded in the same fundamental philosophical ideas of liberal democracy and its relationship to free speech. Traditional U.S. perspectives on the role of free speech in society can be traced back to Enlightenment Era philosophers such as Immanuel Kant, John Locke, and Jean-Jacques Rousseau. When considered in direct relationship to the First Amendment, this reliance on Enlightenment philosophy translates into certain First Amendment values, most notably the need to protect almost all speech to ensure that the search for truth, self-fulfillment, and self-government can occur. In the traditional liberal conception of free speech, the individual is both autonomous and sovereign, and the protection of speech, including hate speech, is viewed with an assumption of intrinsic societal value that leaves little or no room for discussions of possible harm. As a result of this rationale, restrictions on hate speech should be treated just as suspect as government attempts to restrict political speech.

While traditional First Amendment scholars still hold sway with the courts, since the 1980s, other legal scholars have offered and continue to offer critiques of the accepted position. In general, these scholars, whose academic backgrounds cover a wide spectrum including law, ethnic studies, gender studies, religious studies, and communication, question the generally accepted suppositions that democracy is best preserved by protecting virtually all speech. Proponents of hate speech regulation see no value in protecting hateful speech whose only intent is to denigrate and terrorize certain already oppressed groups. They disagree with the traditional view that hate speech causes no real harm, that restricting it would ultimately affect minorities disproportionately negatively, and that society needs to allow hate speech to function as a pressure valve. *Free Speech and Hate Speech in the United States* is placed squarely within this realm of critical theory. Employing an interdisciplinary approach, I attempt to add the complexity needed to address the social and political implications of government-sanctioned protection of hate speech in the United States. Broadly, critical race theory, feminist theory, and other critical theorists such as Michel Foucault inform the premise of my critique. Primarily, I draw on the theory of recognition developed by German philosopher Axel Honneth.[8] Honneth's work on recognition offers a possible way to bridge the gap between where we are now and the development of a free speech strategy for the twenty-first century. Ultimately, this book develops a concrete framework grounded in social justice theory that can be used initially for assessing hate speech restrictions specifically, but also has ramifications for the entirety of free speech theory and First Amendment law.

This book is organized in roughly three parts. The first section, which includes Chapters 1 through 4, addresses the legal landscape regarding hate speech restriction both in the United States and abroad. The second section consists of only one chapter, Chapter 5. It lays out an alternative philosophical and legal approach to combating hate speech within a U.S. context. In the third section, Chapters 6–8, I apply my new framework to various contemporary free speech situations to illustrate what might change if we move forward in the way I am suggesting here.

Chapter 1, "Defining Hate Speech," lays the foundation for a legal category of hate speech. Hate speech is a messy, highly contested concept used in political theory, legal theory, legal documents, and in simple common usage with its meaning changing depending on the context of who is using it and to what ends. Additionally, the term itself is often conflated or confused with other concepts such as hateful speech, racist speech, or harmful speech. Defining the concept of 'hate speech' concretely, then, is a difficult task requiring a clear understanding of the context and purpose at the outset. Before suggesting a constitutionally viable legal test to restrict hate speech, it is necessary to offer a legalistic definition that will work within a U.S. context to enable the courts to think in more complex ways about how they might assess hate speech restrictions.

In Chapter 2, "Favoring Human Rights: The International Response," I offer an overview of the way hate speech is treated outside of the United States. Hate crimes and hate speech happen across the globe, but there is no uniformity in how countries address those offenses. Several counties, however, do have some types of prohibitions against varying levels of hate speech related offenses. The prohibitions may come in the form of local jurisdictions, by statute, or as part of the country's constitution. The punishments range from monetary fines to ten-years imprisonment. Which groups receive protection also vary by country. In addition to these internally produced measures, many countries also abide by overarching international treaties. Many of those international regulations have their foundation in the more general protection of human rights.

Chapter 3, "Favoring Free Speech: The U.S. Response," narrows the focus on hate speech regulation to the United States. In comparison to the international community, the United States is significantly more lenient regarding the protection of hate speech. In the United States, hate speech traditionally has been protected by the First Amendment. In the global arena, this stance on hate speech is even more problematic, with the United States often at odds with international laws. This chapter reviews the nearly 70-years of U.S. Supreme Court rulings pertaining to hate speech. From that review, I highlight an emerging pattern of an historical movement from the successful application of the fighting words doctrine to a reliance on reasoning grounded almost exclusively in content neutrality to the current cases, which depend on the use of true threats and the imminent lawless action standard. By reviewing the movement in its totality, we can begin to see the larger pattern which can enable us to show the flaws in the usefulness of these doctrines to address the problem of hate speech adequately.

Chapter 4, "First Amendment Theories: Arguments and Counter Arguments," discusses the theories and philosophy underpinning First Amendment analysis in general and more specifically its place within the hate speech debate. The Supreme Court's rulings have been and will continue to be informed by theoretical debates in disciplines such as law, philosophy, and sociology. It is important then to situate the previous rulings within the theoretical debates surrounding the role of free speech in society. The normative, traditional perspective grounded in Kantian notions of individual autonomy underscores the Court's rationale for free speech protection. In this chapter, I elaborate on how traditional scholars, starting in the 1940s and continuing through today, have dominated the development and propagation of First Amendment doctrine and principles. However, while the Court continues to operate in line with those views, legal scholars have offered critiques of the accepted position since the 1980s. In general, those scholars, whose academic backgrounds span a wide spectrum (including law, ethnic studies, gender studies, religious studies, and communication), question the accepted suppositions that democracy is best preserved by protecting virtually all speech. While those critical approaches have yet to yield a lasting impact on the Court, several offer promise in developing a constitutionally viable way to restrict some level of hate speech.

Chapter 5, "Social Justice, Recognition Theory and a New Legal Response," demonstrates that due to the lack of nuance in the previous Supreme Court rulings in cases dealing with hate speech, a rather radical departure is required – one that includes the consideration of a certain level of restriction of hate speech in general and of hate speech on the Internet, an area that has since its public debut been heralded as a place for robust and wide-open information sharing. In other words, the problem in restricting hate speech in the United States requires two actions. First, just as the critical theorists discussed in Chapter 4 proposed, one must have a fundamental shift in thinking about speech in society. This shift requires a willingness to question past conceptions of why, when, and how we protect speech and to what end. If the overall reason for speech protection is to promote and foster a free democratic society, then the way that protection is legislated needs to be considered in relation to actual outcomes. Specifically, in Chapter 5, I build from a social justice framework using Axel Honneth's recognition theory to create a more culturally centric approach to thinking about the power of speech in modern society and the role of the First Amendment in harnessing that power. From that philosophical foundation, I incorporate elements from previous critical models to create a new two-tiered framework that will approach hate speech on the Internet with the subtlety necessary to protect both the human rights of members of minority groups and the highest amount of free speech in general.

Chapter 6, "From *R.A.V. v. St. Paul* to *Matal v. Tam*: The Parameters of Restriction," is the first chapter to test the application of the two-tiered framework established in Chapter 5. The intent of this chapter is to illustrate the parameters of what types of speech would be regulable and what types wouldn't under this new approach. While the Supreme Court, of course, has not heard any cases that specifically identify hate speech as such, they have ruled on cases that touch on, to one degree or another, the kinds of speech that is often associated with hate speech. The cases I review in Chapter 6 span a more than 25-year period starting with *R.A.V. v. St. Paul* in 1992. In *R.A.V.*, the U.S. Supreme Court would hear the case concerning legislation that most closely fits within the category of speech I defined in Chapter 1. The case focused on whether fighting words doctrine could be used to support the St. Paul, Minn., Bias Motivated Crime Ordinance, an ordinance that prohibited the display of a symbol "which one knows or has reason to know arouses anger, alarm, or resentment in others on the basis of race, color, creed, religion or gender." In a unanimous opinion, the Supreme Court struck down the ordinance, ruling that it was facially unconstitutional because it was content-based, imposing a special prohibition on particular disfavored subjects of race, color, and creed. Through application of my two-tiered framework, I indicate that the ruling in *R.A.V.* would have been substantially different. The three other cases reviewed in this chapter are: *Virginia V. Black*, the 2003 case in which the Supreme Court decided that an anti-cross burning ordinance was for the most part constitutional; *Snyder v. Phelps*, the 2011 case that focused on whether hateful protests targeting military funerals could be constitutionally restricted; and *Matal v. Tam*, the 2017 trademark case regarding the constitutionality of the disparagement clause in the Lanham Act of 1946. Taken together, these four cases give shape to the regulable category of hate speech that I am recommending.

The final two chapters address areas of significant current tensions involving the free speech versus hate speech debate. In Chapter 7, "Hate Speech on the Internet: *Elonis v. U.S.*," I explore the explosion of hate speech on the Internet. Recent studies indicate that more than half of the U.S. population reports being subject to hate speech and harassment online with a third of them indicating that the attacks were based on "sexual orientation, religion, race, ethnicity, gender identity or disability."[9] The problem is a global one. For example, in October 2019, the United Nations monitors for freedom of expression issued a landmark report indicating the need for governments and companies to establish concrete regulations concerning hate speech restriction with those regulations being based on human rights law.[10] In addition, more recent studies are showing a causal connection between hate speech expressed online and hate-motivated actions in the real world. While the international community has embraced varying levels of restriction, the United States, citing First Amendment concerns, continues to stand alone in its resistance to hate speech regulation on the Internet. Chapter 6 lays out some of the problems with trying to restrict Internet hate speech within the U.S. context. It then applies the new two-tiered framework to *Elonis v. United States* in an attempt to illustrate how permissible restriction might look. Elonis focused on threatening speech on the Internet and, as a result, it is an interesting space to consider regulation.

Chapter 8, "Campus speech: Free Speech v. Hate Speech," delves into one of the most publicized and most contentious areas of the hate speech discussion in the United States today. While the issue of hate speech on college campuses continues to gain attention by the media, lower courts, state legislatures, and even Congress and the president, the U.S. Supreme Court has to date remained silent. One lower court case – *Gilles v. Davis* – serves as an excellent example of the types of debates occurring in the lower courts surrounding the tensions raised by external speakers on campus. In *Gilles*, the Third Circuit Court of Appeals addressed the issue of removal of an off-campus speaker because of that speaker's offensive and hateful messages directed against members of the gay and lesbian community. This case illustrates: (1) the confusion over how to treat the escalating issues of hatred, (2) the conflation of the university as a place for intellectual debate with the protection of all speech, and (3) the way the framework developed in Chapter 4 could help establish clear boundaries that would support both the exchange of ideas and the protection of all students.

Notes

1 Jon Porter, *8chan Returns to the Internet as 8kun*, THE VERGE, November 4, 2019, *available at* https://www.theverge.com/2019/11/4/20947429/8chan-8kun-online-image-board-shooter-gunmen-manifesto [last accessed February 22, 2020].
2 Emily Birnbaum, *U.S. Company Will Stop Support 8chan after El Paso Shooting*, THE HILL, August 4, 2019, *available at* https://thehill.com/policy/technology/456132-us-company-will-stop-supporting-8chan-after-el-paso-shooting [last accessed February 22, 2020].
3 For a discussion of the phrase "the price we pay" in regard to freedom of speech, *see* Laura Lederer and Richard Delgado, THE PRICE WE PAY: THE CASE AGAINST RACIST SPEECH, HATE PROPAGANDA AND PORNOGRAPHY (1995).
4 Melissa Eddy and Aurelien Breeden, *The El Paso Shooting Revived the Free Speech Debate. Europe has Limits*, THE NEW YORK TIMES, August 6, 2019, *available at* https://www.nytimes.com/2019/08/06/world/europe/el-paso-shooting-freedom-of-speech.html [last accessed February 21, 2020].

5 David Barrett, *Hate Crimes Rose 17 Percent Last Year, According to New FBI Data*, WASH. POST, November 13, 2018, *available at* https://www. grandforksherald.com/news/4528492-hate-crimes-rose-17-percent-last-year-according-new-fbi-data [last accessed February 21, 2020]. These numbers have remained relatively the same in the FBI's 2018 report, see 2018 Hate Crime Statistics, *available at* https://www.justice.gov/hatecrimes/hate-crime-statistics [last accessed February 21, 2020].

6 For an in-depth look at recognition theory and its usefulness in framing First Amendment analysis, *see* Chapter 5.

7 Richard Delgado and Jean Stefancic, MUST WE DEFEND NAZIS: HATE SPEECH, PORNOGRAPHY AND THE NEW FIRST AMENDMENT (2018).

8 Some of his works include: THE STRUGGLE FOR RECOGNITION: THE MORAL GRAMMAR OF SOCIAL CONFLICTS (1995); WITH NANCY FRASER, REDISTRIBUTION OR RECOGNITION: A POLITICAL-PHILOSOPHICAL EXCHANGE (2004); THE I IN WE: STUDIES IN THE THEORY OF RECOGNITION (2012) AND FREEDOM'S RIGHT: THE SOCIAL FOUNDATIONS OF DEMOCRATIC LIFE (2014).

9 Jessica Guynn, *If You've been Harassed Online, You Are Not Alone. More than Half of Americans Say They've Experienced Hate*, USA TODAY, February 13, 2019, *available at* https://www.usatoday.com/story/news/2019/02/13/study-most-americans-have-been-targeted-hateful-speech-online/2846987002/ [last accessed February 22, 2020].

10 Office of the High Commissioner, *Governments and Internet Companies Fail to Meet Challenge of Online Hate*, UNITED NATIONS HUMAN RIGHTS, October 21, 2019, *available at* https://www.ohchr.org/EN/NewsEvents/Pages/DisplayNews.aspx?NewsID=25174&LangID=E [last accessed February 22, 2020].

1   Defining Hate Speech

"What we are seeing – and I think it's very much a result of the tenor at the top – is a normalization of hate speech."[1] This usage of the term 'hate speech' by New Jersey Attorney General Gurbir Grewal in a 2019 interview speaks to both the current concern around the topic and also the spaciousness of the term. 'Hate speech' is a messy, highly contested concept used in political theory, legal theory, legal documents, and in simple common usage with its meaning changing depending on the context of who is using it and to what ends. In addition, the term itself is often conflated or confused with other concepts such as hateful speech, racist speech, or harmful speech.[2] Defining the concept of 'hate speech' concretely, then, is a difficult task requiring a clear understanding of the context and purpose at the outset. Defining the term as specifically as possible at the start is of paramount importance for three reasons. First, without proper definition, scholars and lawmakers talk past each other. While words have a defined meaning, that definition is based on assumed context. If each person, however, is applying a different context to the term, then the term's meaning is altered. In the case of hate speech, for example, without a precise definition, the context of the meaning of the term could span from burning crosses to virulent tweets to micro-aggressions, making it impossible to clearly identify a path forward toward regulation. Second, and connected to the first point, lack of clear definition leaves the recommendation of hate speech restriction easily attacked, dismissed, or misrepresented by free speech scholars. This situation allows critiques of hate speech regulation to rely on fears of over-zealous government suppression to reject outright the possibility of any regulation. Finally, if the end goal, as it is here, is to produce a constitutionally regulable category of speech, then the parameters of what constitutes hate speech must be clearly articulated in order to produce effective laws. Candida Harris et al. explained this concern precisely:

> If the role of the law in this context is to impose boundaries on expression, it is essential to be clear on the content or nature of illegitimate or unacceptable expression, and on the boundaries

between thought and opinion which remains either unexpressed or privately expressed, and that which in some way enters the public domain.[3]

In addition, I would include that by developing a concrete definition we can further support the amelioration of the particular evils of hate speech that we are trying to address.

Formulating a definition of hate speech that will hold up to constitutional scrutiny is no easy feat, partly because the term itself is so loaded. However, while many agree that the term is problematic, it remains a useful term to describe the legal concept. As Bhikhu Parekh noted, "Even the term 'hate speech' is unsatisfactory because it stresses hatred, an extremely strong emotion. However, given that it is widely used and there is no obvious alternative, I shall continue to use it..."[4] My intention is to offer a legalistic definition that will work within a U.S. context to enable the courts to think in a more nuanced capacity about how they might assess hate speech restrictions. This definition also requires us to think pointedly about the types of harms caused by hate speech, harms that are distinctly different from the more generic harms treated through incitement or true threats doctrine. Toward that aim, this chapter explores the difficulties and possibilities in developing a constitutionally acceptable approach that will offer meaningful change to the way we treat hate speech in the United States.

Following, I provide an overview of previous work conducted on this topic. While I examine both scholarly interpretations and some legal approaches, this discussion is not intended to be comprehensive, but merely to express the breadth of possible definitions. I focus on three approaches that I think offer some guidance in how we might best proceed. Then, I address the various harms associated with hate speech. Understanding the possible harms that it causes will facilitate refinement of the term to help situate it better within a U.S. free speech context. This positioning also requires an introduction into the foundational principles driving First Amendment analysis to illustrate how hate speech regulation can be reconciled alongside (not in place of) those principles. Finally, I propose a definition of hate speech that I rely on throughout the remaining chapters as the guiding interpretation of the term.

Approaches to Defining Hate Speech

Even within the parameters of the legal definition of the concept, there exist seemingly endless ways of defining the term. For example, one scholar defines it simply as "speech that singles out minorities for abuse and harassment."[5] Another scholar, relying on various international regulations, found the common traits to be "the use of words which are deliberately abusive and/or insulting and/or threatening and/or demeaning directed at members of vulnerable minorities, calculated to stir up hatred against them."[6] Professors Karmen Erjavec and Melita Poler Kovacic pull from earlier race theorist definitions to construct perhaps one of the most encompassing. They contend that

> Hate speech refers to an expression that is abusive, insulting, intimidating, harassing and/or incites to violence, hatred, or discrimination. It is directed against people on the basis of their race, ethnic origin, religion, gender, age, physical condition, disability, sexual orientation, political conviction and so forth.[7]

Political Theorist Jonathan Seglow defined hate speech as speech that "attacks (and is intended to attack) its targets because of their race, ethnicity, gender, sexuality, religion and so on, and which conveys intense feelings of antipathy."[8] While seemingly similar to those offered above, Seglow went on to qualify his definition by noting that in order to have a complete definition, you must consider the legal and moral reasons against it.[9] In other words, we must consider why we think hate speech is morally or socially wrong in order to offer an accurate legal assessment of what should be regulable. For instance, law professor Craig Martin focused on the "dehumanizing" traits of certain hateful language to develop his definition of hate speech.[10] This reliance on the protection of human dignity is embedded in many international and national legal documents outside of the United States. Those pieces of legislation rely on who is targeted, in what circumstances, and through what means.[11] For example, the United Nations requires its members to "condemn all propaganda and all organizations which are based on ideas or theories of superiority of one race or groups of persons of one colour or ethnic origin, or which attempts to justify or promote racial hatred or discrimination..."[12] I address these international approaches in greater depth in Chapter 3.

Several scholars seek to explain the term by creating categories or focusing on characteristics instead of a mere definition. This approach provides the additional complexity needed to develop a workable legal definition. For example, Parekh says that hate speech has three essential features.[13] Gregory S. Gordon posits three discreet categories.[14] Caleb Yong recommends that "hate speech" as a category is too broad, and he breaks it down into four main categories of hate speech.[15] Given the importance of understanding both the intricacies and the variations in these types of characterizations, it is worth the time to take a closer look at a few of them.

In his article focused on prosecuting crimes against humanity, Gordon argued that hate speech might qualify as persecution even if it doesn't directly call for violent action.[16]

> [I]t is problematic to consider 'hate speech' in a vacuum. Unlike incitement to genocide (an inchoate crime), which, as a legal matter, is

not necessarily uttered in the context of simultaneous mass violence, hate speech as persecution must be legally tied to contemporaneous, large-scale violence or inhumane treatment (based on the required "attack").[17]

Context, then, is a driving factor in Gordon's development of categories. His three categories of hate speech are: (1) "general hate speech," which dehumanizes the victim group but is not necessarily directed at any audience in particular; (2) "harassment," which is spoken directly to members of the victim group; and (3) "incitement," which is directed toward third parties and encourages them to take action (whether violent or nonviolent) against members of the victim group.[18] He explained that the first category, general comments not directed at any particular person, is the mildest form of hate speech in which we include racial, ethnic, and religious stereotypes; group libel; and dehumanizing or demonizing members of groups.[19] The second category, comments made directly to someone, are considered "harassment" by Gordon.[20] His third category invokes incitement, which he breaks into two subcategories – incitement toward nonviolent action and incitement toward violent action. Of the prior subcategory, he explained: "Incitement to hatred urges the majority group to develop general feelings of animosity toward the victim group. It is similar to group libel but takes a more active tone in encouraging the majority group to despise the minority."[21] This type of hate speech could take the form of calling on the majority to refuse restaurant service to certain groups or discourage marriage with members of that group. Gordon concluded that we must balance concerns of the negative effects of hate speech against important First Amendment protections. He advises, however, that "an outright ban on charging nonadvocacy hate speech as persecution ignores the extreme importance of such speech in service of mass atrocity."[22]

While Gordon focused specifically on crimes against humanity and on developing a categorization of hate speech that could be legislated based on those persecution concerns, Yong's approach applied more to a general discussion of hate speech in relation to established free speech principles.[23] He identified four main categories of hate speech – targeted vilification, diffuse vilification, organized political advocacy for exclusionary and/or eliminationist policies, and other assertions of fact or value which constitute an adverse judgment on an identifiable racial or religious group.[24] He reviewed those four categories in light of the free speech principle to determine whether the category is not covered by the principle, is covered by the principle but still unprotected speech, or is protected speech.

Through his analysis, he found his category of targeted vilification to not be covered by the free speech principle. He defined targeted vilification as "speech whose dominant intention is to wound, insult or intimidate the audience, motivated by hostility towards or contempt for the audience's racial or religious identity."[25] These incidents could be face-to-face or could include incidents without immediate contact, such as the spraying of a swastika on someone's door or putting a noose on their desk. In the case of targeted vilification, Yong found that "free speech rights are only minimally implicated" because the aim of the speech in question isn't to communicate an idea but rather to induce psychological harm. He found the next two categories – diffuse vilification and organized political advocacy – to be covered under the principle but not necessarily protected. In both cases, Yong argued that compelling interests can outweigh the various justifications embedded within the free speech principle. He offered as an example a Nazi march or a slave auction in blackface. He stated that while those instances are "at some level political speech" because their main intention is to wound or intimidate, the free speech interests are weak and outweighed by the harms. The final category of hate speech – assertions of fact and evaluative opinions – is protected speech because "despite the significant potential harms, this category of speech is protected because of the powerful free speech interests and rights involved."[26] He assessed that some speech, such as speech conflating certain religious or ethnic groups with disease or criminal behavior, can be countered with more speech, so restriction is not necessary.[27]

Parekh also considered his definition in relation to free speech principles, but he privileged competing principles, such as human dignity, equality, freedom from harassment and intimidation, protections of one's good name, and social harmony.[28] He first offered a broad definition of hate speech as speech that "expresses, encourages, stirs up, or incites hatred against a group of individuals distinguished by a particular feature or set of features such as race, ethnicity, gender religion, nationality and sexual orientation."[29] He then identified three essential features of hate speech – it is directed against a specified or easily identifiable individual or group of individuals, it stigmatizes the target group by ascribing undesirable qualities, and it causes the target group to be viewed as legitimate objects of hostility.[30] Taken together, these characteristics both encourage and attempt to justify discrimination, and, as a result, direct threats or incitement are not necessary components for assessing whether or not hate speech is regulable. Parekh explained:

> Although hate speech breathes the spirit of exclusion and violence, it does not necessarily or by definition result in violence or public disorder...What matters is its content – what it says about an individual or group – and its long-term effect on the group and the wider society, rather than its immediate consequences in terms of public disorder.[31]

Instead of violence or public disorder, hate speech, as seen through the prism of his three elements, can be "offensive, angry, abusive, and insulting." It also can be "subtle, moderate, non-emotive, even bland."[32] What matters to Parekh is the content coupled with the long-term effect of the speech. Under his analysis, speech that could be considered regulable hate speech would include shouting racist epithets, statements asking for the removal of an entire population from the country, or calls to vandalize places associated with an identifiable group.[33]

Harms in Hate Speech

For my purposes, I believe that the legal definition needs to consider what specific harms we are seeking to redress. As scholars, Ishani Maitra and Mary Kate McGowan noted:

> [G]etting clear about the harms in question is important, for at least two reasons. First, the kind of empirical evidence that is needed to establish that speech is harmful will vary greatly according to which kind of harm one has in mind. Second…what ought to be done about the harms of such speech depends greatly on what the harms in fact are.[34]

I would add that determining what harms we are talking about is a necessary step to help direct the courts in assessing the constitutionality of possible hate speech restrictions. What those harms might be are themselves dictated by which principles we are privileging. I elaborate on this later in terms of recognition theory in Chapter 5, but for now, note that I will be situating my definition to create a balance between our commitment to free speech and our commitment to equal treatment. My approach differs from approaches based on the Kantian autonomous individual and negative liberties by instead focusing on a social justice/human rights framework, which calls for a level of positive liberty on the part of the government in terms of speech.

Within those parameters, key pieces for me in establishing a regulable category of hate speech are as follows: what harms are we trying to ameliorate, who are we trying to protect, and under what circumstances. Scholars have identified many different harms that result from the hate speech act. These harms range from psychological to physical, immediate to long-term, and individual to societal. They can include, among other things, physical violence, assault to dignity, reinforcing societal prejudice, and stifling political participation. In determining the level of harm of hate speech, additional considerations have been suggested including private versus public instances, the intent of the speaker, and the context of the speech.[35]

The questions of which exact harms hate speech causes and whether or not those harms are significant enough to justify the restriction of hate speech are perhaps the most contentious points of debate. Implied or sometimes stated explicitly by those supporting some level of regulation is a concern for the harms that hate speech can inflict upon individuals, targeted groups, and/or society as a whole. Those opposed to restricting hate speech also address the issue of harm, but find it either overstated by regulation proponents, under-supported by research, or not significant enough to curtail free speech. Both of these positions will be explored in more depth in Chapter 4. However, given the influence of the question of harm in informing how we might best define a regulable category of hate speech, I think it necessary to flesh out exactly what those harms are.

Neither side of the debate disputes the likelihood that certain types of hate speech may lead to physical violence. The sticking point is, rather, a matter of degree. Some regulation proponents address these harms in terms of immediate advocacy of violence, such as calling on a group of people to assault a lesbian walking down the street, while others look to longer-term effects, such as widespread and continual hate speech messages on social media leading to a shooting in a synagogue. Opponents agree that there are times when certain hate speech can lead to immediate acts of violence; however, they feel that these instances can be regulated through pre-existing viewpoint-neutral doctrines such as true threat or fighting words.[36]

Agreement weakens significantly when considering less obvious types of physical harm, such as high blood pressure or heart issues, and virtually no agreement exists on the psychological impact. Legal philosopher Alexander Brown found that in much research supporting the connection between hate speech and psychological harm "the evidence often falls short of demonstrating a causal connection between exposure to hate speech specifically and medium- to long-term psychological and physiological health complications."[37] Law Professor Eric Heinz took an even more critical position. He explained:

> A serious problem is that the evidence thus far supplied by US-based prohibitionists has been published in twentieth- or early twenty-first-century in-house university law journals (or in spin off book publications and reprints from those original pieces), which, throughout those years, have lacked standard scholarly peer review. That defect becomes decisive as to details of empirical or statistical method...Those copious publications fail to cite statistical data that would trace causation from hateful expression within public discourse to cognizable social harms.[38]

Both Brown and Heinz are correct in asserting the importance of data to support the claims. However, they are incorrect in their assessment that research is not being conducted in this area.

Studies from scholars in various disciplines, particularly in the field of psychology, are increasingly finding connections between hate speech and psychological harm. Given the frequent claims made to the contrary, I think that it is important to highlight a few of these studies. For example, one experiment-based psychology study focused on two sets of self-identified Asian American university students.[39] Students were presented with different scenarios designed to vary the nature of insults delivered in a public space.[40] The results of their empirical study showed that "participants were emotionally affected by second-hand accounts of hate speech and suffered a (presumably) temporary reduction in collective self-esteem as a consequence of reading about their own group being disparaged."[41] They hypothesized that direct experience with targeted hate speech would likely result in "more extreme and enduring consequences." However, they stated that more research would need to be conducted based on actual first-hand observations of hate speech by minority group members to prove that claim.[42] Communication scholar Laura Leets in 2002 sought to determine how people experience hate speech.[43] For her study, she chose two groups that are frequent targets – Jewish people and gays and lesbians. The pool of participants included 120 students who volunteered from one public and one private university. The students were given hate speech examples and then asked through a survey a series of questions regarding the examples.[44] The content analysis of those questionnaires revealed several patterns, including that the short- and long-term consequences reflected the three-stage sequence found in other traumatic experiences, and the response to those hateful statements was most often passive.

One final example is a 2013 study that looked at the impact perceived racism has on emotional and physical health.[45] Using the social stress model,[46] Kathryn Freeman Anderson addressed two hypotheses: "that racial minorities will be more likely to experience both emotional and physical stress symptoms from differential treatment on the basis of race as compared to whites" and "that having experienced stress from perceived racism will be a predictor for overall poorer mental and physical health."[47] To examine these hypotheses, she used two items from the Behavioral Risk Factor Surveillance System, which is conducted by the National Center for Chronic Disease Prevention and Health Promotion.[48] Her research demonstrated "being a racial minority is a substantial predictor for experiencing both emotional and physical stress symptoms from discriminatory experiences."[49] She concluded that "these findings demonstrate that experiencing both emotional and physical stress symptoms from perceived racist treatment are related to overall poorer mental and physical health."[50]

These three studies are but a modest sampling of the research being conducted on the psychological and physical impacts of hate speech and prejudice on members of minority groups.[51] So, Brown's concern about the need for more studies focused explicitly on the role of hate speech as an impact factor is somewhat warranted, but Heinz's conclusion that peer-reviewed work is not being conducted in this area is erroneous. Empirical and other types of studies are being conducted, and they are as a whole showing in significant numbers that there is a substantial correlation between hate speech and the mental and physical health of those it targets.

Scholars in fields including psychology, sociology, and anthropology have all noted the dehumanizing effect of hate speech, which not only affects the person targeted but also leads others to believe that the targeted person is less valuable or not deserving of humane treatment. These studies span a range from focusing on hate speech's impact on minority members' place in society to its silencing effects to its ability to impair political participation. While I elaborate on each of these in forthcoming chapters, it remains important to briefly assess them based on the harms that researchers have found them to be.

Those targeted by hate speech, first and foremost, experience a feeling of being left out of or not welcome in society at large. Philosophy Professor Ishani Maitra said that in addition to direct psychological harms of hate speech on targets, it also affects the "positions of the groups to which those targets belong within the social hierarchy."[52] She elaborated on this point by noting that "speech can fix facts about the distribution of social power, including facts about who has this power, and who lacks it."[53] Law Professor Rory Little addressed a similar concern, framing it in terms of the impact to society at large:

> [T]he harms to minority-group targets living within the larger community ought not be ignored: When a society is defaced with anti-Semitic signage, burning crosses and defamatory racial leaflets, [a societal] assurance of security 'evaporates. A vigilant police force and the Justice Department may still keep people from being attacked or excluded,' but the objects of hate speech are deprived of the assurance that the society regards them as people of equal dignity.[54]

The concept of dignity is addressed in extensive detail in Chapters 4 and 5 as it directly relates to my usage of Recognition Theory as a mechanism to reorient the First Amendment in relation to hate speech.

Additional studies also have addressed concerns of inequality and dehumanization.[55] Connected to those harms related to inequality and dehumanization is the ability of hate speech to silence those who are targeted by it. Many scholars, myself included, identify this as one of the most egregious injuries resulting from certain forms of hate speech.[56] This position, which I elaborate on in Chapter 4, asserts that many targets of hate speech are so devastated and traumatized that they are silenced often both in that moment and in the future.[57] This silencing can take the form of a person not responding to directly targeted hate speech, not responding to hate speech targeting a group they are a member in, avoiding places where they might reasonably anticipate being targeted, and/or removing themselves from social and political conversations. First Amendment scholars frequently invoke the response that the answer to speech we don't like is not censorship, but more speech.[58] However, if hate speech silences portions of the population, effectively censoring them, then they are left unable to respond to that speech and likely will be unable to participate in speech venues as well. As a result, the impact of silencing on members of targeted groups is connected to the many harms listed above, but adds an additional element in terms of its impact on democratic participation and self-government.[59] One of the driving principles of the First Amendment is that it protects a high level of speech in order to ensure a well-functioning democratic government.[60] Hate speech, through its silencing function, not only stifles the political participation of those who are targeted by it but also, because of their absence, it effects society as a whole.

A Regulable Definition

The combination of the above harms and the pervasive, pernicious, and escalating incidents of hate speech and hate acts today requires us to revisit our position in the United States on restricting hate speech. I suggest that the category of regulable hate speech should be situated somewhere between protection of human dignity – a laudable goal that will not work within the constructs of the First Amendment – and the viewpoint neutral legal options currently available, which ignore much of what makes hate speech particularly heinous. In other words, a regulable definition of hate speech must be broader in scope than current First Amendment doctrine allows but narrower than other international definitions, most of which focus in some way on the concept of dignity. Both the U.S. and international definitions have a point of overlap – both are fundamentally focused on protecting selfhood as a primary goal – but they differ on how to achieve that goal. On the one hand, the emphasis on dignity privileges human rights but carries with it the risk of eroding freedom of speech and expression. One the other hand, the U.S. approach, with its attachment to viewpoint neutrality, privileges protection of speech but carries with it the risk of under protecting the civil rights and liberties of those who are members of socially disempowered groups. The best regulable definition of hate speech should start where the two approaches overlap – protection of selfhood – and attempt to alleviate as best as possible the risks associated with each.

A legal category of hate speech is best defined by focusing on the characteristics of both the group targeted and the speech itself. As such, my definition of regulable hate speech relies in large part on Parekh's 2012 definition where he illuminates three concrete characteristics of hate speech. Hate speech can be defined as: (1) it is "directed against a specified or easily identifiable individual or ...a group of individuals based on an arbitrary and normatively irrelevant feature," (2) the "hate speech stigmatizes the target group by implicitly or explicitly ascribing to it qualities widely regarded as highly undesirable," and (3) that "the target group is viewed as an undesirable presence and a legitimate object of hostility."[61] This definition requires us to think about the precise harms caused by hate speech, harms that are distinct from the more generic harms treated through fighting words, incitement, or true threats doctrine, and allows for application to Internet hate speech as well. To create a more comprehensive definition of hate speech, I add to the above definition a consideration of additional layers. Building from my earlier work, as well as research conducted by Politics and Public Policy Professor Katharine Gelber, I also consider context, social power, and history in determining the level of harm.[62] Inclusion of these additional factors when defining regulable hate speech will help to establish parameters that will allow the restriction of some hate speech, while also ensuring the protection of the most amount of free speech. In other words, those additional factors will force lawmakers and jurists to be careful and thoughtful about creating proposed hate speech regulations and will, hopefully, keep the government and courts from developing hate speech regulations in such a way that they lack the elasticity needed to work within complex and changing social arenas. Defining regulable hate speech through the combination of Parekh's definition and the additional criteria creates the foundation for a test that the courts could apply when considering anti-hate speech laws. This definition will be used in Chapter 5 as the base for a two-tiered framework for analysis that the courts could apply when assessing the constitutionality of hate speech regulations. That framework will then be tested in multiple areas, including Internet speech in Chapter 7 and speech on college campuses in Chapter 8.

Conclusion

Starting with a clear definition of hate speech is paramount to determining a workable, constitutionally sound path toward some level of restriction. While the term itself is problematic, it is still a viable option for legal purposes so long as it is clearly defined. This chapter reviewed existing definitions of the term hate speech, with most of the emphasis a discussion on those definitions that have some connection to legal application. Following this discussion, I further examined three studies that offered typographies or categories to help us define the term. I then argued that the best legal definition would start from the premise of harm. In other words, what specific harms does hate speech cause? I reviewed studies from various fields, such as law, philosophy, and psychology, to lay out the spectrum of harms. Throughout that review, I touched on some of the counter opinions, many of which will be elaborated on in later chapters. Finally, I offered the definition of hate speech that I think will best protect both targets of hate speech and freedom of speech. Before incorporating that definition into a new framework for case analysis, I will first, in Chapters 2 through 4, layout the current legal and philosophical landscape of hate speech regulation in the United States and internationally, and elaborate both on traditional free speech principles in general and on their relationship to the hate speech debate among legal scholars.

Notes

1 Elizabeth Barber, *The New Jersey A.G. Taking on Trump*, THE NEW YORKER, January 14, 2019, *available at* https://www.newyorker.com/magazine/2019/01/14/the-new-jersey-a-g-taking-on-trump [last accessed September 8, 2019].
2 For additional discussion of these different terms, *see* Clay Calvert, *Hate Speech and Its Harms: A Communication Theory Perspective*, 47 J. COMM. 4, at 4–5 (1997) (conflation of 'hate speech' with 'assaultive speech'); J. David Cisneros and Thomas K. Nakayama, *New Media, Old Racisms: Twitter, Miss America and Cultural Logics of Race*, 8 J. INT'L. INTERCULTURAL COMM. 108 (2015) (racist speech); Steven H. Shiffrin, WHAT'S WRONG WITH THE FIRST AMENDMENT? 35–46 (2016) and *Racist Speech, Outsider Jurisprudence, and the Meaning of America*, 80 CORNELL L. REV. 43 (1994) (racist speech); Alexander Brown, HATE SPEECH LAW: A PHILOSOPHICAL EXAMINATION 453 (2015) (hateful speech); Brian Levin, *Cyberhate: A Legal and Historical Analysis of Extremists Use of Computer Networks in American*, 45 AM. BEHAV. SCIENTIST 958 (2002) (hateful expression); Rao Neomi, *Three Concepts of Dignity in Constitutional Law*, 86 NOTRE DAME L. REV. 183, 251–252 (2011) (hateful speech) George Cherian, *Hate Spin: The Twin Political Strategies of Religious Incitement and Offense-Taking*, 27 COMM. THEORY 156 (2017) (hate spin); Amal Clooney and Philippa Webb, *The Right to Insult in International Law*, 48 COLUM. L. REV. 1 (2017) (insulting speech); Amos N. Guiora, TOLERATING INTOLERANCE: THE PRICE OF PROTECTING EXTREMISM (2014) (extremist speech); Ivan Hare and James Weinstein (eds.), EXTREME SPEECH AND DEMOCRACY (2009) (extreme speech); Brett G. Johnson, *Networked Communication the Reprise of Tolerance Theory: Civic Education for Extreme Speech and Private Governance Online*, 50 FIRST AMEND. STUD. 14 (2016) (extreme speech); Alexander Brown, *Retheorizing Actionable Injuries in Civil Lawsuits Involving Targeted Hate Speech: Hate Speech as Degradation and Humiliation*, 9 ALA. C.R. & C.L. L. REV. 1 (2018) (targeted hate speech); Rosalie Berger Levinson, *Targeted Hate Speech and the First Amendment: How the Supreme Court Should Have Decided Snyder*, 46 SUFFOLK U. L. REV. 45 (2013) (targeted hate speech); and Alexander Tsesis, DESTRUCTIVE MESSAGES: HOW HATE SPEECH PAVES THE WAY FOR HARMFUL SOCIAL MOVEMENTS (2002) (hate propaganda, destructive messages, and biased speech).
3 Candida Harris, Judith Rowbotham and Kim Stevenson, *Truth, Law and Hate in the Virtual Marketplace of Ideas: Perspectives on the Regulation of Internet Content*, 18 INFO. & COMM. TECH. L. 155 (2009).

4 Bhikhu Parekh, *Is There a Case for Banning Hate Speech*, in THE CONTENT AND CONTEXT OF HATE SPEECH: RETHINKING REGULATION AND RESPONSES, 40 (Michael Hertz and Peter Molnar, eds., 2012). For additional discussion of the problem with the term, *see* Eric Heinz, HATE SPEECH AND DEMOCRATIC CITIZENSHIP 22–23 (2016) and Katharine Gelber, *Hate Speech – Definitions & Empirical Evidence*, 32 CONST. COMMENT. 619 (2017).

5 Mark Slagle, *An Ethical Exploration of Free Expression and the Problem of Hate Speech*, 24 J. MASS MEDIA ETHICS 238 (2009).

6 Jeremy Waldron, THE HARM IN HATE SPEECH (2012).

7 Karmen Erjavec and Melita Poler Kovacic, *"You Don't Understand, This Is a New War!" Analysis of Hate Speech in News Web Sites' Comments*, 15 MASS COMM. SOC'Y 899, 900 (2012).

8 Jonathan Seglow, *Hate Speech, Dignity and Self-Respect*, 19 THEORY MORAL PRAC. 1103, 1104 (2016).

9 *Id.* at 1105.

10 Craig Martin, *Striking the Right Balance: Hate Speech Laws in Japan, the United States and Canada*, 45 HASTINGS CONST. L. Q. 455 (2018).

> Before launching into the comparative examination, however, we should pause to consider what, precisely, we mean by "hate speech," and thus what should be prohibited or constrained by so-called hate speech laws, subject to freedom of speech considerations. The answer to this question is, of course, dependent on some of the other aspects of the problem with which we will grapple below, and so to answer that question here may in some ways seem to predetermine the normative arguments to follow... On this view, the more extreme kind of hate speech that should be of concern in democratic societies, is that which vilifies, denigrates, alienates, delegitimizes and even attempts to dehumanize the members of identifiable groups—groups that often have been historically the subject of negative stereotyping, prejudice, and discrimination
>
> (459.)

11 For a more detailed discussion of these laws, *see* Chapter 2. Also, *see* Brown, *supra* note 2, at 19–48 (breaking down laws and regulations around the world); Toby Mendel, *Does International Law Provide for Consistent Rules on Hate Speech?*, in THE CONTENT AND CONTEXT OF HATE SPEECH: RETHINKING REGULATION AND RESPONSES, 40 (Michael Hertz and Peter Molnar, eds., 2012); Katharine Gelber, SPEAKING BACK: THE FREE SPEECH VERSUS HATE SPEECH DEBATE 93–115 (2002) (comparing the United States, the United Kingdom, and Australia); Harris, et al., *supra* note 3 (comparing multiple countries including the United States, the United Kingdom, Germany, and Canada); Jacob Weinrib, *What is the Purpose of Freedom of Expression*, 67 U. TORONTO FAC. L. REV. 165 (2009) (exploring the Canadian Charter in terms of hate speech); Clooney and Webb, *supra* note 2 (focus on international law and treatise); Michel Rosenfeld, *Hate Speech in Constitutional Jurisprudence: A Comparative Analysis*, 24 CARDOZO L. REV. 1523 (2003) (reviewing laws from Canada, Germany, the United Kingdom, as well as international covenants); and Robin Edger, *Are Hate Speech Provisions Anti-Democratic?: An International Perspective*, 26 AM. U. INT'L L. REV. 199 (2011).

12 *International Convention on the Elimination of All Forms of Racial Discrimination*, December 21, 1965, 660 U.N.T.S. 195 [hereinafter ICERD].

13 Parekh, *supra* note 4, at 40–41.

> First, it is directed against a specified or easily identifiable individual or, more commonly, a group of individuals based on an arbitrary and normatively relevant feature...Second, hate speech stigmatizes the target group by

implicitly or explicitly ascribing qualities widely regarded as highly undesirable...Third, because of its negative qualities, the target group is viewed as an undesirable presence and a legitimate object of hostility.

14 Gregory S. Gordon, *Hate Speech and Persecution: A Contextual Approach*, 46 VAND. J. TRANSNAT'L L. 303, 307 (2013).
15 Caleb Yong, *Does Freedom of Speech Include Hate Speech?*, RES PUBLICA, published online July 13, 2011, https://link.springer.com/article/10.1007/s11158-011-9158-y. For other examples, *see* Alexander Brown, *What is Hate Speech? Part 1: The Myth of Hate*, 36 LAW & PHIL. 419, 446 (2017) (says that something is hate speech if "(1) it is speech or expressive conduct, (2) concerns any members of groups or classes of persons identified by protected characteristics, and (3) involves or is intimately connected with emotions, feelings, or attitudes of hate or hatred."); John C. Knechtle, *When to Regulate Hate Speech*, 110 PENN ST. L. REV. 539 (2006) (says there are two factors to consider: historical accounts of discriminatory practices and jurisprudential history) and Harris et al., *supra* note 3, at 168 (discusses three approaches used to define the concept).
16 Gordon, *supra* note 14, at 306.
17 *Id.* at 307.
18 *Id.*
19 *Id.* at 342.
20 *Id.* at 342–343.

> Such statements would be addressed to the collective group (e.g., 'You do not belong here,' or 'You are parasites') or to particular individuals (e.g., 'You filthy residents of the Biryogo are making the rest of society dirty and disease infected. You are destroying our country.').

21 *Id.* at 343–344.
22 *Id.* at 373.
23 Yong, *supra* note 15. He identifies those free speech principles as: discovery of truth, self-fulfillment and personal development, participation in democratic self-government, and autonomy.
24 *Id.*
25 *Id.*
26 *Id.*
27 *Id.* He includes in this category Group Libel, which he deems should be protected speech.
28 Parekh, *supra* note 4, at 43. "Although free speech is an important value, it is not the only one."
29 *Id.* at 40.
30 *Id.*
31 *Id.* at 41.
32 *Id.*
33 *Id.* at 38–39.
34 Ishani Maitra and Mary Kate McGowan, SPEECH AND HARM: CONTROVERSIES OVER FREE SPEECH 5 (2012).
35 William Funk, *Intimidation and the Internet*, 110 PENN ST. L. REV. 579, 591–592 (Internet speech versus in-person speech); Alexander Brown, *Averting Your Eyes in the Information Age: Online Hate Speech and the Captive Audience Doctrine*, 12 CHARLESTON L. REV. 1 (public targeted hate speech with the intent to inflict emotional distress and objective/subjective tests); Knechtle, *supra* note 15, at 626 (context and history are key in determining level of harm).
36 For a more in-depth discussion of both of these positions, *see* Chapter 4.

37 Brown, *supra* note 2, at 57.
38 Heinz, *supra* note 4, at 127–128.
39 *See* Robert Boeckmann and Jeffrey Liew, *Hate Speech: Asian American Students' Justice Judgements and Psychological Responses*, 58 J. OF SOC. ISSUES 363 (2002).
40 *Id.* at 368.

> Specifically, the scenarios described several people standing in a cashier's line in a grocery store. The target of the insult delays the line by using a credit card when he realizes he doesn't have enough money for his purchases. One of the people waiting mutters a slur—"What a fucking fat asshole" (Overweight condition); "What a fucking chink" (Asian American condition); or "What a fucking nigger" (African American condition)—and then when the target of insult makes a nonverbal surprise response, the person continues by shouting a more extensive degrading insult: "I hate you! [You fat asshole you (Overweight); All you chinks (Asian American); All you niggers (African American)] are forever holding up the entire line. If you didn't bring enough cash, you shouldn't come into the store at all! Go back home!"

41 *Id.* at 377.
42 *Id.* at 379. They noted that this type of study would obviously raise ethical concerns and so would need to be designed carefully and include debriefing sessions.
43 Laura Leets, *Experiencing Hate Speech: Perceptions and Responses to Anti-Semitism and Antigay Speech*, 58 J. SOC. ISSUES 341 (2002).
44 *Id.* at 347. Leets explained in her study that all examples were based on actual experiences in order to increase external validity. For example, her stimulus material related to antisemitism included the following statements from Louis Farrakhan and the Nation of Islam: "You wonder why I call it Jew-nited nations…Jew York City…Jew-niversity. Because you [Jews] control it." and "I don't give a damn what you say about me, you bagel-eating, hook-nose, lox-eating…Jew."
45 Kathryn Freeman Anderson, *Diagnosing Discrimination: Stress from Perceived Racism and the Mental and Physical Health Effects*, 83 SOC. INQUIRY 55 (2013).
46 *Id.* at 58.

> Social stress theory emphasizes the social sources of stress factors which may impact mental and physical health outcomes. The theory argues that certain groups within society are in a disadvantaged social position, which leads to an increased exposure to social sources of stress and less resources with which to cope with stress…Social stress theory highlights these 'external circumstances' of social life. These factors can then lead to higher prevalence of health problems within those populations with social disadvantage.

47 *Id.* at 59.
48 *Id.* at 59–60.

> The first item read: 'During the past 30 days, have you felt emotionally upset, for example angry, sad, or frustrated, as a result of how you were treated based on your race?' This item deals with the mental or emotional stress of racist experiences. Based on previous literature, which is more focused on mental health, I expect a greater effect from this item. The second item reads: 'Within the past 30 days, have you experienced any physical symptoms, for example headache, upset stomach, tensing of

your muscles, or a pounding heart, as a result of how you were treated based on your race?' This item addresses the physical stress that one may experience as a result of racism.

49 *Id.* at 78.
50 *Id.*
51 For a few additional studies, *see* Ricci Harris et al., *Racism and Health: The Relationship between Experience of Racial Discrimination and Health in New Zealand*, 63 SCI. & MED. 1428 (2006) (arguing that health effects of racism should be considered when addressing health inequities); Rosalie Berger Levinson, *Targeted Hate Speech and the First Amendment: How the Supreme Court Should Have Decided Snyder*, 46 SUFFOLK U. L. REV. 45, 71–72 (2013) (discussing studies that show "that victims experience psychological and physiological symptoms such as fear, rapid pulse rate, difficulty breathing, nightmares, posttraumatic stress disorder, hypertension, psychosis, and suicide"); Jack McDevitt et al., *Consequences for Victims: A Comparison of Bias- and Non-bias-motivated Assaults*, 45 AM. BEHAV. SCI. 697–713 (2001) (found that "the level of intrusive thoughts, feelings of safety, nervousness, and depression were all significantly higher for bias crime victims"); Timothy Jay, *Do Offensive Words Harm People?*, 15 PSYCH. PUB. POL'Y & L. 84 (2009) (suggesting that negative hate speech directed toward ethnic immigrants in the United States is a significant predictor of suicide rates); Lisa Feldmen Barrett, HOW EMOTIONS ARE MADE: THE SECRET LIFE OF THE BRAIN (2018) (arguing that from the perspective of our brain cells, certain speech is a form of violence). For recent studies focused exclusively on hate speech and social media, *see* Chapter 7.
52 Maitra and McGowan, *supra* note 34, at 7.
53 *Id.*
54 Rory K. Little, *Hating Hate Speech: Why Current First Amendment Doctrine Does Not Condemn a Careful Ban*, 45 HASTINGS CONST. L. QUART. 577, 582 (2018).
55 For example, *see*, Ishani Maitra, *Subordinating Speech*, in SPEECH AND HARM: CONTROVERSIES OVER FREE SPEECH 94 (2012) (interrogating whether hate speech marks the targets as inferior enough to deprive them of basic rights); Fasoli Fabio et al., *Not "just words": Exposure to Homophobic Epithets Leads to Dehumanizing and Physical Distancing from Gay Men*, 46 EUR. J. SOC. PSYCH. 237 (2016) (found a correlation between exposure to anti-gay epithets and dehumanizing of the targets); Katharine Gelber and Luke McNamara, *Evidencing the Harms of Hate Speech*, 22 SOC. IDENTITIES 324 (2016) (conducted interviews and found the negative effects of hate speech to warrant regulation); Gelber, *supra* note 11 (explaining how hate speech reproduces and reinforces inequality); Knechtle, *supra* note 15 (discussing harm in relation to both immediate violence and long-term human dignity); and Brown, *supra* note 35, at 26–27 (explaining the impact of hate speech on the target's autonomy and emotional tranquility).
56 Chris Demaske, MODERN POWER AND FREE SPEECH: CONTEMPORARY CULTURE AND ISSUES OF EQUALITY 87 (2009). For a thorough discussion of the silencing power of hate speech, *see* Gelber and McNamara, *supra* note 55; Brown, *supra* note 2, at 198. For a more in-depth discussion of the origins of silencing concerns, *see* Chapter 4.
57 Gelber, *supra* note 4, at 622.

[H]ate speech acts harm in the saying of them, and that they harm in important ways that silence their targets. This is not to say that every instance of hate speech must silence its target, as clearly some instances of hate speech result in wide public disapprobation, or mobilise counter claims by targets and their allies. But it is to say that hate speech properly understood is capable of harming in these ways, and that these harms ought to be recognized...

58 For a lengthier discussion of this position, *see* Chapter 4, pages 64–67.

59 For additional discussions of this point, *see* Gelber, *supra* note 4, at 625 ("hate speech with historically identifiable and systemic discrimination is key to its success in discursively enacting harm to a sufficient degree that it would imperil a target's ability to participate in the political decision making that affects them."); Weinrib, *supra* note 11, at 178 (hate propaganda circumvents democracy); Kevin Dunn and Jacqueline Nelson, *Challenging the Public Denial of Racism for a Deeper Multiculturalism*, 32 J. INTER-CULTURAL STUD. 587 (2011) (through data collection in Australia found that hate speech can lead to a broader social pathology of unevenness in citizenship).

60 For additional discussions of importance of political participation in defense of the First Amendment, *see* Chapter 4, pages 64–65.

61 Parekh, *supra* note 4.

62 Demaske, *supra* note 56, and Gelber, *supra* note 4.

2 Favoring Human Rights
The International Response

First Amendment law, of course, only governs speech in the United States. However, speech itself is not confined by state borders. Speech regulations in general and hate speech regulations more specifically that happen in other countries impact us. Understanding those legal approaches both reinforces the extent of the problem of current U.S. hate speech protection and introduces some possible alternatives to the U.S. position. Review of laws and regulations in other countries and internationally is a necessary step toward conceiving of legally regulable hate speech restrictions in the United States. This review not only illustrates the impossibility of a U.S.-centric approach – global communication mediums mean that we can no longer isolate ourselves from the rest of the world – but also can serve as a road map to assist the United States in not repeating the same legislative design flaws that other countries are experiencing. As will become apparent during this discussion of those laws and regulations, there is a fundamental difference between the United States and the rest of the world when it comes to free speech. The U.S. focus is on protecting the individual, while the international approach is almost universally tempered by concerns about human dignity. Given the global nature of communication and the increasing instances of hate and hate speech in the United States, I posit that we should rethink our approach to hate speech regulation and should do so in a way that privileges the middle ground between individual rights and human dignity. That new approach will be discussed in depth in Chapter 5, but first, we need to understand what those regulations look like in other countries and within the international community.

In this chapter, I begin with a general overview of hate speech laws in other countries. I then highlight three specific countries – Germany, Japan, and Canada. I chose to highlight these countries for different reasons: Germany, because it has arguably the most restrictive hate speech laws; Japan, because it has passed the most recent country-wide anti-hate speech legislation; and Canada, because it is close to the United States both in proximity and, in many cases, in how it approaches legal issues. From examination of those countries, I turn my attention to various international treaties. Finally, I offer several examples of incidents where U.S. companies and individuals have come into conflict with international or country-based laws around the usage of hate speech.

An Overview of Global Hate Speech Laws

Hate crimes and hate speech happen across the globe, but there is no uniformity in how countries treat those offenses. Most countries (with the exception of the United States) prohibit hate speech-related offenses to varying degrees. The prohibitions may come in the form of regional laws,[1] national statutes,[2] or constitutions.[3] The punishments range from monetary fines to 10-years imprisonment. Which groups receive protection also vary by country. For example, England, Wales, and France all have laws that prohibit incitement on grounds of race, religion, sexual orientation, and disability,[4] while Poland restricts speech that would offend the feelings of religious communities or public speech that insults groups based on national, ethnic, racial, or religious affiliation.[5] Canada covers broadly "any identifiable group."[6] At present, France, Germany, Belgium, Switzerland, and Austria all have laws criminalizing the denial of crimes against humanity. How the offense is defined and criminalized also differs. In addition to incitement, countries have set parameters for restrictions based on the extent to which the speech is threatening, promoting hatred, insulting, ridiculing, defamatory, provoking animosity, or invoking rancor.[7]

Germany

Germany is notable for its expansive hate speech laws that seek to prohibit and criminalize incitement of hatred or attacks on human dignity based on group identification such as race, nationality, or religion. Michel Rosenfeld, professor of law and comparative democracy, explained:

> The contemporary German constitutional system is grounded in an order of objective values, including respect for human dignity and perpetual commitment to militant democracy. As such, it excludes certain creeds and thus paves the way for content-based restrictions on freedom of speech which would be unacceptable under American free speech jurisprudence.[8]

In Germany, freedom of expression is protected under Article 5(1) of the constitution, which reads:

> Every person shall have the right to freely express and disseminate his opinions in speech, writing, and pictures and to inform himself without hindrance from generally accessible sources. Freedom of the press and freedom of reporting by means of broadcasts and films shall be guaranteed. There shall be no censorship.[9]

From that language, it would appear that Germany protects speech with the same vigor as the United States. However, according to the German constitution, those speech rights are subject to provisions under Article 5(2) that limits those rights when balancing them against the protection of young persons and the right of personal honor.[10] The parameters of speech rights protected under Article 5 are established through sections of criminal law, administrative law, and civil codes. For example, the German Federal Penal Code contains efforts meant to restrict freedom of speech with regard to hate speech, including group defamation, use of propaganda by Nazi organizations, and incitement of hatred against minorities.[11] Punishments for violating these provisions can be steep. For example, inciting hatred of a minority is a criminal offense that carries with it a prison sentence of up to five years. Its restrictions apply to hate speech communicated within the country even if that communication originated outside of the country.

Another example of limits to the constitutional protection of speech is the German Penal Code, Section 130, which holds a prison sentence of up to five years if the speech "incites hatred against segments of the population or calls for violent or arbitrary measures against them; or assaults the human dignity of others by insulting, maliciously maligning, or defaming segments of the population."[12] It also addresses instances in which someone:

a   disseminates such written materials;
b   publicly displays, posts, presents, or otherwise makes them accessible;
c   offers, supplies, or makes them accessible to a person under 18 years;
d   produces, obtains, supplies, stocks, offers, announces, commends, undertakes to import or export them, in order to use them or copies obtained from them within the meaning of Nos (a) to (c) or facilitate such use by another; or ... by radio, media services, or telecommunication services shall be liable to imprisonment not exceeding three years or a fine.[13]

In 2017, that language in the German Penal Code led to the passage of the Act to Improve Enforcement of the Law in Social Networks, otherwise known as the Network Enforcement Act (NetzDG).[14] This law is intended to reduce hate speech on social media sites by requiring social media intermediary companies (such as Facebook) to delete or block questionable content within 48 hours of receiving a complaint. Under the law, platforms who fail to comply with valid requests for information removal can be fined up to 50 million euros (approximately 56 million dollars). The Rights, Equality, and Citizenship (REC) Programme of the European Union in its 2018 country report on Germany noted:

NetzDG has been broadly criticized for its vague and overbroad provisions, for its lack of clear definitions, and for privatizing censorship.

There are also challenges to its constitutionality in relation to federal states. Although it does not create new 'hate speech' prohibitions, it compels content removal on the basis of a number of provisions in the Criminal Code...many of these provisions raise serious freedom of expression concerns...moreover, the obligation to remove or block content applies without any prior determination of the legality of the content in issue by a court, and gives no guidance to social networks on respecting the right of freedom of expression in 'hate speech' determinations. Private enterprises are not competent to make these complex factual and legal determinations, and NetzDG provides no recourse to users whose content is blocked or unfairly deleted.[15]

Despite these concerns, Germany continues to crack down on hate speech on social media sites. For example, in June 2019, police in Germany carried out dozens of raids in 13 federal states as part of an orchestrated strike against those violating the country's strict hate speech laws.[16] In July, Germany's Office of Justice found Facebook in violation of NetzDG and fined the company $2.3 million. In December 2019, in response to increasingly violent fascist attacks, Chancellor Angela Merkel double-down on NetzDG, proposing that companies be required to report each instance of hate speech to German authorities.[17]

This firm stance against Internet hate speech is nothing new in Germany. In a 2009 article, Candida Harris et al., noted: "Significant steps have been taken in the German courts to enforce anti-hate speech laws in an Internet context."[18] They offered as examples the 2000 case in which Germany's highest court found that the German law banning "Holocaust denial" material applies to foreigners who post such content on web sites outside of the country, if that material is accessible in Germany,[19] and a 2002 ruling in which the Dusseldorf district government blocked access to several U.S.-based sites because the sites contained content deemed "harmful to adolescents."[20] Even before the passage of NetzDG, those authors warned: "These blocking decrees have 'triggered off a controversy about the providers' legal responsibility in general and especially the access providers' responsibility for web content'."[21]

Japan

In 1947, Japan enacted Article 21 of its constitution in an effort to protect speech in the aftermath of World War II. Prior to this point in time, Japanese citizens had no basic right to freedom of speech or expression. Article 21 reads:

Freedom of assembly and association as well as speech, press and all other forms of expression are guaranteed. No censorship shall be maintained, nor shall the secrecy of any means of communication be violated.[22]

In addition to a constitutional protection of speech, Japan, similar to the United States, had previously raised concerns about Article 4 of The International Convention on the Elimination of all Forms of Racial Discrimination and its possible chilling effect on free speech.[23]

Despite these concerns, Japan became one of the most recent countries to pass anti-hate speech legislation. Japan has a long and contentious history of racism tracing back to the late nineteenth century.[24] In more recent times, much of that racial animosity has been targeted toward Koreans living within the country. During the past decade, Japan has seen increasing hate speech rallies and online attacks. The move toward restricting some of that speech can be traced partly back to two incidents at the Kyoto Korean School. On December 21, 2009, *Zaitokukai*, a group of far- or ultra-right activists, held a hate-filled protest at the Kyoto Chosen Dai-ichi Primary School. The protestors "hurled abusive, discriminatory and intimidating words to the school and people inside as well as Korean residents in general. They also damaged school facilities."[25] On January 14, 2010, despite a court order to desist, the group held another protest at the same location. The protestors used bullhorns and yelled phrases such as "The school is an education organization to foster North Korean spies" and "The school occupied the land by raping and beating women during the way when there were no (Japanese) men in the town."[26] The school filed a lawsuit against Zaitokukai and in December 2013, in what has been hailed as a "historic ruling," the court ordered the group to pay $120,000 in damages for "staging demonstrations using racist slogans."[27]

The Kyoto case is but one example of hate-based demonstrations held in Japan recently.[28] The country enacted the Hate Speech Act of 2016 in order to comply with international treaties and combat increasing incidents of anti-Korean rallies and demonstrations. Germany and Japan serve as polar examples in how restrictive these parameters can be. If Germany can be seen as having some of the most stringent anti-hate speech legislation, then Japan's law may be one of the most lenient. The Hate Speech Act calls attention to discriminatory speech and behavior, declares that it "will not be tolerated," and requires national and local governments to "spread awareness" among the general public about the need to eliminate hate speech.[29] Law Professor Craig Martin called the language in the Act "vapid" and noted, "There is no actual prohibition of either the creation or the dissemination of hate speech, nor any sanctions whatsoever for the communication of hate speech."[30] The lack of penalties or punishments can likely be traced to Japan's constitution, which, much like the United States, contains robust support for freedom of expression.[31]

Despite the timidity of the Act, it remains significant that Japan has taken this step toward some level of restriction on hate speech. While disagreement exists over the effectiveness of the law, political leaders in Japan note both that the law has had some immediate impact in court rulings and it has also led local governments to construct their own, more detailed anti-hate speech legislation.[32] For example, Tokyo's Kunitachi City Council approved an ordinance in late 2018 aimed at banning discriminatory practices and hate speech. Specifically, the bill "prohibits discrimination based on race, ethnicity, gender, occupation and status."[33] Tokyo metropolitan government is also looking into expanding its legislation by restricting the use of its facilities "for potential hate rallies and other hate speech acts."[34] Other areas including Kawasaki, Nagoya, and Kobe are also working on developing hate speech legislation.

Canada

Canada, our closest neighbor to the North, offers an interesting space to study hate speech regulation for a couple of reasons. First, Canadian courts tend to be open to referencing rulings from other countries, including the United States, and while those foreign cases have no jurisdiction, they do (or at least can) inform Canada's multicultural legal approach. Second, Canada's treatment of hate speech at the national and local levels offers a middle ground between the excessive restrictions by Germany, and considerably more lax approach by Japan. Finally, Canada's balancing of human dignity with free speech rights provides a glimpse of the benefits and difficulties associated with trying to meet both goals.[35]

In 1982, the Canadian Charter took effect, offering for the first time constitutional protection for, among other things, freedom of speech.[36] Section 2 of the Canadian Charter reads:

Everyone has the following fundamental freedoms:

a   freedom of conscience and religion;
b   freedom of thought, belief, opinion, and expression, including freedom of the press and other media of communication;
c   freedom of peaceful assembly; and
d   freedom of association.[37]

While these protections seem clearly stated and firmly in support of freedom of speech, other Charter provisions offer significant qualifiers to the scope of protection. For example, Section 1 of the Charter covers the guarantees of rights and freedoms and includes protection of fundamental freedoms and democratic rights, equality rights for all, and Canada's multicultural heritage and Indigenous People's rights.[38] In addition, Section 27 focuses exclusively on the protection of multicultural heritage with a charge to maintain and promote multiculturalism.[39] The rights established in Sections 1 and 27 have to be weighed against the speech rights laid out in Section 2. In other words, unlike the First Amendment, which requires no commitment to balancing, the Canadian Charter "directly invites judicial balancing of rights against other social issues."[40]

In addition to limits set by the Charter, freedom of speech is also re-stricted through other laws and regulations. Three provinces – British Columbia, Alberta, and Saskatchewan – restrict hate speech through their human rights acts. For example, British Columbia has a speech revision, which is similar to the others:

1   A person must not publish, issue, or display, or cause to be pub-lished, issued, or displayed, any statement, publication, notice, sign, symbol, emblem, or other representation that

a   indicates discrimination or an intention to discriminate against a person or a group or class of persons, or
b   is likely to expose a person or a group or class of persons to hatred or contempt because of the race, color, ancestry, place of origin, religion, marital status, family status, physical or mental disability, sex, sexual orientation, gender identity or expression, or age of that person or that group or class of persons.[41]

One of the most recent court cases to focus on those types of human rights laws was the 2013 *Saskatchewan Human Rights Commission v. Whatcott*.[42] In this case, complaints were filed with the Human Rights Commission concerning flyers published and distributed by William Whatcott. The flyers allegedly promoted hatred against people based on their sexual orientation.[43] The *Whatcott* case ultimately led to a Supreme Court ruling that found that while Section 14 (1)(b) of the Sas-katchewan Human Rights Code infringed on Sections 2(a) and 2(b) of the Canadian Charter, it was saved by Section 1 of the Charter.[44]

Finally, the Canadian Criminal Code also limits the Charter protec-tion of speech.[45] As one scholar has noted:

> Canadian criminal law also does not require that the message be offensive. In determining whether the speech conveyed hatred, the judge takes into consideration the speech's audience and its social and historical context, the circumstances in which the speech was given, the manner and tone used, and the persons to whom the mes-sage was addressed.[46]

These legal remedies for restriction of hate speech in the effort of pro-tecting human dignity have led to a series of significant court cases in Canada. A discussion of the key hate speech case, *R. v. Keegstra,* is necessary to illustrate more completely the Canadian approach, and to establish the defining differences between the U.S. and Canadian ap-proaches to hate speech.[47]

In 1990, the Canadian Supreme Court in *Keegstra* ruled on whether or not Section 319(2) of the Criminal Code was constitutional. The facts in the case were as follows: James Keegstra was a high school teacher in Eckville, Alberta. As part of his course curriculum, he included anti-Semitic material. He told students that Jewish people were "treacherous," "sadistic," and "power hungry and child killers."[48] He also claimed that "Jews [had] created the Holocaust to gain sympathy."[49] Students were expected to reproduce this material on exams and their grades were dependent on it.[50] In 1982, Keegstra was fired for failing to follow curriculum guidelines, but it was his charge for violating Section 391 of the Criminal Code that led to the Court ruling. In a severely divided ruling, the Court upheld Keegstra's conviction. In reaching its conclusion, the Court weighed the benefits of protecting hate speech with the possible negative impacts of it on society. Chief Justice Dickson wrote:

> [T]he presence of hate propaganda in Canada is sufficiently substantial to warrant concern. Disquiet caused by the existence of such material is not simply the product of offensiveness, however, but stems from the very real harm which it causes. Essentially, there are two sorts of injury caused by hate propaganda. First, there is harm done to members of the target group...A second effect of hate propaganda which is of pressing concern is its influence upon society at large...It is not inconceivable that the active dissemination of hate propaganda can attract individuals to its cause, and in the process create serious discord between various cultural groups in society.[51]

Before reaching this point in its analysis, the Court first spent ample time discussing how the United States under the First Amendment might address the issue. Dickson reviewed relevant U.S. case law and concluded that the U.S. approach was not one that could be undertaken by Canada due to Canada's focus on multiculturalism and human rights.[52] Ultimately, the Court found that even though Section 319(2) did infringe on some level of freedom of expression, it was a justifiable restriction necessary to protect individuals and society at large from the harms of hate propaganda. The courts have heard other cases regarding the restriction of hate speech during the past 30 years.[53] Most recently, in early 2019, James Sears and LeRoy St. Germaine, both associated with the small publication *Your World News*, were convicted of promoting hatred against women and Jewish people.[54]

Before concluding this look at Canada's treatment of hate speech restrictions, it should be noted that in recent years, Canada has instituted Internet hate speech regulations. Under those regulations, ISPs are protected from criminal prosecution for allowing access to hate speech. However, individual sites that include discriminatory material pertaining to race, relation, or national or ethnic origin are subject to government injunctions. Law professor Jean-Maria Kamatali explained the regulation: "For hate and extremist speech that is posted on the Internet, Canadian law requires the person who posted it to appear, or be represented, before the Canadian court."[55] As is the case in Germany, this rule applies to all people who violate the law, not just those who reside in Canada. Despite the regulations already in place, the House of Commons Standing Committee on Justice and Human Rights recently conducted an exploration into hate speech on social media sites.[56] In June of 2019, the committee offered recommendations that could assist the government to "better mitigate the incitement of hatred through online platforms."[57]

International Treaties

As is illustrated from the previous summary, individual countries have developed a myriad of ways to counterbalance hateful speech. These legal remedies range from local ordinances to national acts and, in some instances, constitutional amendments. In addition to these internally produced measures, many countries also abide by overarching international treaties. At the heart of those treaties is an international commitment to a human rights framework. This commitment can be traced to the period immediately following World War II when "international consensus crystallized around the need to identify the individual rights and liberties which all governments should respect, and to establish mechanisms for both promoting States' adherence to their human rights obligations and for addressing serious breaches."[58] From those concerns, several inter-governmental organizations, such as the United Nations and the Council of Europe, were created to advance human rights around the world. Those organizations would craft both non-binding declarations and binding treaties to further that goal. Many international regulations concerning hate speech have their foundation in this more general protection of human rights. These governing documents, as well as the case law resulting from them, encompasses 70 years and creates an intricate tapestry of legal decisions involving instances of hate speech. The following discussion is not intended to be comprehensive but merely to offer a bird's-eye view of the development of some of these rules and regulations.

Perhaps the earliest attempt at this protection can be found in the Universal Declaration of Human Rights (UDHR), which passed in 1948. That declaration, while not directly addressing hate speech, did focus on the need for the equal treatment of all[59] and emphasized that equal treatment meant a freedom from discrimination in any form.[60] Specifically, Article 7 of the UDHR states: "All are equal before the law and are entitled without any discrimination to equal protection of the law. All are entitled to equal protection against any discrimination in violation of this Declaration and against any incitement to such discrimination."[61] THE UDHR does not call out freedom of expression on its own; however, Article 29(2) could be seen to impact freedom of expression. That article states: "In the exercise of his rights and freedoms, everyone shall be subject only to such limitations as are determined by law solely for the purpose of securing due recognition and respect for the rights and freedoms of others" and of meeting "the just requirements of morality, public order and the general welfare in a democratic society."[62] Clearly, that language does not address hate speech in any specific terms. But, one could argue that Article 29(2) opens the door for the consideration of hate speech regulation when said hate speech runs the risk of impeding "due recognition and respect for the rights and freedoms of others."

The International Convention on the Elimination of all Forms of Racial Discrimination was the first international treaty to address the problem of hate speech directly.[63] CERD, which was adopted by the United Nations General Assembly in 1965, not only expressed concerns about hate speech but also laid out regulations related to various manifestations of hate speech. The items regulated included dissemination of ideas based on racial superiority, dissemination of ideas based on racial hatred, incitement to racial discrimination, and incitement to acts of racially motivated violence. Article 4 of the CERD reads in part:

> States Parties condemn all propaganda and all organizations which are based on ideas or theories of superiority of one race or group of persons of one colour or ethnic origin, or which attempt to justify or promote racial hatred and discrimination in any form, and undertake to adopt immediate and positive measures designed to eradicate all incitement to, or acts of, such discrimination and, to this end, with due regard to the principles embodied in the Universal Declaration of Human Rights and the rights expressly set forth in article 5 of this Convention, inter alia:
>
> a   Shall declare an offence punishable by law all dissemination of ideas based on racial superiority or hatred, incitement to racial discrimination, as well as all acts of violence or incitement to such acts against any race or group of persons of another colour or ethnic origin, and also the provision of any assistance to racist activities, including the financing thereof.[64]

In short, Article 4 of CERD states that all those who sign the treaty agree to make "all dissemination of ideas based on racial superiority or hatred" legally punishable offenses.[65] As of January 2020, there were 182 parties to CERD and 88 signatories.[66] However, many of the countries have made reservations to one or more sections of CERD. The United States, for example, has refused to sign Article 4 citing conflicts with the First Amendment.[67] In 2013, CERD adopted General Recommendation 35, "Combating Racist Hate Speech," in an attempt to offer more direction in determining what constitutes punishable racist speech.[68] GR 35 identified the following as punishable: dissemination of ideas based on racial and ethnic superiority, incite based on grounds of race, color, descent or national or ethnic origin, expression of insults, ridicule or slander, and participation in organizations that promoted and incite racial discrimination.[69]

While CERD might be seen as the most aggressive international covenant calling for hate speech restrictions, other broad international treaties, such as the International Covenant on Civil and Political Rights (ICCPR) and the European Convention on Human Rights (ECHR), also call for some level of repercussion for hate speech, although to a lesser degree than CERD.[70] In terms of the ICCPR, just as it is under Article 19 of the UDHR, freedom of expression is protected by language within the law. Article 19(2) of the ICCPR states, in part:

> Everyone shall have the right to freedom of expression; this right shall include freedom to seek, receive and impart information and ideas of all kinds, regardless of frontiers, either orally, in writing or in print, in the form of art, or through any other media of his choice.[71]

Clearly, this language signals a strong commitment to freedom. However, ICCPR also includes language that hints at admissible hate speech restrictions. First, Section 3 states:

> The exercise of the rights provided for in paragraph 2 of this article carries with it special duties and responsibilities. It may therefore be subject to certain restrictions, but these shall only be such as are provided by law and are necessary: (a) For respect of the rights or reputations of others; (b) For the protection of national security or of public order, or of public health or morals.[72]

From the language in Section 3, it can be inferred that there might be some limitations due to the "special duties and responsibilities" imbued in the practice of freedom of expression. In 1994, the Human Rights Committee expanded on the discussion of freedom of expression under Article 19 and noted: "It is the interplay between the principle of freedom of expression and such limitations and restrictions which determines the actual scope of the individual's right."[73] In other words, freedom of expression is not wholesale protected, but its limits must be carefully constructed. The Committee cautioned that "[W]hen a State party imposes certain restrictions on the exercise of freedom of expression, these may not put in jeopardy the right itself."[74] In short, ICCPR extends some possibility of hate speech restriction. Article 20(2) of the International Covenant on Civil and Political Rights ("ICCPR") provides an additional layer that may lead to the consideration of legal restrictions on hate speech. Specifically, it reads:

1   Any propaganda for war shall be prohibited by law.
2   Any advocacy of national, racial, or religious hatred that constitutes incitement to discrimination, hostility, or violence shall be prohibited by law.[75]

The Human Rights Committee has heard several cases related to the ICCPR and hate speech restrictions and often has ruled that those restrictions do not unduly infringe on free speech. Those convictions included an Italian right-wing militant and publisher who brought back the dissolved Fascist Party,[76] a political group in Canada who used telephone services to arouse hatred against Jewish people,[77] and a French man who claimed that certain parts of the Holocaust didn't happen.[78] Despite those rulings, the Human Rights Committee has consistently voiced that the right to freedom of expression encompasses "even expression that may be regarded as deeply offensive."[79] The Committee also detailed that when a State seeks to justify restrictions on the right to freedom of expression because of a protection of other rights, then the State bears the burden of demonstrating "a direct and immediate connection between the expression and the threat [to others' rights]."[80] The United States has registered reservations concerning Article 20(2) of the ICCPR, citing conflicts with the First Amendment.

At the regional level, restrictions are considered through bodies such as the European Court of Human Rights, which has sustained convictions for hate speech,[81] and the European Commission Against Racism and Intolerance, which adopted a recommendation on combating racism in 2015.[82] The ECRI General Policy Recommendation No. 15 starts by "Reaffirming the fundamental importance of freedom of expression and opinion, tolerance and respect for the equal dignity of all human beings for a democratic and pluralistic society."[83] Protection of freedom of expression remains an important right. However, the ECRI in its recommendation immediately followed that support by stating, "Recalling, however, that freedom of expression and opinion is not an unqualified right and that it must not be exercised in a manner inconsistent with the rights of others."[84] As a result of this position, the ECRI recommends, among other things, that member states ratify the Additional Protocol to the Convention on Cybercrime, the Framework Convention for the Protection of National Minorities, and Protocol No. 12 to the European Convention on Human Rights. In addition, the ECRI asks member states to withdraw any reservations to Article 4 of the CERD and to Article 20 of the ICCPR; perform organized and vigorous measures to raise public awareness about "the importance of respecting pluralism and of the dangers posed by hate speech;" offer support for individuals and groups who are targeted by hate speech; and through regulatory means require media (including Internet providers, online intermediaries and social media) to "promote action to combat the use of hate speech and to challenge its acceptability, while ensuring that such action does not violate the right to freedom of expression and opinion, and accordingly."[85] From just this brief review of measures under CERD, ICCPR, and ECRI, it becomes clear that attempts at restricting hate speech require a thoughtful and careful application, but that it is also possible to create those types of thoughtful legislative schemes.

In addition to broader laws regulating hate speech, international treaties also exist dealing specifically with the Internet and hate speech. Most notably, the Council of Europe developed the Cybercrime Treaty in 2001.[86] This treaty intended to offer a coordinated effort by the international community to deal with many of the problems emerging due to the networked global communication system. Concerns addressed in the initial 2001 treaty included, among other elements, illegal access, interception or interference of information, computer-related fraud, and offenses related to child pornography and copyright. To date, the document has received 49 ratifications or accessions, including the United States and several non-European Council members.[87] Beginning in 2001, the European Council revisited its concerns about global communication and developed the Additional Protocol to the Convention on Cybercrime, concerning the criminalization of racist and xenophobic acts committed through computer systems.[88] This provision requires that signatories create domestic laws criminalizing any online materials distributed internationally that promote racist or xenophobic ideas or that threaten or insult individuals because of their group affiliation based on race, color, national or ethnic origin, or religion.[89] The United States refused to sign the provision, citing conflicts with the First Amendment.

Global Actions, Local Implications

While the U.S. government can cite the First Amendment when refusing to participate in global legal initiatives combating hate speech, U.S. companies must still contend with various laws in other countries concerning hate speech on the Internet. Throughout the past two decades, companies such as Yahoo, Google, Twitter, and Facebook have all found themselves attempting to reconcile their content with varying rules and regulations within the international community. For example, in one of the earliest conflicts, Yahoo found itself clashing with French officials over what those officials deemed to be hate speech content on the service provider's site.[90] In that case, the French anti-Nazi group LICRA brought action against Yahoo for allegedly violating French law by making Nazi memorabilia available through its site. The incident resulted in a ruling by a French Court against Yahoo, a U.S. District Court ruling in favor of the company, and a Ninth Circuit Court of Appeals ruling overturning the district court ruling.[91] In the end, Yahoo removed the Nazi memorabilia from its French site. Recently, French officials have begun cracking down more vigorously on hate speech, including Internet hate speech. Spurred by the deadly attacks on the satirical weekly *Charlie Hebdo* in 2015, French President Francois Hollande declared that he would make fighting racism a personal cause. The French government dedicated 72 million euros over a three-year period to this end, which included a new unit dedicated to monitoring and fighting hate speech online.[92] While no legal actions have been taken since then against U.S. Internet companies, concerns remain that these new laws could, in effect, make companies like Google and Facebook accomplices in hate speech cases.[93]

American citizens and companies also have experienced issues in Germany. As previously noted, under Germany's Federal Penal Law, hate speech is restricted within the country regardless of where the speech originated. In two rather famous cases, the United States refused to extradite men wanted in Germany for violating their anti-hate speech laws. One case involved Ernst Zundel, a German-born Holocaust denier.[94] Zundel moved to Canada in his late teens in 1958. There, he became political, writing pro-German materials under his own name and Nazi propaganda under a pseudonym. He moved to the United States in 2000. At the time, he was under investigation by the Canadian Human Rights Commission for promoting hatred against Jewish people. He left Canada before the Commission had completed its hearings. In addition, at that time, he was wanted by German authorities to stand trial for violating their laws concerning Holocaust denial. The United States is extremely reluctant to extradite a U.S. citizen for behavior that is legal in the United States. In the case of Zundel, the United States did not extradite him to Germany, but eventually sent him back to Canada for violating U.S. immigration laws.[95] In another example, Gary Lauck, an American citizen known as the "Farm Belt Fuhrer," was wanted in Germany during the 1990s for disseminating hate literature, tapes, and paraphernalia into Germany from his home state of Nebraska.[96] Under the principle of double criminality, the United States refused to extradite him to Germany to face the charges.[97] Lauck would eventually serve time in Germany, but only because he traveled outside of the United States and was then extradited to Germany from Denmark. He served four years in prison and upon his release in 1999 was deported back to the United States.[98]

While countries deliberate over who has the legal authority to restrict hate speech on the World Wide Web, corporations are taking the lead in addressing the issue. Legal scholar Jeff Rosen reviewed the 2012 global incident concerning the anti-Islamic YouTube video "Innocence of the Muslims" and the subsequent fallout from its presence on the web.[99] Despite President Obama's public support of free speech rights, U.S. government offices asked YouTube to remove the video. Google refused, stating that the video did not violate its definition of hate speech. However, Google did decide to temporarily block access to the video in Libya and Egypt, based on what Google called "the very difficult situation" in those countries.[100] Rosen noted,

> The incident confirmed a lesson that is transforming our global debates about free speech: today, lawyers at Google, YouTube,

Facebook, and Twitter have more power over who can speak and who can be heard than any president, judge or monarch.[101]

In other words, in the United States, private companies are given the power to determine if, when, and how much speech to protect or restrict in the global arena. For example, during his April 2018 appearance before the U.S. Congress, Facebook CEO Mark Zuckerberg said that within ten years, Facebook will have the technology to detect hate speech using artificial intelligence.[102] There was no acknowledgment in his comments about the difficulty (and importance) of defining hate speech at the outset, and definitely no mention of who would set those parameters. It seems from his statement that he sees Facebook, not governmental bodies, as having the power to make those types of content decisions. This power is likely misplaced, though, as evidenced by the recent uses of Facebook to spread targeted advertising toward hate groups and to interfere with U.S. elections.[103] In addition, while the United States may be happy giving total control to Internet companies to police hate speech on the web, other countries are not as generous, as is probably best displayed through Germany's NetzDG law. German authorities contend that Facebook underreported complaints about illegal hate speech and that by counting only certain categories of hate speech, it skewed the number of incidents on its site.[104] Both at the global level and in the United States, these recent incidents lend strong support to the position that decisions impacting important social concerns such as human rights should not be left to the purview of corporations.

Conclusion

While the United States is not bound by the speech laws governing the international community, it is impacted by them due to the global nature of communication today. Those approaches to hate speech restriction stand in stark contrast to the overly permissible stances taken in the United States. In this chapter, I reviewed various hate speech restrictions at the national and international levels. I focused more specifically on the regulations in three countries (Germany, Japan, and Canada) and two international treaties (CERD and ICCPR) to illustrate the variety and breadth of restrictive approaches adopted throughout the world. Through that review, it becomes evident that one philosophical position unites the world and leaves the Unite States on the outside, and that is the reliance on or care given to the protection of human dignity over the protection of sweeping freedom of expression rights. Those opposing positions are discussed in considerable detail in Chapters 4 and 5. However, before looking at the broader philosophy driving the conceptualization of hate speech and hate speech regulation, Chapter 3 explores the history of hate speech regulation in the United States focusing on its treatment by the Supreme Court throughout the past 70 years.

Notes

1 For example, in Australia, in addition to the Federal Racial Discrimination Act of 1975, several areas including Tasmania, New South Wales, Queensland, and Victoria have regional legislation as well.

2 For example, New Zealand, Singapore and the United Kingdom all have national statutes limiting hate speech. *New Zealand Human Rights Act 1993, Section 61, available at* http://www.legislation.govt.nz/act/public/1993/0082/latest/DLM304643.html [last accessed January 14, 2019]; *Singapore Maintenance of Religious Harmony Act, available at* https://sso.agc.gov.sg/Act/MRHA1990; *United Kingdom Racial and Religious Hatred Act 2006, available at* http://www.legislation.gov.uk/ukpga/2006/1/contents [last accessed January 14, 2019].

3 For example, Serbia, Brazil, and South Africa all have constitutional provisions related to hate speech. *Republic of Serbia Constitution, available at* http://www.ustavni.sud.rs/page/view/en-GB/235-100028/constitution#d2; *Brazil's Constitution of 1988, available at* https://www.constituteproject.org/constitution/Brazil_2014.pdf; *The Constitution of the Republic of South Africa, available at* https://www.gov.za/documents/constitution/constitution-republic-south-africa-1996-1 [last accessed January 14, 2019].

4 Audrey Guichard, *Hate Crime in Cyberspace: The Challenges of Substantive Criminal Law*, 18 INFO. & COMM. TECH. L. 201 (2009).

5 Rights, Equality and Citizenship Programme of the European Union, *Poland: Responding to 'Hate Speech': 2018 Country Report, available at* https://www.article19.org/wp-content/uploads/2018/04/Poland-Hate-Speech.pdf [last accessed September 8, 2019].

6 Jeremy Waldron, THE HARM IN HATE SPEECH 8 (2012).

7 For a detailed discussion of these types of laws, *see* Alexander Brown, HATE SPEECH LAW: A PHILOSOPHICAL EXAMINATION (2015).

8 Michel Rosenfeld, *Hate Speech in Constitutional Jurisprudence: A Comparative Analysis*, 24 CARDOZO L. REV. 1523, 1550 (2003).

9 *Germany: Basic Law for the Federal Republic of Germany [Germany]*, May 23, 1949, *available at* http://www.refworld.org/docid/4e64d9a02.html [last accessed August 22, 2019].

10 *Id.*

11 Candida Harris, Judith Rowbotham & Kim Stevenson, *Truth, Law and Hate in the Virtual Marketplace of Ideas: Perspectives on the Regulation of Internet Content*, 18 INFO. & COMM. TECH. L. 155, 168 (2009).

12 *Strafgesetzbuch* [StGB] [Penal Code] art. 130, reprinted in GERMAN LAW ARCHIVE, *available at* https://germanlawarchive.iuscomp.org/?p=752 [last accessed July 8, 2019].

13 *Id.*

14 *The Network Enforcement Act* (NetzDG), reprinted in GERMAN LAW ARCHIVE, *available at* https://germanlawarchive.iuscomp.org/?p=1245 [last accessed July 8, 2019].

15 Rights, Equality and Citizenship Programme of the European Union, *Germany: Responding to Hate Speech, 2018 Country Report, available at* https://www.article19.org/wp-content/uploads/2018/07/Germany-Responding-to-%E2%80%98hate-speech%E2%80%99-v3-WEB.pdf [last accessed August 22, 2019]. For additional discussions about NetzDG, *see*

Rebecca Zipursky, *Nuts about Netz: The Network Enforcement Act and Freedom of Expression*, 42 FORDHAM INT'L L.J. 1325 (2019) (reviewing free speech concerns regarding the NetzDG and offering remedies); Dawn Carla Nunziato, *The Marketplace of Ideas Online*, 94 NOTRE DAME L. REV. 1519 (2019) (reviewing the specifics of NetzDG and its possible impact on the global community); Imara McMillan, *Enforcement Through the Network: The Network Enforcement Act and Article 10 of the European Convention on Human Rights*, 20 CHI. J. INT'L L. 252 (2019) (exploring the conflict between state-described freedom of expression and the autonomy of social media companies to regulate content on their platforms); Catherine O'Regan, *Hate Speech Online: an (Intractable) Contemporary Challenge?*, 71 CURRENT LEGAL PROBLEMS 403 (2018) (comparing current rules for regulating hate speech online in four countries); and Jack M. Balkin, *Free Speech is a Triangle*, 118 COLUM. L. REV. 2011 (2018) (outlining four objections to government programs such as NetzDG).

16 *Dozens of Raids over Online Hate Speech*, DW.COM, *available at* https://www.dw.com/en/germany-dozens-of-raids-over-online-hate-speech/a-49080109 [last accessed August 22, 2019].

17 Kate Brady, *Germany Announces Plans to Combat Far-Right Extremism and On-Line Hate Speech*, DW AKADEMIA, *available at* https://www.dw.com/en/germany-announces-plans-to-combat-far-right-extremism-and-online-hate-speech/a-51049129 [last accessed February 17, 2020].

18 Harris, et al., *supra* note 11, at 168.

19 *Id*. at 168.

20 *Id*. at 168–169.

21 *Id*. at 169.

22 *Article 21, The Constitution of Japan*, May 3, 1947, *available at* https://japan.kantei.go.jp/constitution_and_government_of_japan/constitution_e.html [last visited August 22, 2019].

23 *International Convention on the Elimination of all Forms of Racial Discrimination*, March 7, 1966, updated status April 3, 2016, *available at* https://web.archive.org/web/20160304195652/https://treaties.un.org/Pages/ViewDetails.aspx?src=TREATY&mtdsg_no=IV-2&chapter=4&lang=en#EndDec [last accessed August 22, 2019]. Japan signed CERD but with a reservation that stated:

> In applying the provisions of paragraphs (a) and (b) of article 4 of the [said Convention] Japan fulfills the obligations under those provisions to the extent that fulfillment of the obligations is compatible with the guarantee of the rights to freedom of assembly, association and expression and other rights under the Constitution of Japan, noting the phrase 'with due regard to the principles embodied in the Universal Declaration of Human Rights and the rights expressly set forth in article 5 of this Convention' referred to in article 4.

24 Hiroshi Fukurai and Alice Yang, *The History of Japanese Racism, Japanese American Redress, and the Dangers Associate with Government Regulation of Hate Speech*, 45 HASTINGS CONST. L.Q. 533, 534 (2018):

> After the Western concept of race was first introduced in Japan in the late nineteenth century, state planners and political elites incorporated its concept to construct a set of "racialized" ideologies to promote a new nation-state building project. These manufactured ideologies included an imagined national unity based on its divine cultural roots in the "three-thousand-year history" of the imperial family, a myth of racial

homogeneity of its national subject, and claims of Japanese racial superiority over other Asian races.

25 Asia-Pacific Human Rights Information Center, *Rise of Hate Speech in Japan*, 74 Focus 2013, *available at* https://www.hurights.or.jp/archives/focus/section2/2013/12/rise-of-hate-speech-in-japan.html [last accessed February 20, 2020].

26 Park Ji-won, Hate Speech against Koreans Still Active in Japan, THE KOREAN TIMES, March 3, 2019, *available at* https://www.koreatimes.co.kr/www/nation/2019/03/120_265876.html [last accessed February 20, 2020].

27 *Id.*

28 For details on these incidents, *see* Ayako Hatano, *The Internationalization of International Human Rights Law: The Case of Hate Speech in Japan*, 50 N.Y.U. J. INT'L L. & POL. 637 (2018): "Data from the Japanese Ministry of Justice show that between April 2012 and September 2015 there were at least 1,152 hate-based demonstrations," at 638.

29 For English translation *see*, http://www.moj.go.jp/ENGLISH/m_jinken04_00001.html [last accessed September 10, 2019].

30 Craig Martin, *Striking the Right Balance: Hate Speech Laws in Japan, the United States and Canada*, 45 HASTINGS CONST. L. Q. 455, 466 (2018).

31 For a lengthy discussion of the constitution and its relationship to hate speech protection, *see* Junko Kotani, *Proceed with Caution: Hate Speech Regulation in Japan*, 45 HASTINGS CONST. L. Q. 603 (2018).

32 *Three Years after Enactment of Japan's Hate Speech Law, Politicians Call for Increased Efforts to Eradicate Discrimination*, THE JAPAN TIMES, May 31, 2019, *available at* https://www.japantimes.co.jp/news/2019/05/31/national/three-years-enactment-hate-speech-law-politicians-call-increased-efforts-eradicate-discrimination/#.XVGUBZNKjow [last accessed August 22, 2019].

33 Lee Tae-hee, *Anti-Korean Hate Speech to be Prohibited by Law in Japan*, THE KOREAN HERALD, December 13, 2018, *available at* http://www.koreaherald.com/view.php?ud=20181213000712 [last visited August 22, 2019].

34 *EDITORIAL: Continued Action Needed to Totally Root out Hate Speech in Japan*, THE ASAHI SHIMBUN, June 17, 2019, *available at* http://www.asahi.com/ajw/articles/AJ201906170023.html [last accessed August 22, 2019].

35 For a comparison of the U.S. and Canadian approaches to hate speech, *see* Michel Rosenfeld, *Hate Speech in Constitutional Jurisprudence: A Comparative Analysis*, 24 CARDOZO L. REV. 1523 (2003) (reviewing laws and international covenants from Canada, Germany, and the United Kingdom). He noted:

> Under the American view, there seems to be a greater likelihood of harm from the suppression of hate speech that falls short of incitement to violence than from its toleration. From a Canadian perspective, on the other hand, dissemination of hate propaganda seems more dangerous than its suppression as it is seen as likely to produce enduring injuries to self-worth and to undermine social cohesion in the long run.

36 *Canadian Charter of Rights and Freedoms*, April 17, 1982, *available at* https://laws-lois.justice.gc.ca/eng/Const/page-15.html [last accessed August 22, 2019].

37 *Id.*

38 For discussion of these rights, see *Guide to the Canadian Charter of Rights and Freedoms*, GOVERNMENT OF CANADA, *available at* https://www.

canada.ca/en/canadian-heritage/services/how-rights-protected/guide-canadian-charter-rights-freedoms.html#a2aId [last accessed August 22, 2019].

39 *Id.*

40 Ronald J. Krotoszynski, Jr., The First Amendment in Cross-Cultural Perspectives: A Comparative Legal Analysis of the Freedom of Speech 28 (2006).

41 *Section 7, Discriminatory Publication,* Human Rights Code, *available at* http://www.bclaws.ca/Recon/document/ID/freeside/00_96210_01#section7 [last visited August 22, 2019].

42 Saskatchewan Human Rights Commission v. Whatcott, 1 S.C.R. 467 (2013), *available at* https://scc-csc.lexum.com/scc-csc/scc-csc/en/item/12876/index.do [last accessed August 22, 2019].

43 The text on the flyers included "Keep Homosexuality out of Saskatoon's Public Schools!" and "Sodomites in our Public Schools."

44 Saskatchewan Human Rights Commission v. Whatcott, 1 S.C.R. 467 (2013), *available at* https://scc-csc.lexum.com/scc-csc/scc-csc/en/item/12876/index.do [last accessed August 22, 2019].

45 *Section 319, Public Incitement to Hatred,* Canadian Criminal Code, *available at* https://laws-lois.justice.gc.ca/eng/acts/c-46/section-319.html [last accessed August 22, 2019]. Section 319 reads: Public incitement of hatred: 319 (1) Every one who, by communicating statements in any public place, incites hatred against any identifiable group where such incitement is likely to lead to a breach of the peace is guilty of (a) an indictable offence and is liable to imprisonment for a term not exceeding two years; or (b) an offence punishable on summary conviction.

Willful promotion of hatred: (2) Every one who, by communicating statements, other than in private conversation, willfully promotes hatred against any identifiable group is guilty of (a) an indictable offence and is liable to imprisonment for a term not exceeding two years; or (b) an offence punishable on summary conviction.

46 Jean-Marie Kamatali, *The Limits of the First Amendment: Protecting American Citizens' Free Speech in the Era of the Internet & the Global Marketplace of Ideas,* 33 Wis. Int'l L. J. 587, 593 (2016).

47 R. v. Keegstra, 3 S.C.R. 697 (1990).

48 *Id.* at 714.

49 *Id.*

50 *Id.*

51 *Id.* at 746.

52 *Id* at 738–744.

> [T]he international commitment to eradicate hate propaganda and, most importantly, the special role given equality and multiculturalism in the Canadian constitution necessitate a departure from the view, reasonably prevalent in America at present, that the suppression of hate propaganda is incompatible with the guarantee of free expression
>
> (743.)

53 To review some of those cases, *see,* Mugesera v. Canada (Minister of Citizenship and Immigration), 2 S.C.R. 100 (2005); R. Krymowski, 1 S.C.R. 101 (2005); R. v. Zundel, 2 S.C.R. 731 (1992), R. v. Andrews, 3 S.C.R. 870 (1990); and Canada (Human Rights Commission) v. Taylor, 3 S.C.R. 892 (1990).

54 Mack Lamoueux, *James Sears, Editor of Canada's Most Racist Paper, Guilty of Hate Charges,* Vice, January 24, 2019, *available at* https://www.

vice.com/en_ca/article/qvypjp/james-sears-editor-of-canadas-most-racist-paper-guilty-of-hate-charges [last accessed August 13, 2019].

55 Kamatali, *supra* note 40, at 593.

56 *Canadian Parliament Explores Internet, Social Media and Hate Speech*, BAHA'I WORLD NEWS SERVICE, April 18, 2019, *available at* https://news.bahai.org/story/1321/ [last accessed August 13, 2019].

57 *Id.*

58 *Overview of Human Rights Framework*, INT'L JUST. RESOURCE CTR., *available   at*   https://ijrcenter.org/ihr-reading-room/overview-of-the-human-rights-framework/ [last accessed February 20, 2020].

59 *See*, Article One, *UN General Assembly, Universal Declaration of Human Rights*, December 10, 1948, 217 A (III), *available at* http://www.refworld.org/docid/3ae6b3712c.html [last accessed August 19, 2016].

60 *Id.* at Article 2.

61 *Id.* at Article 7.

62 *Id.* at Article 29(2).

63 *International Convention on the Elimination of All Forms of Racial Discrimination*, December 21, 1965, 660 U.N.T.S. 195 [hereinafter CERD].

64 *Id.* at 220.

65 *Id.*

66 For a more detailed discussion of CERD, *see* Onder Bakircioglu, *Freedom of Expression and Hate Speech*, 16 TULSA J. COMP. & INT'L L. 1, 27–31 (2008).

67 For a lengthier discussion of the U.S. reasoning, *see* Lisa Herndon, *Why Is Racial Injustice Still Permitted in the United States?: An International Human Rights Perspective of the United States' Inadequate Compliance with the International Convention on the Elimination of All Forms of Racial Discrimination*, 31 WISC. INT'L. L.J. 322, 343–344 (2013). For the latest recommendations to the United States from the United Nations concerning this issue, *see* Committee on the Elimination of Racial Discrimination, *Concluding Observations on the Combined Seventh to Ninth Periodic Reports of the United States of America*, CERD/C/USA/CO/7-9, 4 (2014).

68 UN Committee on the Elimination of Racial Discrimination (CERD), General Recommendation No. 35: Combating racist hate speech, September 26, 2013, CERD/C/GC/35, *available at* https://www.refworld.org/docid/53f457db4.html [last accessed February 20, 2020].

69 *Id.*

70 European Union, *Council Framework Decision 2008/913/JHA of 28 November 2008 on combating certain forms and expressions of racism and xenophobia by means of criminal law*, *available at* http://eur-lex.europa.eu/legal-content/EN/TXT/?uri=uriserv%3Al33178 [last accessed August 22, 2019].

71 *International Covenant on Civil and Political Rights*, December 16, 1996, *available   at*   https://www.ohchr.org/en/professionalinterest/pages/ccpr.aspx [last accessed August 22, 2019].

72 *Id.*

73 General Comment 10, Article 19, HUMAN RIGHTS COMMISSION, Nineteenth Session, 1883, *available at* http://hrlibrary.umn.edu/gencomm/hrcom10.htm [last accessed August 22, 2019].

74 *Id.*

75 *International Covenant, supra* note 63.

76 M.A. v. Italy, Communication No. 117/1981 (September 21, 1981), U.N. Doc. Supp. No. (A/39/40) at 190 P 13.3 (1984).

77 Malcom Ross v. Canada, Communication No. 736/1997, U.N. Doc. CCPR/C/70/D/736/1997 P 11.5 (October 18, 2000).

78 Robert Faurisson v. France, Communication No. 550/1993, U.N. Doc. CCPR/C/58/D/550/1993 P 9.6 (November 8, 1996).

79 *General Comment No. 34*, HUMAN RIGHTS COMMITTEE, September 12, 2011, *available at* https://www2.ohchr.org/english/bodies/hrc/docs/gc34.pdf [last accessed August 22, 2019].

80 *Id.*

81 European Court of Human Rights, *Hate Speech: Fact Sheet*, March 2019, *available at* https://echr.coe.int/Documents/FS_Hate_speech_ENG.pdf [last visited August 8, 2019].

82 *ECRI General Policy Recommendation No. 15 on Hate Speech*, December 8, 2015, *available at* https://rm.coe.int/ecri-general-policy-recommendation-no-15-on-combating-hate-speech/16808b5b01 [last accessed August 22, 2019].

83 *Id.* at 3.

84 *Id.*

85 *Id.* at 5–10.

86 Convention on Cybercrime (2001) Budapest, 23 XI 2001, *available at* http://www.coe.int/en/web/conventions/full-list/-/conventions/treaty/185 [last accessed August 23, 2016].

87 Council of Europe, Chart of signatures and ratifications of Treaty 185, *available at* https://www.coe.int/en/web/conventions/full-list/-/conventions/treaty/185/signatures [last accessed August 26, 2016].

88 Council of Europe, Convention on Cybercrime, November 23, 2001, *available at* http://www.refworld.org/docid/47fdfb202.html [last accessed August 24, 2016].

89 *Id.* For an extended discussion, *see* Jessica S. Henry, *Beyond Free Speech: Novel Approaches to Hate on the Internet in the United States*, 18 INFO. & COMM. TECH. L. 235, 240 (2009).

90 Harris, et al., *supra* note 11, at 169.

91 For details about these cases, *see* Yahoo!, Inc. v. La Ligue Contre Le Racisme et L'Antisemitisme, 169 F.Supp.2d 1181, 1194 (N.D.Cal.2001) and Yahoo! Inc. v. La Ligue Contre Le Racisme et l'antisemitisme (LICRA), 433 F.3d 1199 (9th Cir. 2006).

92 Angelique Chrisafis, *France Launches Major Anti-racism and Hate Speech Campaign*, THE GUARDIAN, Friday, April 17, 2015, *available at* https://www.theguardian.com/world/2015/apr/17/france-launches-major-anti-racism-and-hate-speech-campaign [last accessed July 4, 2016].

93 Timothy J. Seppala, *French Law Would Make Google, Facebook Accomplices to Hate Speech*, ENGADGET, January 28, 2015, *available at* https://www.engadget.com/2015/01/28/french-law-would-make-google-and-facebook-accomplices-to-hate/ [last accessed July 4, 2016].

94 For a more in-depth discussion of the Zundel case, see Raphael Cohen-Almagor, *Freedom of Expression v. Social Responsibility: Holocaust Denial in Canada*, 28 J. MASS MEDIA ETHICS 42 (2013); Robert M. O'Neil, *Hate Speech, Fighting Words, and Beyond – Why American Law is Unique*, 76 ALB. L. REV. 467, at 203–208 (2012/2013); Henry, *supra* note 89, at 240–241 (2009); and Krotoszynski, *supra* note 40, at 64–66.

95 In 2005, Canada deported Zundel back to Germany where he was tried, convicted and sentenced to serve the maximum five-year imprisonment under the law restricting the dissemination of Holocaust denial materials.

96 Henry, *supra* note 89.

97 For further explanation of "double criminality," *see Double Criminality Law and Legal Definition*, USLegal.com, *available at* https://definitions. uslegal.com/d/double-criminality/ [last accessed August 22, 2019].

98 *'Farmbelt Fuhrer' is Deported After Serving Four-year Sentence*, JEWISH TELEGRAPHIC AGENCY, March 24, 1999, *available at* https://www.jta. org/1999/03/24/archive/farmbelt-fuhrer-is-deported-after-serving-four-year-sentence-2 [last accessed August 22, 2019].

99 Jeff Rosen, *Who Decides? Civility v. Hate Speech on the Internet*, 13 IN-SIGHTS ON L. & SOC'T MAG. (2013) *available at* http://www.americanbar. org/publications/insights_on_law_andsociety/13/winter_2013/who_ decides_civilityvhatespeechontheinternet.html [last accessed August 26, 2016].

100 Claire Cain Miller, *As Violence Spreads in Arab World, Google Blocks Access to Inflammatory Video*, NEW YORK TIMES, September 13, 2012, *available at* http://www.nytimes.com/2012/09/14/technology/google-blocks-inflammatory-video-in-egypt-and-libya.html?_r=0 [last accessed August 26, 2016]. Google was not the only company dealing with internet hate speech. For additional discussions, *see*, O'Neil, *supra* note 94, at 469. He wrote

> A few weeks later, Twitter was reported to have blocked German Twitter users from accessing an account of the activities of a neo-Nazi group that is banned in Germany. The following day, however, a French Jewish group reported that Twitter had removed the anti-Semitic postings and had reopened access even to German users.

101 Rosen, *supra* note 99.

102 Dave Gershgorn, *Mark Zuckerberg Just gave a Timeline for AI to take Over Detecting Internet Hate Speech*, QUARTZ, April 10, 2018, *available at* https://qz.com/1249273/facebook-ceo-mark-zuckerberg-says-ai-will-detect-hate-speech-in-5-10-years/ [last accessed August 22, 2019]. Zuckerberg said,

> Hate speech—I am optimistic that over a five-to-10-year period we will have AI tools that can get into some of the linguistic nuances of different types of content to be more accurate, to be flagging things to our systems, but today we're just not there on that. Until we get it automated, there's a higher error rate than I'm happy with.

103 *See*, Sapna Maheshwari and Mike Isaac, *Facebook Vows More Human Oversight of Ad Targeting*, NEW YORK TIMES, September 20, 2017, *available at* https://www.nytimes.com/2017/09/20/business/media/facebook-racist-ads.html [last accessed August 22, 2019] and Mike Isaac and Scott Shane, *Facebook's Russia-linked Ads Came in Many Disguises*, October 2, 2017, NEW YORK TIMES, *available at* https://www.nytimes. com/2017/10/02/technology/facebook-russia-ads-.html [last accessed August 22, 2019].

104 Thomas Escritt, *Germany Fines Facebook for Under-Reporting Complaints*, REUTERS, July 2, 2019 *available at* https://www.reuters.com/ article/us-facebook-germany-fine/germany-fines-facebook-for-under-reporting-complaints-idUSKCN1TX1IC [last accessed August 22, 2019].

3   Favoring Free Speech
The U.S. Response

In comparison to the international community, the United States is significantly more lenient regarding hate speech. In the United States, hate speech traditionally has been protected by the First Amendment. As Kent Greenawalt explains in "Fighting Words: Individuals, Communities and Liberties of Speech," hate speech finds protection in the First Amendment because of a basic premise in free speech doctrine to not restrict speech based on the message or content:

> The fundamental idea is that some messages should not be favored over others. Certain differences in content are a permissible basis of distinction; a message directly urging someone to commit a crime may be treated differently from a message urging someone to obey the law. But, in general, differences in viewpoint are not a permissible basis for distinction.[1]

In the global arena, this stance on hate speech is even more problematic, causing the United States often to be at odds with international laws. By looking at current U.S. rulings pertaining to hate speech and the United States' lack of commitment to international Internet laws, it is easy to see that there is "a fundamental and inescapable difference between the legal treatment afforded racist and xenophobic speech under the First Amendment and U.N., E.U. and German law."[2]

As I elaborate on in this chapter, hate speech has a long history of contentious court rulings in the United States and has generated much debate about whether it should be protected by the First Amendment in all circumstances, some circumstances, or not at all. This debate takes on urgency as we become globally connected through technology and as we see an increasingly virulent and divisive political landscape emerging in the United States. In this chapter, I explore the history of the legal treatment of hate speech restrictions through U.S. Supreme Court rulings. Following that review, I highlight and discuss the implications of the key legal doctrines that the Court has relied upon in those cases.

U.S. Hate Speech: Legal Perspectives

Hate speech continues to be an area with little to no attention paid to it by the Supreme Court. While some cases have tangentially touched on the topic, such as *Terminiello v. Chicago, Brandenburg v. Ohio, Snyder v. Phelps*, and *Walker v. Sons of the Confederate Veterans*, only a few have addressed on the issue directly.[3] Following is a historical review of the cases restricting some form of hate speech. From those cases, I extrapolate the essential doctrines employed and begin to illustrate the limitations of current free speech analysis, especially those limitations concerning social equality in general and with hate speech specifically.

Beauharnais v. Illinois (1952)

In 1952, the U.S. Supreme Court heard its first case pertaining to the constitutionality of restricting speech that targets people based on their race. In this case, Joseph Beauharnais, president of the short-lived White Circle League,[4] was arrested and subsequently found guilty and fined $200 for violating an Illinois law that made it illegal to distribute any publication that "exposes the citizens of any race, color, creed or religion to contempt, derision or obloquy."[5] He had published a leaflet that warned, "If persuasion and the need to prevent the white race from becoming mongrelized by the negro will not unite us, then the aggressions ... rapes, robberies, knives, guns and marijuana of the negro, surely will."[6] The Illinois State Supreme Court upheld his conviction. Beauharnais appealed, claiming that the law violated his First Amendment rights of free speech and press and that it should be void for vagueness.[7] The Court, in a 5-4 plurality opinion, first acknowledged that the Illinois law in question was a "form of criminal libel law."[8] Justice Frankfurter, relying on the language from *Chaplinsky v. New Hampshire*, noted:

> There are certain well-defined and narrowly limited classes of speech the prevention and punishment of which has never been thought to raise any Constitutional problem. These include the lewd and obscene, the profane, the libelous, and the insulting or 'fighting' words – those which, by their very utterance, inflict injury or tend to incite an immediate breach of the peace.[9]

Frankfurter and the plurality found that the language in Beauharnais' leaflets constituted a form of group libel, holding up an entire race to ridicule and abuse.[10]

Although the Court recognized that this law could be enforced abusively through silencing political discourse by "prohibiting libel of a political party," it nevertheless determined that the state should be able to "adopt measures against criminal libels sanctioned by centuries of Anglo-American law."[11] The law was sufficiently narrow and well-defined, such that there were "adequate standards" in place to guide enforcement.[12]

National Socialist Party of America v. Skokie (1977)

Although this case only warranted a short per curium opinion by the U.S. Supreme Court, *National Socialist Party of America v. the Village of Skokie* remains one of the key court rulings in the hate speech debate.[13] In 1977, members of the National Socialist Party of America (NSPA) asked permission to hold a demonstration in Skokie, Illinois, a 70,000 resident community that was nearly two-thirds Jewish. The NSPA has been described as a group "dedicated to the incitation of racial and religious hatred directed principally against individuals of Jewish faith or ancestry and non-Caucasians."[14] The party requested permission from Skokie officials to march in front of the village hall, carrying signs stating "Free Speech for the White Man" and "Free Speech for White America."[15] Because of the high population of Jewish people, village leaders enjoined the demonstration, an action that eventually resulted in a split Supreme Court decision and a lifting of the injunction. The circuit court issued the original order enjoining the party from "marching, walking or parading in the uniform of National Socialist Party of America," displaying the swastika, or distributing pamphlets promoting hatred against Jewish people.[16] The appellate court modified the order, allowing the group to demonstrate but not display the swastika during the demonstration.[17] The question before the State Supreme Court, then, was whether the appellate court order concerning the swastika was a violation of the party's First Amendment rights.[18]

The court first established that "public expression of ideas may not be prohibited merely because the ideas are themselves offensive to some of their hearers."[19] The listener's feelings cannot be considered as valid reasons for prohibiting speech, but the court also noted that there are certain categories of speech – obscenity, defamation, fighting words, for example – which can be restricted because of the content of the speech. In these cases, the government still maintains "the heavy burden of justifying the imposition of a prior restraint upon the defendant's right of freedom of speech."[20] To decide the case, the court looked at the category of fighting words to see if the restraint on speech could be considered constitutional:

> The display of the swastika, as offensive to the principles of a free nation as the memories it recalls may be, is symbolic political speech intended to convey to the public the beliefs of those who display it. It does not, in our opinion, fall within the definition of 'fighting words,' and that doctrine cannot be used here to overcome the heavy presumption against the constitutional validity of a prior restraint.[21]

The court concluded that the government could not choose what was acceptable public discourse based merely on the fact that certain symbols cause anger or resentment on the part of the listener. The swastika could not be considered fighting words, nor could the audience's reaction be a justifiable reason for restricting speech.[22]

R.A.V. v. St. Paul (1992)

The question of using the fighting words doctrine to support hate speech regulation would be revisited in 1992 in what would be the first of two highly significant cases related to hate speech. The case, *R.A.V. v. St. Paul*, focused on an incident in which several teenagers taped broken chair parts together to form a crudely made cross and proceeded to burn the cross inside the fenced yard of a black family.[23] The teenagers were subsequently charged under the St. Paul, Minn., Bias Motivated Crime Ordinance. This ordinance prohibited the display of a symbol "which one knows or has reason to know arouses anger, alarm or resentment in others on the basis of race, color, creed, religion or gender."[24]

R.A.V. claimed that the ordinance was overbroad and impermissibly content-based and as such was unconstitutional. The trial court, agreeing with R.A.V., dismissed the charges on the grounds that the ordinance prohibited expressive conduct, which violated the First Amendment. The Minnesota Supreme Court, however, reversed the ruling. Finally, in a ruling that seemed to close the door on any constitutionally acceptable hate speech regulation, the Supreme Court in a 9-to-0 opinion, struck down the St. Paul ordinance, ruling that it was facially unconstitutional because it was content-based, imposing a special prohibition on particular disfavored subjects of race, color, or creed.[25]

Justice Antonin Scalia, writing for the Court, stated: "The dispositive question in this case, therefore, is whether content discrimination is reasonably necessary to achieve St. Paul's compelling interest; it is not."[26] He wrote that, while "burning a cross in someone's front yard is reprehensible," the city had options available to prevent such acts "without adding the First Amendment to the fire."[27] The Court found that the St. Paul ordinance was impermissibly content-based because while it restricted proscribable fighting words, it only restricted a subset of fighting words based solely on the content of the speech. He found that content-based regulations are presumptively invalid under the First Amendment unless the speech being regulated fits into a proscribable category, such as obscenity, fighting words, or defamation.

The Court held that even inside of the proscribable categories established by the Court, there are two reasons why speech might still be protected: (1) if the reason for the speech being restricted is based on content discrimination not related to the proscribable content of the category, and (2) if the speech is being restricted only because of secondary effects.[28] Scalia stated that while the categorical approach is used, the Court does not apply an all-or-nothing approach to speech restriction or protection within categories.[29] Based on this reasoning, the Court asserted that fighting words are not worthless or undeserving of First Amendment protection in every instance. Such speech may sometimes warrant protection because, "[W]e have not said that [fighting words] constitute 'no part of the expression of ideas,' but only that they constitute 'no essential part of any expression of ideas.'"[30] In this sense, the proscribed categories of speech such as fighting words are content-neutral categories because in restricting the speech, neither the specific words themselves nor the ideas they expressed are important. Instead, fighting words, according to the majority, can be restricted based on the mode of expression. Justice Scalia wrote,

> Another valid basis for according differential treatment to even a content-defined subclass of proscribable speech is that the subclass happens to be associated with particular 'secondary effects' of the speech, so that the regulation is 'justified without reference to the content of the...speech.'[31]

He offered, for example, that sexual derogatory fighting words might get incidentally restricted under Title VII's prohibition against sexual discrimination.[32] To further explain this distinction, the majority compared the regulation of fighting words with the regulation of the volume of a noisy sound truck:

> [B]oth can be used to convey an idea; but neither has, in and of itself, a claim upon the First Amendment. As with the sound truck, however, so also with fighting words: The government may not regulate use based on hostility—or favoritism—to the underlying message expressed.[33]

The government may restrict speech based on the time, place, or manner of the speech, but not based on the particular ideas expressed. In the case of the sound truck, the noise element can be restricted, but the government cannot restrict based on the particular messages that the different sounds might convey. According to the Court, prohibition in the category of fighting words follows a similar line of reasoning. Fighting words can be restricted not because of their content, but, instead, based on "essentially a non-speech element of communication."[34]

Looking specifically at the St. Paul ordinance, the Court first found the ordinance to be content-based. The St. Paul ordinance applied only to that speech that caused "alarm, anger or resentment" of people based on their "race, color, creed, religion, or gender." These restrictions only applied to hateful epithets spoken to certain disempowered groups with no explanation as to why those groups should be protected, but not other groups such as gays and lesbians.[35] Justice Scalia wrote:

> Displays containing abusive invective, no matter how vicious or severe, are permissible unless they are addressed to one of the specified disfavored topics. Those who wish to use 'fighting words' in connection with other ideas—to express hostility, for example, on the basis of political affiliation, union membership, or homosexuality—are not covered.[36]

According to the Court, it was this selectivity that made the St. Paul ordinance content-based. It found that because the St. Paul ordinance relied specifically on "messages of racial, gender or religious intolerance," the ordinance directly conflicted with the rationale for the content neutrality principle in First Amendment law. Justice Scalia wrote: "Selectivity of this sort creates the possibility that the city is seeking to handicap the expression of particular ideas."[37] This content discrimination, according to the Court, is not permissible, even in a proscribable class such as fighting words.

The majority concluded that the Minnesota Supreme Court erred in finding that despite possible content discrimination, the discrimination was justified because of compelling state interest in ensuring "the basic human rights of members of groups that historically have been subjected to discrimination."[38] The Court asserted that while the state does have an interest in this area, that interest does not override the "danger of censorship" that this content-based statute brought with it.[39]

Virginia v. Black (2003)

The second significant hate speech case would be decided by the Supreme Court just a little more than a decade after *R.A.V.* In 1998, Barry Black held a Ku Klux Klan rally on his private property, a rally that culminated in the burning of a cross approximately 300–350 yards away from a public road and within the vicinity of eight–10 houses. Black was subsequently charged with violating a Virginia statute that made it unlawful for a person to burn a cross "with the attempt to intimidate any person or group."[40] Also in 1998, Richard Elliot and Jonathan O'Mara were charged under the Virginia cross-burning statute. Elliot and O'Mara burned a cross in their African-American neighbor's yard after the neighbor had complained about loud target practice at the Elliot and O'Mara yard. Black, Elliot, and O'Mara all were found guilty by trial and had their convictions upheld by the Court of Appeals of Virginia. Each respondent appealed to the Supreme Court of Virginia, arguing the statute was facially unconstitutional. The State Supreme Court combined the cases and overturned the lower courts' rulings, finding that the statute was "analytically indistinguishable from the ordinance found unconstitutional in *R.A.V.*"[41] The court found the statute to be content-based because it singled out cross burnings and overbroad because the prima facie provision enhanced the possibility of conviction and ultimately chill free expression. The U.S. Supreme Court granted certiorari in the case, and in an extremely divided ruling in 2003, affirmed in part and remanded in part.

Justice Sandra Day O'Connor wrote the plurality opinion in which it was found that Virginia could prohibit cross burning without violating the First Amendment. To establish this point, Justice O'Connor first described why cross burnings constitute true threats, distinguishing the Virginia statute from the one struck down in *R.A.V.* Relying on *Watts v. United States*,[42] the Court defined true threats as "those statements where the speaker means to communicate a serious expression of an intent to commit an act of unlawful violence to a particular individual or group of individuals."[43] In addition, the plurality noted that the speaker need not intend to commit the violence but that the individuals being targeted feel fear of violence.[44] Justice O'Connor wrote a lengthy history of the role of cross burning in the United States to establish that

> while a burning cross does not inevitably convey a message of intimidation, often the cross burner intends that the recipients of the message fear for their lives. And when a cross burning is used to intimidate, few if any messages are more powerful.[45]

As a result, the state can restrict cross burnings that are used for intimidation, but cross burnings do not automatically constitute intimidation. While cross burning can be used to intimidate, it also can be used "as potent symbols of shared group identity and ideology."[46] The plurality concluded that the cross burned by Black and other KKK members was for ideological reasons, and so overturned his conviction. In respect to Elliot and O'Mara, the judgment was vacated and the case remanded for consideration minus the *prima facie* clause.[47]

In the plurality opinion, Justice O'Connor also distinguished *Black* from *R.A.V,* explaining that in *R.A.V.*, the Court found the Minnesota statute unconstitutional because it allowed the city to "impose special prohibitions on those speakers who express views on disfavored subjects."[48] However, this ruling did not mean "the First Amendment prohibits all forms of content-based discrimination within a proscribable area of speech."[49] Justice O'Connor outlined several areas from *R.A.V.*, such as threats against the president, that the Court noted could be constitutionally restricted true threats. Also, while the statute in *R.A.V.* focused on specified targets of the hate speech, the statute in *Black* focused instead on a specific subset of intimidating messages.[50]

Matal v. Tam (2017)

Although not directly a hate speech case, *Matal v. Tam* dealt with the issue of disparaging speech. While there is a difference between hate speech and merely offensive speech, this 2017 ruling strongly reinforced the Court's application of the viewpoint neutrality principle.[51] In an 8-0 opinion, the Court found the Disparagement Clause in the Lanham Act of 1946 to be invalid under the First Amendment because it was viewpoint-based and not narrowly tailored to serve a substantial state interest.[52] The clause prohibited trademarks containing matter that may "'disparage...or bring...into contempt or disrepute' any 'persons, living or dead.'"[53] Justice Samuel Alito began the opinion with a succinct statement concerning the act: "It offends a bedrock First Amendment principle: Speech may not be banned on the ground that it expresses ideas that offend."[54] Directly addressing the viewpoint question, the Court found the clause to be a violation of that principle despite the fact that the clause would apply to disparagement against members of any group. The Court explained:

> It denies registration to any mark that is offensive to a substantial percentage of the members of any group. But in the sense relevant here, that is the viewpoint discrimination: Giving offense is a viewpoint. We have said time and again that "public expression of ideas may not be prohibited merely because the ideas are themselves offensive to some of their hearers."[55]

In a concurring opinion, Justice Anthony Kennedy, joined by Justices Ruth Bader Ginsburg, Sonia Sotomayor, and Elena Kagan, also addressed the viewpoint neutrality position finding that the clause "reflects the Government's disapproval of a subset of messages it finds offensive" and that this is "the essence of viewpoint discrimination."[56] He wrote that, "[b]y mandating positivity, the law here might silence dissent and distort the marketplace of ideas."[57] Finally, in terms of viewpoint neutrality, Justice Kennedy expressed concern about the dangers of government intervention in that marketplace. He noted:

> The danger of viewpoint discrimination is that the government is attempting to remove certain ideas or perspectives from a broader debate. That danger is all the greater if the ideas or perspectives are ones a particular audience might think offensive, at least at first hearing. An initial reaction may prompt further reflection, leading to a more reasoned, more tolerant position.[58]

Both Justice Alito's opinion and Justice Kennedy's concurrence reinforce the deep-seated commitment by the Court to uphold viewpoint neutrality in First Amendment cases.

Key Legal Doctrines

A pattern emerges in Supreme Court hate speech related cases that illustrates the historical movement from the successful application of the fighting words doctrine to a reliance on reasoning grounded almost exclusively in content neutrality and true threats doctrine. This review shines a spotlight on the larger pattern, enabling me to show the flaws in the usefulness of these doctrines to combat social inequities. Following is a breakdown of those key doctrines.

Fighting Words

Early on, the category of fighting words seemed to hold some promise as a vehicle for the restriction of hate speech. The doctrine, first introduced in *Chaplinsky v. New Hampshire*, gained traction in *Beauharnais* when the Court used it to uphold a law explicitly designed to deal with hate speech. Forty years later, the Court would move away from its initial application of the fighting words doctrine. In *R.A.V. v. St. Paul*, the Court reviewed an ordinance whose language closely mirrored the language in the ordinance ruled on in *Beauharnais*.[59] Despite the similarities in language, the Court unanimously found the ordinance to be unconstitutional, and went so far as to construct an argument making it impossible to constitutionally use the fighting words doctrine to support hate speech restrictions. As a result, *R.A.V.* did not actually close the door on hate speech restrictions, but it did close the door on the use of fighting words doctrine as a vehicle to justify those types of restrictions. It was also this case that introduced the reliance on the concept of content neutrality as a driving factor in assessing hate speech laws.

Content Neutrality

While the application of content neutrality in hate speech cases can be tied to *R.A.V.*, the concept of content neutrality is pervasive across First Amendment jurisprudence. The focus on content neutral restrictions in First Amendment jurisprudence can be traced to the 1930s[60] and can be defined in this way:

> Content-neutral restrictions limit communication without regard to the message conveyed. Laws that prohibit noisy speeches near a hospital, ban billboards in residential communities, impose license fees for parades and demonstrations, or forbid the distribution of leaflets in public places are examples of content-neutral restrictions. Content-based restrictions, on the other hand, limit communication because of the message conveyed. Laws that prohibit seditious libel, ban the publication of confidential information, forbid the hiring of

teachers who advocate the violent overthrow of government, or out-
law the display of the swastika in certain neighborhoods illustrate
this type of restriction.[61]

While the intent behind the concept is laudable, its application is often
less than praiseworthy. The intent is to ensure that the government does
not unnecessarily restrict speech based on its favoritism or dislike of
the message being expressed. In other words, content neutrality is intended to protect the most amount of speech in an effort to ensure that
all views, particularly unpopular ones, will be protected. In terms of
hate speech restrictions, the content neutrality principle offers a broad
umbrella that sweeps under it most hate speech restrictions. With the
exception of the cross-burning ordinance in *Virginia v. Black*, the Court
has consistently found any hate speech restrictions to be content-based
and, as such, unconstitutional. The application of this principle is problematic for multiple reasons, including a lack of consensus by the Court
about what it means to be content neutral, but also, as an analytical tool
it is one-dimensional.

   R.A.V. serves as a perfect illustration of the inherent problem in relying on content neutrality as the defining legal tool in First Amendment
analysis. Writing for the majority, Justice Scalia contended that while
the Court has sometimes found that certain categories of expression are
outside the protection of the First Amendment, it did not mean this lit-
erally.[62] For example, while the government may restrict libel, it cannot
make an additional content distinction within that subset of speech and
also restrict only libel critical of the government.[63] In his concurrence,
Justice Byron White agreed with the majority that the St. Paul ordinance
was facially overbroad. However, he found the majority's application of
content neutrality to proscribable categories of speech to be a radical
departure from precedent and concluded that the approach was "trans-
parently wrong."[64] Justice White wrote:

> [T]his Court has long held certain discrete categories of expression
> to be proscribable on the basis of their content...Today, however, the
> Court announces that earlier Courts did not mean their repeated
> statements that certain categories of expression are "not within the
> area of constitutionally protected speech."[65]

In these categories, decisions are based on content, but the speech is
proscribable because "the evil to be restricted so overwhelmingly out-
weighs the expressive interest."[66] Justice White explained that the majority's logic concerning a subset of protected speech in those categories
was contradictory. The contradiction is that if a proscribable category
is created because "the content of the speech is evil" then a subset of
that evil speech would be "by definition worthless and undeserving

of constitutional protection."[67] To Justice White, there is no question that content restrictions are permissible in the case of non-proscribable speech.[68]

Justice White then endorsed a reliance on content neutrality but disagreed with the way the majority interpreted its application. He further endorsed the concept of content neutrality by explaining that this content-based approach in First Amendment decision-making has "provided a principled and narrowly focused means for distinguishing between expression that the government may regulate freely and that which may regulate on the basis of content only upon a showing of compelling need."[69] White's critique, one could argue, serves as support that indeed this principle is not narrowly focused and does not aid the government (or the courts) in determining boundaries for the regulation of speech. He accused the majority of creating a "simplistic, all-or-nothing approach" that conflates protection of viewpoint with protection of content. However, perhaps it is the current all-or-nothing reliance on the concept of content neutrality that is one-dimensional and thus problematic.[70]

This confusion as to the best way to apply content neutrality also was addressed by Justices Harry Blackmun and John Paul Stevens. In his concurring opinion, Justice Blackmun raised concerns that the Court's interpretation of content neutrality application in *R.A.V.* would weaken the long-standing categorical approach, specifically taking issue with Justice Scalia's discussion of fighting words and content-neutral categories.[71] Justice Stevens offered the most nuanced discussion concerning how to interpret and apply content neutrality. Despite dicta in certain cases to the contrary, he wrote, content-based distinctions are "far from being presumptively invalid" and "are an inevitable and indispensable aspect of a coherent understanding of the First Amendment."[72] He wrote that, in fact, "[O]ur entire First Amendment jurisprudence creates a regime based on the content of speech."[73] He offered, as an example, that merely deciding what speech falls into a proscribable or a non-proscribable category must be determined by its content. For Justice Stevens, the content must be judged to some degree on the situation in which it is being used. In the case of hate speech, he finds that specific circumstances may lead to the need for special rules.[74] In other words, sometimes it is the content distinction itself that should drive and support the speech regulation. He called for "a more subtle and complex analysis" that could include both content- and viewpoint-based restrictions, so long as the state meets the strict standard of scrutiny.[75]

Reliance on the content neutrality principle would continue in future hate speech-related cases, including *Virginia v. Black*. In *Black*, however, the Court sidestepped some of the inherent problems with the application of content neutrality by also focusing on the true threats doctrine. Use of this doctrine, of course, brought with it a new host of difficulties, particularly concerning how the courts might deal with regulating so-called "threatening" speech online. The Court's recent ruling in *Matal v. Tam* illustrates how entrenched the concept of content neutrality is in First Amendment analysis.

True Threats

One of the more recent hate speech cases decided by the U.S. Supreme Court, *Virginia v. Black*, illustrates where we are today in terms of the First Amendment and hate speech regulation. *Black* added a new area of free speech doctrine into the mix. With fighting words doctrine no longer an option and content neutrality an unsatisfactory one, the Court instead relied on true threats to determine the constitutionality of the Virginia statute restricting cross burning. Of the various doctrines invoked in hate speech cases, true threats doctrine works to some degree better than the others. However, it still falls short because (1) it does not directly address the hate speech problem – the doctrine is based on content neutrality, (2) it is still subjective and confusing in its application, and (3) because true threats have often been interpreted by the Court to be imminent, then it will have little to no application on Internet speech where the speaker of the threat is likely not in the same physical locality as the person being threatened.

The true threats doctrine has origins in a case that dealt neither with hate speech nor with the Internet. In *Watts v. United States*, the Supreme Court ruled on a case in which an 18-year-old was convicted of violating a 1917 statute after he made allegedly threatening comments toward the president at an anti-war rally.[76] The Court struck a balance between the language in the statute and

> the background of a profound national commitment to the principle that debate on public issues should be uninhibited, robust, and wide-open, and that it may well include vehement, caustic, and sometimes unpleasantly sharp attacks on the government and public officials.[77]

It concluded that Robert Watts' comments did not constitute a true threat; they were merely a "very crude offensive method of stating a political opposition to the President."[78] In other words, while the true threats standard articulated in *Watts* offered a more contemporary and complex approach than its clear and present danger predecessor, the new standard still raised concerns predominantly because of its lack of precise direction.

The *Watts* case clarified that political hyperbole could not be considered a true threat and left further definition to later courts. In *Virginia v. Black*, the Court augmented the definition of true threats.[79] Justice O'Connor, writing for the majority, found that true threats

> encompass those statements where the speaker means to communi-
> cate a serious expression of an intent to commit an act of unlawful

violence to a particular individual or group of individuals. The speaker need not actually intend to carry out the threat.[80]

Despite this additional language in *Black*, true threats doctrine still does not offer sufficient guidance in determining the possible constitutionality of broader hate speech legislation.

First, the application in *Black* was narrowly focused on one type of hate speech – cross burnings – with the majority opinion relying on an extensive history of that one type of speech as justification for restriction. Second, despite the language stating that the speaker "need not actually intend to carry out the threat,"[81] subsequent courts have focused on proximity as a key element in determining the level of threat, making it difficult to imagine application of the true threats standard in the realm of the Internet. The lower courts have added to this confusion.[82] Specifically, lower courts have struggled between determining whether or not an objective standard or a subjective standard should steer their rulings. Simply put, should the proof of threat be based on whether the speaker intended to carry out the threat or whether a reasonable person when hearing the statements would find them threatening?[83]

Most recently, in *Elonis v. United States*, the Supreme Court missed an opportunity to weigh in on the true threats standard. In an 8-to-1 opinion, the Court overturned the appellate court ruling, finding that the lower court had applied the wrong standard when determining whether or not the comments posted by Anthony Elonis qualified as legally proscribable threats. The Third Circuit Court of Appeals applied a reasonable person standard, a standard that focuses on whether or not a reasonable person reading those posts would find them threatening.[84] The Supreme Court, however, discounted that reasoning, instead relying on a question of whether or not Elonis intended the comments as actual threats.[85] As a result of this line of reasoning, the majority did not address the true threats standard developed in First Amendment jurisprudence.

The explication here of the legal doctrines relied on in past hate speech-related cases serves as a necessary starting point to illustrate the lack of consistency in application in current case analysis. From that review, one thing becomes glaringly apparent: Whether one favors hate speech restrictions or opposes them, the Court's decisions to date raise more questions than offer answers, and none of the reasoning applied so far is adequate to deal with Internet hate speech. This review also illustrates the Court's unwavering reliance on content and viewpoint neutrality as guiding principles in First Amendment analysis.

Conclusion

The U.S. Supreme Court has been struggling with the issue of hate speech restriction since the 1950s, when it first ruled in *Beauharnais* that the text in the leaflet in question constituted group libel because it upheld an entire race to ridicule. That case, while seeming to start the United States on a course similar to the one taken in the international community, turned out instead to be more an anomaly than a foundation. Subsequent rulings would hold that only in the case of viewpoint-neutral true threats could we restrict hate speech in any way at all. This chapter reviewed those key cases in the development of the U.S. legal approach to hate speech restriction. This chapter also drew attention to the spectrum of First Amendment doctrine used in deciding those cases, illustrating a trajectory that started with application of fighting words doctrine and ended where we are today with reliance on the doctrines of content neutrality and true threats.

In the next chapter, Chapter 4, I examine the philosophical underpinnings of traditional legal approaches to speech protection in general and in relation to hate speech more specifically and examine the counterpositions that scholars in the Unite States began asserting in the late 1980s. In Chapter 5, I introduce a new framework for analysis that calls for a shift in how we think about speech protection and ultimately leads to a new legal approach.

Notes

1 Kent Greenawalt, FIGHTING WORDS: INDIVIDUALS, COMMUNITIES, AND LIBERTIES OF SPEECH 16 (1995).
2 Eric t. Eberwine, *Sound and the Fury Signifying Nothing? Juren Bussow's Battle Against Hate Speech on the internet*, 49 N.Y. L. SCH. L. REV. 353, 375 (2004/2005).
3 *See*, Terminiello v. Chicago, 337 U.S. 1 (1949) (held that speech designed to stir up anger and provoke disputes is protected by the First Amendment); Brandenburg v. Ohio, 395 U.S. 444 (1969) (speech can be prohibited if it is "directed at inciting or producing imminent lawless action" and it is "likely to incite or produce such action."); Snyder v. Phelps, 562 U.S. 443 (2011) (the First Amendment shields those who stage protests at the funeral of a military service member from liability); and Walker v. Sons of the Confederate Veterans, 135 S. Ct. 2239 (2015) (state license plates constitute government speech and so messages on them can be restricted).
4 The White Circle League of America was founded in 1949 Illinois with a goal "to keep white neighborhoods free from negros." The group's charter was revoked by a circuit court in 1950 and the group became inactive in 1952.
5 343 U.S. 250 (1952).
6 *Id.* at 252.
7 *Id.* at 251.
8 *Id.* at 253.
9 *Id.* at 255–256 (quoting Chaplinsky v. New Hampshire, 315 U.S. 568, at 572 (1942)).
10 *Id.* at 257–258. "No one will gainsay that it is libelous falsity to charge another with being a rapist, robber, carrier of knives and guns and user of marijuana."
11 *Id.* at 264.
12 *Id.*

13 National Socialist Party of America v. Village of Skokie, 432 U.S. 43 (1977) and Village of Skokie v. National Socialist Party of America, 373 N.E.2d 21 (Ill. 1978).

14 373 N.E.2d 21, 22 (Ill. 1978).

15 *Id.*

16 *Id.*

17 *Id.*

18 *Id.* at 23.

19 *Id.* at 21.

20 *Id.* at 23.

21 *Id.* at 24.

22 *Id.* at 26.

23 R.A.V. v. City of St. Paul, Minnesota, 505 U.S. 377 (1992).

24 *Id.*

25 *Id.*

26 *Id.* at 395.

27 *Id.* at 396.

28 *Id.* at 389.

29 *Id.* at 383–384:

> We have sometimes said that these categories of expression are "not within the area of constitutionally protected speech" or that "the protection of the First Amendment does not extend" to them. Such statements must be taken in context, however, and are no more literally true than is the occasionally repeated shorthand characterizing obscenity "as not being speech at all." What they mean is that these areas of speech can, consistently with the First Amendment, be regulated because of their constitutionally proscribable content (obscenity, defamation, etc.) – not that they are categories of speech entirely invisible to the Constitution, so that they may be made vehicles for content discrimination unrelated to their distinctly proscribable content.

30 *Id.* (quoting Chaplinsky v. New Hampshire, 315 U.S. 568, at 572 (1942)).

31 *Id.* at 389.

32 *Id.*

33 *Id.* at 386.

34 *Id.* at 388.

35 *Id.* at 391. Scalia explained:

> Although the phrase in the ordinance, "arouses anger, alarm or resentment in others," has been limited by the Minnesota Supreme Court's construction to reach only those symbols or displays that amount to "fighting words," the remaining, unmodified terms make clear that the ordinance applies only to "fighting words" that insult, or provoke violence, "on the basis of race, color, creed, religion or gender." Displays containing abusive invective, no matter how vicious or severe, are permissible unless they are addressed to one of the specified disfavored topics.

36 *Id.*

37 *Id.* at 394.

38 *Id.* at 395.

39 *Id.*

40 Virginia v. Black, 583 U.S. 343, 344 (2003).

41 *Id.* at 351.

42 349 U.S. 705 (1969).

43 *Id.* at 359.

44 *Id.* at 360 (Justice O'Connor explained: "Intimidation in the constitutionally proscribable sense of the word is a type of true threat, where a speaker directs a threat to a person or group of persons with the intent of placing the victim in fear of bodily harm or death.").

45 *Id.* at 357.

46 *Id.* at 356.

47 *Id.* at 563–567 (Justice O'Connor offers an in-depth review of the prima facie clause in the statute).

48 *Id.* at 360.

49 *Id.*

50 *Id.* at 362.

51 137 S. Ct. 1744 (2017).

52 *Id.* Justice Neil Gorsuch did not join the Court in time to participate.

53 *Id.* at 1751.

54 *Id.*

55 *Id.* at 1763.

56 *Id.* at 1766 (Kennedy, J., concurring).

57 *Id.* (Kennedy, J., concurring).

58 *Id.* at 1767 (Kennedy, J., concurring).

59 The ordinance in *Beauharnais* made it a crime to exhibit in any public place any publication which "portrays depravity, criminality, unchastity, or lack of virtue of a class of citizens, of any race, color, creed or religion" which "exposes the citizens of any race, color, creed or religion to contempt, derision, or obloquy." 343 U.S. 250, 251 (1952). The ordinance in question in *R.A.V.* made it a crime to display any material that "arouses anger, alarm or resentment in others on the basis of race, color, creed, religion or gender." 505 U.S. 377, 380 (1992).

60 While the Supreme Court would not specifically identify content neutrality until Police Department of Chicago v. Mosley, 408 U.S. 92 (1971), its development can be traced to the Court's reasoning in public forum cases such as the 1939 case Schneider v. New Jersey, 308 U.S. 147.

61 Geoffrey R. Stone, *Content Regulation and the First Amendment*, 25 Wm. & Mary L. Rev. 189 (1983).

62 R.A.V. v. St. Paul, 505 U.S. 377, 383 (1992). For critiques of Justice Scalia's read of proscribable and non-proscribable speech in *R.A.V., see* Michael S. Degan, *Adding the First Amendment to the Fire: Cross Burning and Hate Crime Laws*, 26 Creighton L. Rev. 1109 (1993); Jonathan Holdowsky, *Out of the Ashes of the Cross: The Legacy of R.A.V. v. St. Paul*, 30 New England L. Rev. 1115 (1996); and Jerome O'Callaghan, *Free Speech by the Light of a Burning Cross*, 42 Clev. St. L. Rev. 215 (1994).

63 *Id.* at 384.

64 *Id.* at 377 (White, J., concurring).

65 *Id.* at 400 (quoting Roth v. United States, 354 U.S. 476, 485 (1957)) (White, J. concurring).

66 *Id.* (White, J., concurring).

67 *Id.* at 401 (White, J., concurring).

68 *Id.* at 400 (White, J., concurring).

69 *Id.* (White, J., concurring).

70 I am not suggesting that the concept of content neutrality should be abandoned in First Amendment analysis, but instead that it should not be the only element considered.

71 *Id.* at 415 (Blackmun, J., concurring). ("If all expressive activity must be accorded the same protection, that protection will be scant...If we are forbidden to categorize, as the Court has done here, we shall reduce protection across the board.").

72 *Id.* at 419 (Stevens, J. concurring).

73 *Id.* (Stevens, J., concurring).

74 *Id.* at 416

> Lighting a fire near an ammunition dump or a gasoline storage tank is especially dangerous; such behavior may be punished more severely than burning trash in a vacant lot. Threatening someone because of her race or religious beliefs may cause particularly severe trauma or touch off a riot...such threats may be punished more severely than threats against someone based on, say, his support of a particular athletic team. There are legitimate, reasonable, and neutral justifications for such special rules.

75 *Id.* at 428–431 (Stevens, J., concurring).

76 Watts v. United States, 394 U.S. 705 (1969).

77 *Id.* at 708 (quoting New York Times v. Sullivan, 376 U.S. 254, 270 (1964)).

78 *Id.*

79 538 U.S. 343, at 359 (2003).

80 *Id.*

81 *Id.* at 360.

82 For a more detailed discussion of the fallout of the *Virginia v. Black* decision, *see* Jennifer Elrod, *Expressive Activity, True Threats and the First Amendment*, 36 CONN. L. REV. 541, 561 (2003/2004) (explaining that development of relevant test factors has been the role of the lower federal courts).

83 For examples of this doctrinal confusion, *see* United States v. Elonis, 730 F.3d 321, 329 (3rd Cir. 2013) ("[W]e read 'statements where the speaker means to communicate a serious expression of an intent to commit an act of unlawful violence' to mean that the speaker must intend to make the communication. It would require adding language the Court [in *Virginia v. Black*] did not write to read the passage as 'statements where the speaker means to communicate [and intends the statement to be understood as] a serious expression of an intent to commit an act of unlawful violence....'); United States v. Cassel, 408 F.3d 622 (9th Cir. 2005) (determining that "speech may be deemed unprotected by the First Amendment as a 'true threat' only upon proof that the speaker subjectively intended the speech as a threat"); Porter v. Ascension Parish School Board, 393 F.3d 608, 616 (5th Cir. 2004) (stating that the protected status of threatening speech is not determined by whether the speaker had the subjective intent to carry out the threat; rather, to lose the protection of the First Amendment and be lawfully punished, the threat must be intentionally or knowingly communicated to either the object of the threat or a third person.); Planned Parenthood of Columbia/Willamette Inc. v. American coalition of Life Activists, 290 F.3d at 1058, at 1088 (9th Cir. 2002) (en banc) (defining true threats as statements made when a "reasonable person would foresee that the statement would be interpreted by those to whom the maker communicates the statement as a serious expression of intent to harm").

84 730 F.3d 321, 329–330 (3rd Cir. 2013).

85 Elonis v. United States, 135 S. Ct. 2001, 2012 (2015).

> In light of the foregoing, Elonis' conviction cannot stand. The jury was instructed that the Government need prove only that a reasonable person would regard Elonis' communications as threats, and that was error. Federal criminal liability generally does not turn solely on the results of an act without considering the defendant's mental state. That understanding 'took deep and early root in American soil' and Congress left it intact here: Under Section 875(c), wrongdoing must be conscious to be criminal.

4 First Amendment Theories
Arguments and Counter Arguments

The U.S. approach to free speech protection is significantly different than those of the international community or other countries, particularly regarding hate speech. Often these differences are attributed to the existence of the First Amendment. American scholars, jurists, and commentators proudly boast of the First Amendment as proof positive that the United States is the only country to truly protect speech. However, those declarations are seldom followed by any discussion whatsoever of other countries' legal approaches or, if there is some mention, it is often skewed with a focus on those countries that are most restrictive, or on moments where countries' commitments to free speech have failed. As I have already established in Chapter 2, this is not the case. The majority of countries do have some level of commitment to free speech, with several of them approaching the same level as the United States. The difference between the United States and other countries is not so much a variation on the ideal of free speech, but a difference on how to balance the commitment to protect speech against other human rights and liberties. It's not the mere existence of the First Amendment that matters, it is the interpretation of the role of speech in society that is the major distinguishing characteristic.

Understanding the philosophical foundation underpinning free speech protection can help explain why the United States seems to be out of step with the rest of the world, and also illuminate the difficulties in shifting the U.S. position to be more in line with the international community. In Chapter 5, I develop an argument for how the United States might be able to constitutionally consider an approach to hate speech restriction that incorporates some of the focus on human dignity and equality practiced by the international community, while still adhering to its foundational commitments to liberty and freedom. Before entertaining some options that might offer a more modern and coherent legal approach, it is first important to situate the previous court rulings within the theoretical debates surrounding the role of free speech in society.

In this chapter, I first review the normative, traditional conception of free speech in general, focusing specifically on key First Amendment scholars. On the whole, their perspectives underscore the Court's rationale for free speech protection. From that broad discussion of free speech theory, I narrow into a review of the hate speech debate. I concentrate first on a review of the rationale offered by opponents of hate speech restriction before turning my attention to counter arguments established predominantly by critical race theorists and critical legal scholars. These alternative readings of the First Amendment could help facilitate the United States accepting a new way of thinking about the role of hate speech in society and the need for a new interpretation of the First Amendment.[1] Finally, I conclude by synthesizing these various positions into three historical phases in an attempt to help better explain where we are now in relation to hate speech and what the next steps might be.

Traditional Views on Speech Protection

Traditional U.S. perspectives on the role of free speech in society can be traced back to Enlightenment Era philosophers such as Immanuel Kant, John Locke, and Jean-Jacques Rousseau.[2] Most notably, though, it is the work of John Stuart Mill that has had the greatest impact on the Court's interpretation. In *On Liberty*, Mill called for an almost absolutist approach to free speech and certainly a complete protection of political speech.[3] He wrote:

> If all mankind minus one, were of one opinion, and only one person were of the contrary opinion, mankind would be no more justified in silencing that one person, than he, if he had the power, would be justified in silencing mankind…But the peculiar evil of silencing the expression of an opinion is, that it is robbing the human race; posterity as well as the existing generation; those who dissent from the opinion, still more than those who hold it. If the opinion is right, they are deprived of the opportunity of exchanging error for truth: if wrong, they lose, what is almost as great a benefit, the clearer perception and livelier impression of truth, produced by its collision with error.[4]

In other words, to Mill, all speech, no matter what, should be protected because all opinions, no matter what, are deserving of protection. Restricting the expression of any opinion would have negative consequences – both for the individual and society and for current and future generations. Without "collision with error," truth has no actual meaning. Mill articulated four arguments in favor of free expression – the suppressed opinion might be true; the expressed opinion, even if partly wrong, might contain elements of truth; by engaging in debate over our opinions, the truth comes to be more than our personal feelings; and false opinions are needed to keep the truth from becoming dead dogma. Particularly, two main points raised by Mill would become foundational in the legal interpretations of free speech. First was Mill's view that only through open discussion would truth be discovered:

> We can never be sure that the opinion we are endeavoring to stifle is a false opinion; and if we were sure, stifling it would be an evil still...the opinion which it is attempted to suppress by authority may possibly be true. Those who desire to suppress it, of course deny its truth; but they are not infallible...To refuse a hearing to an opinion, because they are sure that it is false, is to assume that their certainty is the same thing as absolute certainty.[5]

Protecting all opinions is essential because we can never be entirely certain of the truth or falsity of an opinion without some debate or discussion. Without allowing the opinion to be stated, we risk the possibility of not hearing expressions of truth. Additionally, protecting free expression facilitates an important human process:

> Wrong opinions and practices gradually yield to fact and argument: but facts and arguments, to produce any effect on the mind, must be brought before it...In the case of any person whose judgment is really deserving of confidence, how has it become so? Because he has kept his mind open to criticism of his opinions and conduct. Because it has been his practice to listen to all that could be said against him; to profit by as much of it as was just, and expound to himself, and upon occasion to others, the fallacy of what was fallacious.[6]

To clarify, for Mill, protecting expression not only protects the liberty of the speaker but also enables both the speaker and the listener to grow as human beings. The process of discerning truth from fallacy strengthens the capabilities of those involved in the debate and, as a result, also promotes greater knowledge development. While I address this more in the following chapters, it should be noted here that Mill does not address the possible downsides or negative consequences of unfettered free speech.[7] Even in his discussion of the harm principle, he does not seem to attend to the possible social harm that speech could cause. First Amendment scholars and jurists would follow suit, relying on Mill's assertion of allowing almost complete free expression, and ignoring or dismissing the question of possible harm. Mill also would be used to support the "marketplace of ideas" dicta found in many U.S. Supreme Court rulings.[8] In short, this reasoning holds that just as the economic marketplace best adjusts itself with little to no government intervention, so will the metaphorical one. In summary, Mill's impact on First Amendment theory and jurisprudence established the following as facts: individuals and society will benefit from the collision of truth and falsity; expression of false information causes no real harm, or at least in most circumstances not enough harm to justify speech restriction; speakers and listeners are autonomous individuals capable of rationally assessing information; and rational thought and behavior will prevail when those autonomous individuals are asked to deliberate on the truth or falsity of an expression.

Current traditional First Amendment theory has its basis in the seminal work of free speech scholar Thomas Emerson. In the 1960s, Emerson became the first scholar to add sufficient theoretical depth to the discussion of the function of free speech in a democratic society.[9] He postulated that the value of free speech in the United States could be grouped into four categories: (1) a means of assuring individual self-fulfillment; (2) a means of attaining the truth; (3) a method for securing citizen participation in the political and social process; and (4) a means of maintaining the balance between stability and change in society. Emerson's argument moves beyond the political nature of the protection of speech and into the realm of speech protection as a way to enhance the assurance of certain intrinsic "human" values. According to Emerson's theory, the freedom to speak one's mind is a necessary precursor for creating fully realized individuals.[10] He argued that the "suppression of belief, opinion and expression" is "an affront to the dignity of man, a negation of man's essential nature."[11] According to Emerson's reasoning, every person – in the development of their personality – must have the right to form their own opinions and beliefs, and, as such, they must be free to express themselves. Otherwise, forming an opinion is of little consequence. In other words, free expression is a necessary element in promoting personal development and is "an integral part of the development of ideas, of mental exploration and of the affirmation of self."[12] He asserted that when the government acts "to cut off [a person's] search for the truth," the government "elevates society and the state to a despotic command over him and places him under the arbitrary control of others."[13] For Emerson, all speech that supports one of the four categories he identified should be free from censorship, regardless of any competing rights or liberties that might be in play.

Emerson's work is significant for multiple reasons. He is the first person to offer an attempt at a unified theory of free speech. His impact on First Amendment theory continues today as scholars invoke his work in areas as wide-ranging as homeschooling, prisoner's rights, and armed protests.[14] His rationale for the protection of speech also has informed Supreme Court rulings.[15] Finally, and perhaps most importantly, he set the foundation for the discussion of free speech in the United States for First Amendment scholars for the next six decades, and likely beyond. Two notable examples of Emerson's influence are C. Edwin Baker and Martin Redish. Baker, in a similar fashion to Emerson, contended that the First Amendment protects the expression of speech for the benefit of individual growth, not the content of speech itself.[16] As such, "[s]peech is protected [by the First Amendment] not as a means to a collective good but because of the value of speech conduct to the individual."[17] According to his reasoning,

> the Constitution should protect all expressive conduct, whether or not intended to communicate propositions or attitudes to others, that involves individual self-expression or attempts at creation, unless the conduct operates coercively, physically obstructs others' activities, or otherwise interferes with others' legitimate decision-making authority.[18]

In short, speech should be privileged above other liberties and only restricted in extreme situations. Ultimately, Baker found that the First Amendment protects "not a marketplace, but rather an arena of individual liberty." He collapsed Emerson's four categories into two – protection of speech to assure individual self-fulfillment and as a means of maintaining the balance between stability and change in society.[19] Redish took a similar approach, but found that the First Amendment protection of speech serves only one purpose – "individual self-realization."[20] Redish did acknowledge the existence of other values – such as the "checking function" on government and the "marketplace of ideas" concept – however, he considered them to be sub-values.[21]

Writing in the period just before Emerson, Alexander Meiklejohn also proffered a theory of free speech that pulled from Mill and was applied, debated, and modified by later scholars.[22] However, while Emerson focused most on the issue of personal autonomy, Meiklejohn focused exclusively on political participation. He believed that free speech is constitutionally valuable because of the significant role it has in producing an informed citizenry. By protecting speech, the First Amendment was helping to secure the ability of people to govern themselves. He wrote: "To be afraid of ideas, any ideas, is to be unfit for self-government. Any such repression of ideas about the common good, the First Amendment condemns with its absolute disapproval."[23] His position, then, was not the pluralistic version offered by Emerson, nor was it tied to any sense of self-fulfillment or self-realization. Meiklejohn was not the only scholar to adopt this politics-centric approach to evaluating the importance of the First Amendment. For example, prolific legal scholar Robert C. Post, who has written extensively on First Amendment issues over the past several decades, adopted a democracy-based theory of free speech protection but offered a more nuanced explanation of what that should look like.[24] Post criticizes Meiklejohn for offering a theory that reflects "an insufficiently radical conception of the reach of self-determination."[25] He postulated that Meiklejohn's model ignores the autonomy of public discourse necessary for democratic self-government.[26] He noted: "Although citizens may not agree with all legislative enactments, although there may be no determinate fusion of individual and collective will, citizens can nevertheless embrace the government as rightfully 'their own' because of their engagement in these communicative processes."[27] In other words, Post subscribed to a more participatory model that sees open and unfettered speech as a key component in the democratic process. Unlike Meiklejohn's tidy town hall model, which assumes the acceptability of government structuring of speech, Post saw the process as significantly messier.[28]

Vincent Blasi, Cass Sunstein, and Owen Fiss also advanced democratic governance as the essential factor driving the protection of speech. Blasi believed that because of the serious threat of government abuse, free speech should be protected to keep that threat at bay.[29] He coined this option the "checking value" and noted, "Indeed, if one had to identify the single value that was uppermost in the minds of the persons who drafted and ratified the First Amendment, this checking value would be the most likely candidate."[30] All other values, according to him, could be subsumed under the importance of this one. Sunstein raised concerns about the direction that the First Amendment seemed to be taking in the 1990s, lamenting that theory and practice had gotten off course.[31] For Sunstein, speech protection needed to be firmly anchored to the principle of popular sovereignty. He stated: "The extraordinary protection now accorded to political speech can well be understood as an elaboration of the distinctive American understanding of sovereignty."[32] In other words, our ability to self-govern and the purpose of the First Amendment are intertwined. He explained:

> The belief that politics lies at the core of the amendment is an outgrowth of the more general structural commitment to deliberative democracy. The concern for ensuring the preconditions for deliberation among the citizenry is closely associated with this commitment.[33]

Any other approach to conceptualizing the role of free speech in U.S. society runs the risk of invalidating efforts to support popular sovereignty. Fiss perhaps took the most extreme position against the self-realization approach.[34] Like Sunstein, he critiqued the traditional free speech approach for focusing on the autonomy of the speaker. He explained his position:

> On the whole, does it enrich public debate? Speech is protected when (and only when) it does, and precisely because it does, not because it is an exercise of autonomy. In fact, autonomy adds nothing, and if need be, might have to be sacrificed, to make certain that public debate is sufficiently rich to permit true collective self-determination. What the phrase 'the freedom of speech' in the first amendment

refers to is a social state of affairs, not the action of an individual or institution.[35]

He argued that the Supreme Court has created a problematic and "inadequate" free speech doctrine by relying on the self-realization reading of the meaning of the First Amendment.[36]

These two schools of thought – Emerson's reliance on individual autonomy and Meiklejohn's focus on political engagement – offer a broad view of the traditional arguments made for why we do or should protect speech. Other scholars offer varying reasons for why free speech is essential in a liberal democracy such as ours but, despite their differences in justifications, their call to action remains the same: in most cases, there is more danger in restricting speech than in the danger allowing it would cause.[37]

Opponents of Hate Speech Restriction

Under the reasoning put forward by the likes of Emerson, Meiklejohn, and company, harm can be considered as a valid justification for speech restriction, but only in extreme circumstances. In most cases, speech is to be privileged based on its possible value in general, not restricted because of its possible harmful impacts. As a result of this rationale, restrictions on hate speech should be treated as just as suspect as government attempts to restrict political speech. As one recent scholar noted:

> American First Amendment scholars have argued that words cannot damage people; that there is not tangible evidence to show that words can truly hurt people; that to suggest that hateful words are equivalent to physical harm is sophistry of the highest order and that there is no objective evidence of the damage inflicted on the target group.[38]

If there is no actual harm, then the targets of the hateful speech can merely respond to hateful speech by exercising their free speech rights within the marketplace of ideas. Restricting hate speech, under this reasoning, runs three risks. The first being the slippery slope concern, a concern that passing one law restricting speech will ultimately take us down a slippery path to more limiting laws.[39] Second, the repercussions could mean that the social, economic, or political majority would use those very restrictions to silence dissident or minority groups.[40] Finally, many traditional scholars contend that restricting hate speech will only mask the hatred between groups, not dissipate it.

The question of whether or not some level of hate speech should be restricted can be traced back to the 1940s, when scholars and jurists began considering the issue under the auspice of group libel laws.[41] Starting in the late 1970s, scholars began to re-engage with the topic, this time because of the *Skokie* case.[42] Scholars and jurists saw an increased interest in proposed hate speech restrictions throughout the 1980s and early 1990s, often in regard to campus speech codes.[43] Legal interest in the subject skyrocketed following the ruling in *R.A.V. v. St. Paul* and continues today.[44] While many traditional free speech scholars have touched on the topic of hate speech, all end up with a similar conclusion: better to protect it and thus the integrity of the sanctity of the First Amendment than to restrict it and run the risk of unnecessary government suppression of speech. The list of scholars weighing in against restricting hate speech is long and covers the spectrum of arguments from those on the liberal left to the conservative right. While I will address a few of those scholars throughout the next several pages, this discussion is nowhere near comprehensive. My intention here, instead, is to offer examples of some of the more prominent arguments made, particularly those relying on traditional perspectives of freedom of speech.[45]

One of the earlier works directly addressing hate speech is Lee Bollinger's 1988 book *The Tolerant Society: Freedom of Speech and Extremist Speech*, in which he critiqued classical approaches to free speech theory, finding them to be inadequate on multiple levels.[46] Instead of free speech protection being grounded in the search for truth and self-s governance, he argued that the dominant foundation for speech protection should be tolerance. Freedom of speech, according to Bollinger, is less about individual freedom and more about its role in creating and shaping community. He explained:

> In this view the social function of free speech is to provide a focus on the mind behind the act of intolerance [that moves to suppress expression] rather than to protect the activity of speech itself as something that possesses independent value.[47]

Specifically, Bollinger proposed that we must tolerate all extremist speech so that we teach ourselves to be more tolerant throughout "the whole tapestry of social intercourse."[48] In short, we must tolerate extremist speech, which includes hate speech, in order to protect our democratic society.

Robert Post also found the protection of hate speech a necessity for democracy to flourish. In 1991, in response to increasing calls for hate speech restrictions on university campuses, Post came out firmly against any restrictions in favor of treating "the distinct harms caused by racist expression."[49] In reviewing hate speech legislation and placing it within the context of American society, Post concluded that it is and should be impossible to restrict hate speech within the confines of the First Amendment. He noted, "The incompatibility of this logic with even the most elementary standards of freedom of speech is obvious. Any communication can potentially express the racist self, and thus no communication can ever be safe from legal sanction."[50] In other words, we must be most wary of the slippery slope of speech restriction and of conflating the expression of dislike with the expression of hate. Post acknowledged the concerns over racism in the U.S. context, but proposed other routes to combating it that do not infringe on the free speech clause of the First Amendment. He resolved:

> To the extent that we care about first amendment values, therefore, we must make do with more modest aspirations. The possibility of effecting a reconciliation between principles of freedom of expression and restraints on racist speech depends upon deflecting our focus away from its spontaneous target, which is the racism of our cultural inheritance, and toward the redress of particular and distinct harms caused by racist expression. The specification of these harms will lead to the definition of discrete forms of speech, the legal regulation of which can then be assessed in light of relevant first amendment values.[51]

One example Post used to illustrate what might be regulable is workplace speech. He wrote: "There is a significant difference between proscribing racial insults directed towards individuals in the workplace and proscribing them in a political discussion or debate."[52] The former is regulable, and the latter is not. Post listed several of the possible harms of hate speech but ultimately found that legal regulation is difficult, if not impossible, in most circumstances, particularly those where the speech in question is related to democratic self-governance and public discourse.[53]

Since the early 1990s, Post has continued to articulate his concerns about hate speech regulation,[54] first in his work on the theory of public discourse, and in a 2009 book chapter where he demonstrated why American society must treat hate speech differently than European countries do.[55] In both cases, he relied heavily on the concept of the autonomous individual and the special role of that individual in the U.S. version of democracy and democratic participation. He contends that any attempts to restrict hate speech that occurs as part of public discourse will have severe negative social consequences.[56]

Other recent scholars continue to emphasize the role of unfettered free speech protection in relation to hate speech restriction. For example, Eric Heinz, in his 2016 book, *Hate Speech and Democratic Citizenship*, rejects both the classical liberal defenses of free speech as well as the newer libertarian contributions.[57] Instead, he starts by defining "longstanding, stable and prosperous democracies (or LSPDs)" and then argues that in those types of democracies, of which the United States is one example, freedom of expression serves as one of the "legitimating

expressive conditions" of democracy. Simply put, only unstable or un-
derdeveloped democracies might need to restrict speech to protect their
citizenry. James Weinstein also relies on the importance of an almost
absolutist approach to free speech in his critique of recent calls for hate
speech restrictions.[58] Weinstein acknowledges anti-discrimination laws
as "an essential means by which modern liberal democracies promote
equality and protect human dignity."[59] However, he contends that hate
speech restrictions not only fail to support those equality goals but instead, they "undermine the legitimacy of antidiscrimination laws."[60]
Relying heavily on Ronald Dworkin,[61] Weinstein argues that any restrictions based on the expression of viewpoints erode democracy and
signal the movement toward an "illegitimate autocracy."[62] Ultimately, he
finds hate speech regulation stifling to political debate and, as a result of
that silencing, damaging to political legitimacy and counter-productive
to the goals of anti-discrimination laws.

Most recently, former ACLU president Nadine Strossen published a
new book on the topic, which picks up with the same line of argument
she has presented in her previous works on the subject.[63] Strossen focuses on the terms 'hate speech' and 'hate crimes,' proclaiming them to
be words that "demonize and call for punishing a broad array of expression, including political discourse that is integral to our democracy."[64]
According to Strossen's book, our commitment to free speech requires
an expansive protection of speech – especially of speech that we don't
like. Reviewing laws and court cases from around the world, she con-
cludes that despite potential harms, "it would be more harmful to both
individuals and society to empower the government to suppress speech
for that reason."[65] Her response to the problem of hate speech is to restrict hateful behavior and to counter hateful speech with more speech.

Proponents of Hate Speech Restriction

While the Court continues to operate in line with the traditional views
of the role of free speech in society, since the 1980s, other legal scholars
have offered and continue to offer critiques of the accepted position.
In general, these scholars, whose academic backgrounds span a wide
spectrum including law, ethnic studies, gender studies, religious studies,
and communication, question the generally accepted suppositions that
democracy is best preserved by protecting virtually all speech. Proponents of hate speech regulation see no value in protecting hateful speech
whose only intent is to denigrate and terrorize certain already oppressed
groups. They disagree with the traditional view that hate speech causes
no real harm, that restricting it would ultimately affect minorities disproportionately negatively, and that protecting hate speech functions as
a pressure valve that allows tensions to dissipate so actions won't occur.
Much of this early critique can be tied to concerns about hate speech on

college campuses and the research conducted by a handful of critical race theorists, including Mari Matsuda, Charles Lawrence, and Richard Delgado.[66] While each made a distinct contribution to the scholarship in this area, Delgado's work – published both single-authored and with his wife, Jean Stefancic – continues to be a driving force in attempts to restrict hate speech.[67]

In 1992, Delgado published one of the first law review articles to call for regulation of racist speech. In "Words That Wound: A Tort Action For Racial Insults, Epithets, and Name-Calling," he proposed a way in which hate speech regulation could be written in accordance with the free speech clause.[68] He began with a detailed account of the psychological, sociological, and political effects of racial insults. For example, in terms of the psychological issue, he noted:

> The psychological responses to such stigmatization consist of feelings of humiliation, isolation, and self-hatred. Consequently, it is neither unusual nor abnormal for stigmatized individuals to feel ambivalent about their self-worth and identity. This ambivalence arises from the stigmatized individual's awareness that others perceive him or her as falling short of societal standards, standards which the individual has adopted. Stigmatized individuals thus often are hypersensitive and anticipate pain at the prospect of contact with "normals."[69]

The psychological damage can be both short-term (immediate anxiety or fear) or long-term (prolonged mental illness). In addition to psychological harm, Delgado identified physical damage from hate speech effects as well: He found that "there is evidence that high blood pressure is associated with inhibited, constrained, or restricted anger, and not with genetic factors, and that insults produce elevation in blood pressure."[70] Relying heavily on social scientific data, he outlined the harm caused to the individual by racism and racist speech and then, much like the reasoning presented in *Brown v. Board of Education*[71] favoring desegregation, made the connection between problems of the individual and the larger effect these problems have on a democratic society. Delgado explained:

> Racism is a breach of the ideal of egalitarianism, that 'all men are created equal' and each person is an equal moral agent, an ideal that is cornerstone of the American moral and legal system. A society in which some members are regularly subjected to degradation because of their race hardly exemplifies this ideal.[72]

In effect, according to Delgado, hate speech is anti-democratic and reinforces inequalities, and because of the harms it inflicts on its victims and society in general, there is a need for judicial intervention. He argued that the issue could be remedied through tort law where, in order for the plaintiff to be successful, they:

> should be required to prove that Language was addressed to him or her by the defendant that was intended to demean through reference to race; that the plaintiff understood as intended to demean through reference to race; and that a reasonable person would recognize as a racial insult.[73]

He concluded that this type of judicial recognition would affirm "the right of all citizens to lead their lives free from attacks on their dignity and psychological integrity."[74]

Delgado not only made his arguments in favor of hate speech regulation but also addressed the possible counter-arguments, especially those based in the First Amendment. For example, he dispelled the position that allowing hate speech functions as a safety valve, permitting anger to be expressed verbally instead of through violence.[75] In addition, he found that instead of promoting self-realization and political participation, protecting hate speech has the counter-effect on both the targets and those speaking the hate speech. He determined that hate speech can and should be regulated under the fighting words doctrine, and then applied Emerson's four values of speech to racial insults. He concluded that regulation of these types of insults would be in keeping with the basic tenets of First Amendment theory.

Lawrence and Matsuda also added to those early discussions of possible legal interventions into the restriction of hate speech. Lawrence, focusing on the debate concerning hate speech on college campuses, argued that through racist speech, racism is encouraged and the liberties of those who are not white are restricted.[76] He acknowledged the importance of protecting speech but raised concerns about the all-or-nothing approach. He noted:

> I fear that by framing the debate as we have – as one in which the liberty of free speech is in conflict with the elimination of racism – we have advanced the cause of racial oppression and have placed the bigot on the moral high ground, fanning the rising flames of racism.[77]

He asserted that the ideals underpinning the First Amendment offer the support for (not against) hate speech restriction.[78] Specifically, he pointed to the speaker's intention as problematic when viewed through the lens of traditional First Amendment principles. He wrote:

> Assaultive racist speech functions as a presumptive strike. The racial invective is experienced as a blow, not a proffered idea, and once the blow is struck, it is unlikely that dialogue will follow. Racial insults

are undeserving of first amendment protection because the perpe-
trator's intention is not to discover truth or initiate dialogue, but to
injure the victim.[79]

As a result of this impact, Lawrence argued for the regulation of some
face-to-face racial speech on college campuses.[80]

Much like Lawrence, Matsuda focused on the harms of racist speech.[81]
She contended that:

> The negative effects of hate messages are real and immediate for
> the victims. Victims of vicious hate propaganda experience physi-
> ological symptoms and emotional distress ranging from fear in the
> gut to rapid pulse rate and difficulty in breathing, nightmares, post-
> traumatic stress disorder, hypertension, psychosis and suicide...
> Victims are restricted in their personal freedom. To avoid receiving
> hate messages, victims have to quit jobs, forgo education, leave their
> homes, avoid certain public places, curtail their own exercise of
> speech rights and otherwise modify their behavior and demeanor.[82]

The damage caused by hate speech, according to Matsuda, impacts individuals and society in a multitude of ways. As such, just like Lawrence, she
dissected the intricacies between the First Amendment protections of speech
and the role of hate speech in a racist culture. Unlike Lawrence, though,
who did not offer a specific legal solution, Matsuda did. She suggested the
creation of legal doctrine that would define regulable hate speech through
the application of a three-tiered test that defined hate speech as (1) a message
of racial inferiority; (2) a message directed against a historically oppressed
group; and (3) a message that is persecutory, hateful, and degrading.[83]

Those early race theorists broke new ground in First Amendment scholarship by questioning the very foundation of free speech assumptions.
Delgado and others "flipped" stock arguments that assumed an intrinsic
value in speech that surpassed any possible harm.[84] In addition, those
scholars expanded the theoretical toolkit for assessing free speech in society. In the past decade, scholars from various academic backgrounds
have continued this legacy, building off of earlier works in an attempt to
find a constitutionally sound way to restrict some level of hate speech. For
example, constitutional law scholar Alexander Tsesis suggested that hate
speech is dangerous not just when it poses an immediate threat or harm,
but can lead to large-scale, long-term negative actions.[85] He first noted:

> History is littered with examples of harmful social movements, in
> various countries and cultures, employing violent racist rhetoric.
> Such hate-filled ideologies lie at the heart of human tragedies such
> as the Holocaust, U.S. slavery in the antebellum South, nineteenth
> century Indian removal, and present-day slavery in Mauritania.[86]

Through historical analysis of those events, he illustrated a causal link between hate speech and negative large-scale social wrongs, such as slavery and genocide. He found that hate speech denies members of target groups their supposed guaranteed civil rights and liberties. He proposed that "social contract obligations require governments both to protect fundamental rights and to increase social well-being."[87] As a result of the impact of hate speech and the requirement of the government to protect members of its citizenry, hate speech can "never be part of a universal rule of reciprocal action."[88] Ultimately, Tsesis maintained that hate speech should be criminally restricted.[89] This recommendation would move beyond incitement to violence and would punish "anyone inciting others to discriminate, persecute, oppress, or commit any similar acts against members of an identifiable group."[90] He offered two model criminal laws that could be imposed against hate speech which would impose prison sentences up to three years and mandatory community service.[91]

Steven Heyman applied a liberal humanist perspective in his study and found that hate speech targeted at specific individuals "often violates their rights of personal security, personality, and equality."[92] Focusing on cases of public hate speech, such as Nazi marches, he argued that those instances might need to be restricted in an effort to protect other rights. "Under the rights-based approach, one should first ask whether the march would infringe the rights of other individuals or the community, and then consider whether it should nevertheless be protected because of its political character."[93] Balancing free speech principles against possible harms, he concluded that the current treatment of hate speech within the U.S. context should be reconsidered. He found that the U.S. Supreme Court erred in its ruling in *R.A.V. v. St. Paul,* when it held (1) that hate speech could only be regulable if it is subsumed under an entire category of unprotected speech and (2) that political hate speech should not be protected at all.[94]

In 2008, I called for restricting some level of hate speech.[95] I used post-structural feminist theories of societal power and individual agency to create a new conception of freedom of speech and a testable, concrete framework for case analysis of speech involving disempowered groups. I found that "Focusing on the relational nature of modern power complicates – and ultimately invalidates – traditional notions of the First Amendment, particularly traditional notions of autonomy."[96] The framework I developed both deconstructed liberal conceptions of autonomy in case law and dispelled the discourse in those free speech areas that sidestepped or ignored issues of power and agency. Additional arguments have been made in the past several years supporting some level of hate speech restriction in the United States.[97] The specific test I developed is discussed in greater detail in Chapter 5.

Much of the recent scholarship focusing on legal responses to restricting hate speech is coming from international researchers.[98] For example,

Katharine Gelber, Australian Professor of Politics and Public Policy, has produced scholarship relating to hate speech and Australian law for nearly 20 years.[99] Gelber's work relies on a similar understanding of the harm that is present in the work of U.S. scholars, emphasizing that hate speech does more than just hurt people's feelings, it creates and maintains systematic inequality.[100] She studied Australian hate speech legislation and found it lacking, predominantly because of how liberty and free speech are defined in relation to each other. She wrote, in reference to the legislation, that "[T]hese arguments suffer from a central weakness in terms of their application to free speech policy: they share an emphasis on free speech policy which posits an absence of restraint on the speech liberty as the central policy goal."[101] She laid claim instead to a "broader, positive conception of liberty" that would allow for the possibility of the government promoting speech.[102] Relying on Martha Nussbaum's capability theory, she called for a capabilities-oriented hate speech policy. In short, capability theory holds as its central tenet that human capabilities are a requisite for the pursuit of the good life.[103] Building from that central position, Gelber found that hate speech serves to interfere with that process, and so government interference is necessitated to promote good human experiences for everyone. As a result, she suggested:

> [C]apabilities theory is able to integrate the two, previously counterposed, goals of speech policy. The goal of allowing free speech and the goal of ameliorating the harms of hate speech may both be considered when devising speech policy. Furthermore, they may both be ameliorated via the same mechanism – the provision of assistance to those whose ability to speak may be hindered by the speech of others.[104]

Ultimately, in her 2002 book, *Speaking Back: The Free Speech versus Hate Speech Debate*, Gelber suggested that speech policy should be designed to facilitate victims' ability to speak back against hate speech, as opposed to policy that punishes hate speakers.[105] Her later works support this position that hate speech laws do not contradict free speech principles and that the existence of these types of laws can have a positive impact on individuals and communities.[106]

UK researcher Alexander Brown serves as another example of this international scholarly interest in studying hate speech. Recently, he has been prolific with nearly a dozen publications (including one book) on the subject since 2015.[107] His works on hate speech run the gambit from purely philosophical to political theory and finally, and most interestingly to me, the use of philosophy and political theory to consider the legality of hate speech restrictions. In his book, *Hate Speech Law: A Philosophical Examination*, he offered an ambitious attempt to dissect philosophical arguments and legal approaches condoning or condemning hate speech bans and creating his own legal response.[108] He explained that hate speech restrictions are created in context:

> More often than not, if institutional authorities decide to enact or enforce a certain hate speech law in a given context, they are bound to be honoring some normative principles but sacrificing others. But if they choose instead to refrain from enacting or enforcing a certain hate speech law in a given context, they are also bound to be honoring some normative principles while sacrificing others.[109]

Much of his book breaks down what he saw as those normative principles at play, such as basic morality, personal development, and cultural development. Much like other scholars who argue for some level of hate speech restriction, Brown also discussed the relationship between freedom of expression and personal development and the need to consider the restriction of the former sometimes to protect the latter.[110] Ultimately, he suggested that hate speech restrictions should be dependent on what he calls "principled compromise." He explained: "Principled compromise is characterized not merely by compromise over matters of principled concern but also by compromise that is itself governed by ideas of moral conduct. The ideals I have in mind are reciprocity, equality and mutual respect."[111] In other words, Brown reviewed legal approaches both internationally and within a U.S. context and, using a list of possible principles, determined that using the approach of principled compromise will best protect both speech rights and the rights of those targeted by hate speech.

In 2018, Brown considered civil lawsuits as a way to deal with what he refers to as "targeted hate speech."[112] He proposed two legal tests – one for determining whether the speech degraded the plaintiff and another for whether or not it humiliated the plaintiff – that could be employed by courts.[113] Using human dignity as his baseline, Brown set out his criteria for evaluating degradation and humiliation and recommended a civil tort approach that would balance human dignity with free speech rights.[114] Brown also addressed the specific issue of Internet hate speech.[115] In one article, he noted that because of differences in communication on-line versus in-person, hate speech occurs differently, finding that "the nature of on-line communication encourages forms of cyberhate that are more spontaneous and, therefore, unconsidered."[116] Despite these differences, he concluded that the problem of online hate speech might be better handled by Internet companies working closely with intergovernmental organizations and national governments.[117] In another article, he considered the application of captive theory doctrine as a possible response to hate speech on the Internet.[118] In applying what has to date been an offline doctrine to online speech, Brown explained: "Captivity is not a matter of being unable to avoid unwelcome speech altogether. Rather, it is a matter of being unable to both avoid unwelcome speech and avoid unreasonable burdens whilst doing so."[119] In terms of the Internet in contemporary culture, he contended that it is unreasonable to suggest that simply logging off is an acceptable solution. In other words, Internet users are, in effect, members of a captive audience.

Often the work by these and other international scholars is ignored by First Amendment researchers, due to the difference in legal support of free speech in other countries. However, there has been considerable discussion among both U.S. and international legal scholars about Jeremy Waldron' 2012 book, which offered a metacritique of free speech absolutism and developed an argument for some level of restriction based off of a need for a commitment to human dignity.[120] According to Waldron, hate speech undermines the very fabric of a well-functioning society by stripping individuals of their dignity and thereby reducing their ability to be productive and successful members of society.[121] As a result, he found that "there is something socially and legally significant at stake" in choosing to restrict or not restrict hate speech.[122] His work heavily emphasized protection of human dignity, and his focus remained on possible restrictions outside of the U.S. context.[123]

Drawing from John Rawls, as well as from a host of other critical legal scholars, Waldron concluded:

> Will hate be tolerated by law in a well-ordered society? We have already considered one response: yes, it will be tolerated as part of the energizing diversity of a free market of ideas. Another response goes as follows: a society cannot be well-ordered if people are advocating racial or religious hatred.[124]

He emphasized that creating and maintaining ordered societies cannot be achieved through a hands-off approach. According to Waldron, "Societies do not become well-ordered by magic. The expressive and disciplinary work of law may be necessary as an ingredient in the change of heart within its racist citizens that a well-ordered society presupposes."[125] Hate speech interferes with the well-ordered society by denying members of targeted groups the sense of public assurance of their dignity and consequently robbing them of equal social status.[126] He explained:

> But in the real world, when people call for the sort of assurance to which hate speech laws might make a contribution, they do so not on the controversial details of someone's favorite conception of justice, but on some of the fundamentals of justice: that all are equally human, and have the dignity of humanity, that all have an elementary entitlement to justice and that all deserve protection from the most egregious forms of violence, exclusion, indignity, and subordination.

Hate speech or group defamation involves the expressed denial of those fundamentals with respect to some groups in society. And it seems to me that if we are imagining a society on the way to becoming well-ordered, we must imagine ways in which these basic assurances are given, even if we are not yet in a position to secure a more detailed conception on justice.[127]

Given this position, Waldron posited that we not only can, but must, restrict some level of hate speech, particularly speech that undermines a person's dignity.[128] And, these restrictions must be specifically addressed to hate speech per se, not simply swept up under other speech restriction categories such as fighting words or incitement because it is the very distinct harms from hate speech that must be restricted.[129]

Understanding the Big Debates

While much attention is being paid to hate speech today by First Amendment scholars, it is important to recognize that this legal and philosophical debate has been in motion for a century. We can bring the bigger picture into clearer focus by looking at what I consider to be three phases of thought concerning the development of the relationship between the First Amendment and hate speech restriction. By doing so, we not only can see the continual attention paid to the question of legalizing some level of hate speech restriction, but we also can better understand where we are today and what our next steps might be.

Phase One, which I will call *Autonomy in the Marketplace*, begins with the trilogy of sedition cases in the early 1900s – *Debs v. United States*,[130] *Schenck v. United States*,[131] and *Abrams v. United States*.[132] These cases mark the first attempt by the Supreme Court to give shape to the values underpinning the First Amendment. While those cases focused specifically on the issue of seditious libel, they also began to set the parameters for when and why we protect speech in any context. Justice Holmes in *Abrams* established a new concept in First Amendment case analysis – the marketplace of ideas – that still drives much analysis today. Holmes wrote:

But when men have realized that time has upset many fighting faiths, they may come to believe even more than they believe the very foundations of their own conduct that the ultimate good desired is better reached by free trade in ideas – that the best test of truth is the power of the thought to get itself accepted in the competition of the market, and that truth is the only ground upon which their wishes safely can be carried out. That at any rate is the theory of our constitution.[133]

Holmes' language set the stage for later theorists to focus on unfettered protection of free expression as a means to attain truth. For example,

Zachary Chaffee, the scholar credited with creating the "seminal legal scholarship"[134] on the First Amendment, wrote:

> The true meaning of freedom of speech seems to be this. One of the most important purposes of society and government is the discovery and spread of truth on subjects of general concern. This is possible only through absolutely unlimited discussion.[135]

As discussed, later scholars such as Meiklejohn, Emerson, Baker, and Post continued this adherence to the search for truth but added other elements such as self-realization and the ability to foster means for democratic self-governance. Throughout all of that early discourse, the focus remained on the speech rights of the autonomous individual with the answer to problematic speech being more speech and not government restriction, no matter the type or level of harm caused by the speech. In terms of hate speech specifically, the culmination of this line of reasoning in Phase One can be seen through the rulings in the Skokie cases.[136] Here, when faced with a Nazi march in a town full of Holocaust survivors, the state Supreme Court determined that the swastika did not constitute fighting words, and it reinforced previous court rulings emphasizing that the impact on the listener could not be considered as grounds for speech restriction.

Phase Two, *From Autonomy to Agency*, can be traced to the introduction of critical race theory, critical legal studies, and feminist legal theory. Beginning in the 1980s and building momentum in the 1990s and early 2000s, those schools of thought shone a critical light on the U.S. legal system in general and First Amendment jurisprudence and scholarship more specifically. Scholars such as Delgado, Matsuda, and Lawrence, in critiquing the treatment of hate speech under the First Amendment, offered a broader critique of legal principles in general. For example, in requesting that some level of hate speech be restricted, they in effect raised concerns about the long-time distinction between negative and positive liberty. First Amendment jurisprudence, as well as traditional free speech theory, supposes a negative liberty within First Amendment protections. That is to say, the government cannot restrict speech, but it has no responsibility, indeed has no right, to promote the speech rights of members of its citizen, no positive liberty.[137] While the First Amendment before this time had been seen as only a negative liberty, critics argued that because of the nature of speech, recognition of a positive liberty might be necessary. This claim can be seen in Delgado's seminal hate speech article asking for a tort remedy. Central to Delgado's position is that because hate speech reinforces inequalities in society, the government is obligated through the judicial system to help offset the negative impacts of that speech. Matsuda raised a similar harm-based argument in the development of her suggested three-tier legal test.

Critical race scholars in Phase Two introduced a second conversation to free speech theory by bringing to the forefront the tension between freedom and equality. As already discussed in this chapter, scholars in Phase One emphasized the importance of freedom of expression as a way to ensure the best democratic system and the most open society. However, scholars in Phase Two would point to the issue of the silencing nature of hate speech and find that because of its ability to silence certain parts of the citizenry, the current application of the First Amendment served to impede freedom for some as opposed to ensuring freedom for most. Those scholars posited that the prerequisite for freedom is equality and not the other way around.

A third major critique raised during this phase came from scholars from diverse academic backgrounds who questioned the notion of the autonomous individual. In Phase One, scholars relied on this autonomous individual as the essence of humanity. Protecting speech rights meant protecting the ability for this individual to form their thoughts and opinions, become self-realized individuals, and help them stave off government imposition into their lives. Phase Two scholars would begin to question the very existence of this autonomous individual and would argue, much as I did in my earlier work, that instead of autonomy, people operate from varying levels of agency, with those levels often informed by social and political standing.[138] In relation to hate speech specifically, this argument laid claim that in certain circumstances, the government may need to restrict the speech rights of some in order to protect and/or promote the speech rights of those with less agency. This approach is illustrated in the Bias Motivated Crime Ordinance that was in question in *R.A.V. v. St. Paul*. That ordinance, which I will discuss in depth in Chapter 6, attempted to restrict speech that "arouses anger, alarm or resentment in others on the basis of race, color, creed, religion or gender."[139] The main focus of that ordinance was on protecting members of marginalized groups from being targeted by certain types of speech.

Phase Three, the *Human Dignity Phase*, is where we are currently. This phase started less than a decade ago and, I would argue, came about for two reasons. First, following the rulings in *R.A.V.* and *Black* in Phase Two, scholars needed to regroup and consider other avenues through which to attack the problem of legally promoting hate speech restrictions under existing First Amendment doctrine. Second, and perhaps of even greater impact, was the explosion of the World Wide Web, and in particular social media. The United States can no longer reasonably take a separatist position with respect to free speech protection. We now exist in the global community, and as such, must begin to take into account how other countries' approaches to speech protection or restriction might impact us. For example, as I stressed in the introduction, the United States has become a safe haven for hate groups due in large part to our lack of hate speech restriction on the Internet. This third phase does not mark a completely new path. It is informed by both the (still predominant) normative conceptions of free speech introduced in Phase One and the (still viable) counter-arguments raised in Phase Two. One point of departure, particularly between Phase Two and Phase Three, is that the focus has shifted from discussions of autonomy and agency to a consideration of human dignity, and more contemporary notions of social justice have replaced conceptualizations of equality. Waldron's book serves as a perfect illustration of this new perspective. My work here fits squarely into this new phase as well, which will be elaborated on in detail in the following chapter. In terms of case law, the U.S. Supreme Court has not yet applied this approach in free speech cases but, as was discussed at length in Chapter 2, it is the approach employed in most international laws regulating hate speech.

Conclusion

Key to understanding the current U.S. position on hate speech protection is understanding the philosophical values underpinning those Supreme Court opinions. To this end, this chapter set out to present a history of First Amendment theory in the United States. This history looked first at the development of general theoretical models by scholars such as Thomas Emerson, C. Edwin Baker, and Robert Post. Through the discussion, we can see the lasting impact of the Enlightenment Theorists, most notably John Stuart Mill, on how the United States treats free expression today. This chapter then drilled down to look specifically at those theorists engaged in the hate speech restriction debate. The possibility of restricting hate speech was first introduced in the 1940s in relation to group libel, and then expanded in the 1980s and 1990s as college campuses and communities across the United States had speech codes and ordinances moved through the court system. While the Supreme Court continued to reaffirm its position on the need to protect hate speech, scholars from a multitude of disciplines raised challenges to both the application by the Court and the interpretation by key First Amendment scholars.

This chapter concluded by identifying three discreet phases in the development of the hate speech restriction debate within the United States. By illuminating these phases, this chapter emphasized not only the longevity and persistence of the concerns about the societal harms of permitting hate speech, but it also helped to establish how the conversation has evolved. In Chapter 5, I elaborate on Phase Three, *The Human Dignity Phase,* and offer my suggestion for where the next step should be in the legal treatment of hate speech restriction under the First Amendment.

Notes

1 This review of the theoretical debates is not meant to be comprehensive, highlighting only a few of the key arguments.
2 See, Immanuel Kant, KANT'S POLITICS OF WRITING (Hans Reiss ed., 1970) Jacques Rousseau, THE SOCIAL CONTRACT AND DISCOURSES (1913); and John Locke, TWO TREATISES ON GOVERNMENT (1821).
3 John Stuart Mill, ON LIBERTY (1859) (reprinted Batoche Books, 2001).
4 *Id.* at 18.
5 *Id.* at 19.
6 *Id.* at 21–22.
7 For an extended discussion of Mill's lack of attention to possible negative consequence of speech protection of false ideas, *see* Frederick Schauer, *Social Epistemology, Holocaust Denial, and the Post-Millian Calculus*, in THE CONTENT AND CONTEXT OF HATE SPEECH: RETHINKING REGULATION AND RESPONSES 59 (Michael Hertz and Peter Molnar, eds. 2012) and Alexander Brown, HATE SPEECH LAW: A PHILOSOPHICAL EXAMINATION 117–120 (2015)
8 For a few examples, *see* Abrams v. U.S., 250 U.S. 616, 630 (1919) ("The best test of truth is to get itself accepted in the competition of the market."); Time, Inc. v. Hill, 385 U.S. 374, 406 (1967) ("'The marketplace of ideas' where it functions still remains the best testing ground for truth."); FCC v. Pacifica, 438 U.S. 726, 745 (1978) ("For it is a central tenet of the First Amendment that the government must remain neutral in the marketplace of ideas.") Texas v. Johnson, 491 U.S. 397, 418 (1989) ("The First Amendment does not guarantee that other concepts virtually sacred to our nation as a whole...will go unquestioned in the marketplace of ideas."); and Reed v. the Town of Gilbert, 135 S. Ct. 2218 (2015) ("I also concede that, whenever government disfavors one kind of speech, it places that speech at a disadvantage, potentially interfering with the free marketplace of ideas...").
9 Thomas Emerson, Toward a General Theory of Free Speech (1963).
10 *Id.* at 3.
11 *Id.* at 5.
12 Thomas Emerson, *Toward a General Theory of the First Amendment*, 72 YALE L.J. 878 (1963).
13 Emerson, *supra* note 9, at 6.
14 In just the last five years, multiple legal scholars have invoked Emerson in defense of their positions. A few of those include Clay Calvert et al., *Access to Information about Lethal Injections: A First Amendment Theory Perspective on Creating a New Constitutional Right*, 38 HASTINGS COMM. & ENT. L.J. 1 (2016) (arguing that First Amendment theory demands public and inmate access to details about the drugs, procedures, and personnel involved in lethal-injection executions); Clay Calvert, *The First Amendment Right to Record Images of Police in Public Places: The Unreasonable Slipperiness of Reasonableness & Possible Paths Forward*, 3 TEX. A&M L. REV. 131(2015) (calling on the Supreme Court to quickly consider a right-to-record case to uphold an established First Amendment right for people to record police); Emmanuel Hiram Arnaud, *The Dismantling of Dissent: Militarization and the Right to Peaceably Assemble*, 101 CORNELL L. REV. 777 (2016) (arguing that ritualized use of extreme police force on peacefully assembled groups is a violation of the Assembly Clause): G. Edward White, *The Evolution of First Amendment Protection for Compelled Commercial Speech*, 29 J. L. & POLITICS 481 (2014) (suggesting that the Court is using the Autonomy rationale in deciding compelled commercial speech cases);

R. George Wright, *Public Fora and the Problem of Too Much Speech*, 106 KY. L. J. 409 (2017) (addressing the question of whether there is too much private speech on public fora); Victoria Smith Ekstrand, *Democratic Governance, Self-Fulfillment And Disability: Web Accessibility Under The Americans With Disabilities Act And The First Amendment*, 22 COMM. L. & POL'Y 427 (2017) (arguing that making the Internet a "place of public accommodation" under the ADA is supported by First Amendment principles of democratic governance and self-fulfillment); Katlyn E. DeBoer, *Clash of the First and Second Amendments: Proposed Regulation of Armed Protests*, 45 HASTINGS CONST. L.Q. 333 (2018) (finding that doctrinal strictures of the First Amendment and the theoretical understandings of its purpose both support a call to state legislatures to enact reasonable regulation to prohibit open carry during protest demonstrations); and Jennifer Karinen, *Finding a Free Speech Right to Homeschool: An Emersonian Approach*, 105 GEO. L.J. 191 (2016) (arguing that the First Amendment should be employed when considering the legality and regulation of homeschooling).

15 *See, e.g.*, First Nat'l Bank of Boston v. Bellotti, 435 U.S. 765, 777 n.11 (1978) ("Freedom of expression has particular significance with respect to government because '[i]t is here that the state has a special incentive to repress opposition and often wields a more effective power of suppression.'"); Procunier v. Martinez, 416 U.S. 396, 427 (1974) (Marshall, J., concurring) ("The First Amendment serves not only the needs of the polity but also those of the human spirit – a spirit that demands self-expression. Such expression is an integral part of the development of ideas and a sense of identity. To suppress expression is to reject the basic human desire for recognition and affront the individual's worth and dignity"); and Branzburg v. Hayes, 408 U.S. 665, 726 (1972) (Stewart, J., dissenting) ("Enlightened choice by an informed citizenry is the basic ideal upon which an open society is premised, and a free press is thus indispensable to a free society.").

16 C. Edwin Baker, *The Process of Change and the Liberty Theory of the First Amendment*, 55 S. CAL. L. REV. 293, 342–343 (1982).

17 C. Edwin Baker, *Scope of the First Amendment Freedom of Speech*, 25 UCLA L. REV. 964, 966 (1978).

18 *Id.* at 333.

19 C. Edwin Baker, HUMAN LIBERTY AND FREEDOM OF SPEECH (1989).

20 Martin Redish, THE VALUE OF FREE SPEECH (1974).

21 Other scholars to utilize Emerson's reliance on individual autonomy include David A.J. Richards, *Free Speech and Obscenity Law: Toward a Moral Theory of the First Amendment*, 123 U. PA. L. REV. 45 (1974) and Thomas Scanlon, *A Theory of Freedom of Expression*, 1 PHIL. & PUB. AFF. 204 (1972). Richards suggests that the core of free expression lies in the "human capacity to create and express symbolic systems, such as speech, writing, pictures, and music, intended to communicate in determinate, complex and subtle ways," at 62. Scanlon argues that being able to express oneself is an aspect of autonomy and that it is important for human beings to be autonomous regardless of the consequences. He explains:

> An autonomous person cannot accept without independent consideration the judgment of others as to what he should believe or what he should do. He may rely on the judgment of others, but when he does so he must be prepared to advance independent reasons for thinking their judgment likely to be correct, and to weigh the evidential value of their opinion against contrary evidence

(216.)

22 Alexander Meiklejohn, Political Freedom: The Constitutional Powers of the People (1960).

23 *Id.* at 28.

24 Some of his works focusing on the First Amendment include: Citizens Divided: Campaign Finance Reform and the Constitution (2014); Democracy, Expertise, Academic Freedom: A First Amendment Jurisprudence for the Modern State (2012); Constitutional Domains: Democracy, Community, Management (1995); *Understanding the First Amendment*, 87 Wash. L. Rev. 549 (2012); *Participatory Democracy and Free Speech*, 97 Virginia L. Rev. 477 (2011); *Hate Speech*, in Extreme Speech and Democracy, 123 (Ivan Hare and James Weinstein, eds., 2009); *Reconciling Theory and Doctrine in First Amendment Jurisprudence*, 88 Calif. L. Rev. 2353 (2000); *Community and the First Amendment*, 29 Arizona St. L. J. 473 (1997); *Equality and Autonomy in First Amendment Jurisprudence*, 95 Michigan L. Rev. 1517 (1997); *Recuperating First Amendment Doctrine*, 47 Stan. L. Rev. 1249 (1995); *Meiklejohn's Mistake: Individual Autonomy and the Reform of Public Discourse*, 64 U. Colorado L. Rev. 1109 (1993); *Outrageous Speech and the Constitution: Thoughts on Hustler Magazine v. Falwell*, Dissent, Summer 1990, at 367; and *Cultural Heterogeneity and Law: Pornography, Blasphemy, and the First Amendment*, 76 Calif. L. Rev 297 (1988).

25 Robert Post, *Meiklejohn's Mistake: Individual Autonomy and the Reform of Public Discourse*, 64 U. Colo. L. Rev. 1109, 1118 (1993).

26 Robert Post, *Managing Deliberation: The Quandary of Democratic Dialogue*, 103 Ethics 654 (1993).

27 *Id.* at 111.

28 *Id.* at 1117

Meiklejohn's model of the town meeting, however, precisely violates this necessary indeterminacy of public discourse. While acknowledging that "the voting of wise decisions" must be kept free from government interference, it nevertheless authorizes the censorship of public discourse on the basis of assumptions about function and procedure.

29 Vincent Blasi, *The Checking Value in First Amendment Theory*, 2 Amer. B. Found. Res. J. 523 (1977).

One basic value seems highly relevant to these newer claims, yet has not been accorded a central place in our articulated theory of the First Amendment. This is the value that free speech, a free press, and free assembly can serve in checking the abuse of power by public officials. Consider the most important ways in which the First Amendment has made a difference in recent years. But for the peace marches and other protests, the Johnson administration might very well have escalated the war in Vietnam after the Tet offensive and the Nixon administration might have attempted to sustain a wider war after the Cambodian 'incursion,'

(527.)

30 *Id.* a 527.

31 Cass R. Sunstein, *Free Speech Now*, 59 U. Colorado L. Rev. 255, 263 (1992).

32 *Id.* at 257.

33 *Id.* at 314.

34 Owen M. Fiss, *Free Speech and Social Structure*, 71 Iowa L Rev. 1405 (1986).

35 *Id.* at 1411.

36 *Id.* at 1408.

37 There is a substantive body of traditional First Amendment scholarship covering the past 50 plus years. For some of the more widely discussed, *see* Lee Bollinger, THE TOLERANT SOCIETY: FREEDOM OF SPEECH AND EXTREMIST SPEECH (1986); Harry Kalven Jr., A WORTHY TRADITION: FREEDOM OF SPEECH IN AMERICA (1988); STEVEN SHIFFRIN, INJUSTICE AND THE MEANINGS OF AMERICA (1999); Steven Shiffrin, THE FIRST AMENDMENT, DEMOCRACY AND ROMANCE (1990), Rodney Smolla, FREE SPEECH IN AN OPEN SOCIETY (1992); and James Weinstein, *Participatory Democracy as the Central Value of American Free Speech Doctrine*, 97 VA. L. REV. 49 (2011).

38 Raphael Cohen-Almagor, *Freedom of Expression v. Social Responsibility: Holocaust Denial in Canada*, 28 J. MASS MEDIA ETHICS 42, 48 (2013).

39 For a more detailed discussion of the slippery slope reasoning in law, *see* Eric Lode, *Slippery Slope Arguments and Legal Reasoning*, 87 CAL L. REV.1469 (1999).

40 Nadine Strossen, DEFENDING PORNOGRAPHY: FREE SPEECH, SEX, AND THE FIGHT FOR WOMEN'S RIGHTS 31 (1995). Strossen contends that "all censorship measures throughout history have been used disproportionately to silence those who are relatively disempowered."

41 *See*, Loren P. Beth, *Group Libel and Free Speech*, 39 MINN. L. REV. 167 (1955); Riesman, *Democracy and Defamation: Control of Group Libel*, 42 COLUM. L. REV. 727 (1942); Richard B. Wilson, *Beauharnais v. Illinois, Bulwark or Breach?*, 14 CURRENT ECON. COMMENT 59 (1952); Note, *Statutory Prohibition of Group Defamation*, 47 COLUM. L. REV. 595 (1947); Edward E. Kallgren, *Group Libel*, 41 CALIF. L. REV. 290 (1953); and James J. Brown and Carl L. Stern, *Group Defamation in the U.S.A.*, 13 CLEV.-MAR. L. REV. 7 (1964). Also, see discussion of Beauharnais v. Illinois, 343 U.S. 250, 258–263 (1952) in Chapter 3, pages 40–41.

42 For example, *see* Kenneth Karst, *Equality as a Central Principle in the First Amendment*, 43 U. CM. L. REV. 20 (1975); David Downs, NAZIS IN SKOKIE (1985); David Hamlin, THE NAZI/SKOKIE CONFLICT: A CIVIL LIBERTIES BATTLE (1980); and Lee Bollinger, *The Skokie Legacy: Reflections on an "Easy Case" and Free Speech Theory*, 80 MICH. L. REV. 617 (1982).

43 For a more in-depth discussion of the hate speech versus free speech debate on college campuses, *see* Chapter 8.

44 A search on Lexus/Nexus for the term "hate speech" showed only nine entries between January 1, 1985, and December 31, 1989. The next five years would show an additional nearly 450 articles. Today, the number is just shy of 6,000. These numbers only account for law review articles cataloged through Lexus/Nexus and do not include other academic journals or books.

45 For additional discussions, *see*, Edward J. Eberle, *Hate Speech, Offensive Speech, and Public Discourse in America*, 29 WAKE FOREST L. REV. 1135 (1994) (concluding that government should refrain from regulating speech itself and instead focus only on problematic conduct); Joseph W. Bellacosa, *The Regulation of Hate Speech by Academe vs. the Idea of a University: A Classic Oxymoron*, 67 ST. JOHN'S L. REV. 1 (1993) (finding that "while a narrowly drafted regulation may qualify under some bare exceptional circumstances and analysis, it is in any event counterproductive, rife with frustration, and unwise"); Cary Nelson, *Hate Speech and Political Correctness*, 1992 U. ILL. L. REV. 1085 (1992) (arguing that efforts to regulate hate speech are ultimately more dangerous than their benefits warrant); Jon M. Blim, *Undoing Our Selves: The Error of Sacrificing Speech in the Quest for Equality*, 56 OHIO ST. L.J. 427 (1995) (stating that "If efforts made in a quest for social equality are permitted to impinge on the freedom

of speech, those efforts will prove to be, in more senses than one, self-defeating"); Charles R. Calleros, *Paternalism, Counterspeech, and Campus Speech Codes: A Reply to Delgado and Yun*, 27 ARIZ. ST. L.J. 1249 (1995) (claiming that Delgado and Yun "understate the efficacy of community education and counterspeech, omitting discussion of recent examples of successful counterspeech and of counterproductive measures to suppress offensive speech"); C. Edwin Baker, *Hate Speech*, in THE CONTENT AND CONTEXT OF HATE SPEECH: RETHINKING REGULATION AND RESPONSES 59 (Michael Herz and Peter Molnar, eds. 2012) (claiming that any hate speech regulations are likely to backfire); and George Cherian, *Hate Spin: The Twin Political Strategies of Religious Incitement and Offense-Taking*, 27 COMM. THEORY 156, 159 (2015) ("Hate speech should trigger legal intervention only if it amounts to a call to action that would clearly cause objective harms to the targeted group").

46 Lee Bollinger, THE TOLERANT SOCIETY: FREEDOM OF SPEECH AND EXTREMIST SPEECH (1986).

47 *Id.* at 140.

48 *Id.* at 119.

49 Robert C. Post, *Racist Speech, Democracy and the First Amendment*, 32 WM. & MARY L. REV 267, 270 (1991).

50 *Id.*

51 *Id.* at 270.

52 *Id.* at 302.

53 *Id.* at 327. Post concluded by offering an either-or-scenario for the future:

> The strict implication of this essay, then, is not that racist speech ought not to be regulated in public discourse, but rather that those who advocate its regulation in ways incompatible with the value of deliberative self-governance carry the burden of moving us to a different and more attractive vision of democracy. Or, in the alternative, they carry the burden of justifying suspensions of our fundamental democratic commitments. Neither burden is light.

54 Robert C. Post, CONSTITUTIONAL DOMAINS: DEMOCRACY, COMMUNITY, MANAGEMENT (1995); *Hate Speech*, in EXTREME SPEECH AND DEMOCRACY, 123 (Ivan Hare and James Weinstein, eds., 2009).

55 Robert C. Post, CONSTITUTIONAL DOMAINS: DEMOCRACY, COMMUNITY, MANAGEMENT (1995) and Robert C. Post, *Hate Speech*, in EXTREME SPEECH AND DEMOCRACY, 123 (Ivan Hare and James Weinstein, eds., 2009); and *Participatory Democracy and Free Speech*, 97 VIRGINIA L. REV. 477 (2011); *Interview with Robert Post*, in THE CONTENT AND CONTEXT OF HATE SPEECH: RETHINKING REGULATION AND RESPONSES 11 (Michael Hertz and Peter Molnar, eds. 2012).

56 *Hate Speech*, in EXTREME SPEECH AND DEMOCRACY, 123 (Ivan Hare and James Weinstein, eds., 2009) at 136:

> When law uses community norms to restrict participation in public discourse, it limits the capacity of persons to contribute to the formation of 'that public opinion which is the final source of government in a democratic state.' This may have significant negative social consequences if a society is heterogeneous and encompasses distinct communities with district norms.

57 Eric Heinz, HATE SPEECH AND DEMOCRATIC CITIZENSHIP (2016).

58 James Weinstein, *Hate Speech Bans, Democracy, and Political Legitimacy*, 35 CONST. COMMENT. 527 (2017). For Weinstein's earlier work in

this area, *see*, Hate Speech, Pornography, and the Radical Attack on Free Speech Doctrine (1999).

59 *Id.* at 527.

60 *Id.* at 528.

61 *Id. See also*, Ronald Dworkin, Forward to Extreme Speech and Democracy, vii (Ivan Hare and James Weinstein eds., 2009).

62 *Id.* at 530.

63 Nadine Strossen, Hate Speech: Why We Should Resist It With Free Speech, Not Censorship (2018); Defending Pornography: Free Speech, Sex, and the Fight for Women's Rights (2000, 1995); and *Regulating Racist Speech on Campus: A Modest Proposal*, 1990 Duke L.J. 484 (1990).

64 *Id.* at 1.

65 *Id.* at 4.

66 Mari Matsuda, *Public Response to Racist Speech: Considering the Victim's Story*, 87 Michigan L. Rev. 2320, (1989); Charles Lawrence, *If he Hollers Let Him Go: Regulating Racist Speech on Campus*, 1990 Duke L.J. 431 (1990); and Richard Delgado, *Words that Wound: A Tort Action for Racial Insults, Epithets and Name-Calling*, 17 Harv. C.R.-C.L. L Rev. 133 (1992).

67 Richard Delgado is the author of more than 180 articles and 29 books. Some of his writings about the topic of hate speech include *Words that Wound: A Tort Action for Racial Insults, Epithets and Name-Calling*, 17 Harv. C.R.-C.L. L Rev. 133 (1982); with Laura Lederer, The Price We Pay: The Case Against Racist Speech, Hate Propaganda and Pornography (1995); with Jean Stefancic, Must We Defend Nazis: Hate Speech, Pornography and the New First Amendment (2018, 1997); with Jean Stefancic, Understanding Words that Wound (2004); with Jean Stefancic, *Four Observations About Hate Speech*, 44 Wake Forest L. Rev. 353 (2009); with Jean Stefancic, *Hate Speech in Cyberspace*, 49 Wake Forest L. Rev. 319 (2014).

68 Richard Delgado, *Words that Wound: A Tort Action for Racial Insults, Epithets and Name-Calling*, 17 Harv. C.R.-C.L. L Rev.133 (1992).

69 *Id.* at 137.

70 *Id.* at 139. He explained that "American blacks have higher blood pressure levels and higher morbidity and mortality rates from hypertension, hypertensive disease, and stroke than do white counterparts."

71 347 U.S. 483 (1954).

72 Delgado, *supra* note 68, at 140.

73 *Id.* at 179.

Thus, it would be expected that an epithet such as "You damn nigger" would almost always be found actionable, as it is highly insulting and highly racial. However, an insult such as "You incompetent fool," directed at a black person by a white, even in a context which made it highly insulting, would not be actionable because it lacks a racial component. "Boy," directed at a young black male, might be actionable, depending on the speaker's intent, the hearer's understanding, and whether a reasonable person would consider it a racial insult in the particular context. "Hey, nigger," spoken affectionately between black persons and used as a greeting, would not be actionable. An insult such as "You dumb honkey," directed at a white person, could be actionable under this formulation of the cause of action, but only in the unusual situations where the plaintiff would suffer harm from such an insult.

74 *Id.* at 181.

75 *Id.* at 140.

76 Charles Lawrence, *If he Hollers Let Him Go: Regulating Racist Speech on Campus*, 1990 DUKE L. J. 431 (1990).

77 *Id.* at 436

78 *Id.* at 452: "If the purpose of the first amendment is to foster the greatest amount of speech, then racial insults disserve that purpose."

79 *Id.*

80 *Id.* at 481.

81 Mari Matsuda, *Public Response to Racist Speech: Considering the Victim's Story*, 87 MICHIGAN L. REV. 2320 (1989).

82 *Id.* at 2336–2337.

83 *Id.* at 2357.

84 Richard Delgado and Jean Stefancic, MUST WE DEFEND NAZIS: HATE SPEECH, PORNOGRAPHY AND THE NEW FIRST AMENDMENT 44 (1997)

> We are beginning to flip stock arguments. Until now, the following argument has been determinative: the First Amendment condemns that; therefore, it is wrong. We are raising the possibility that the correct argument may sometimes be: the First Amendment condemns that; therefore, the First Amendment (or the way we understand) is wrong.

85 Alexander Tsesis, DESTRUCTIVE MESSAGES: HOW HATE SPEECH PAVES THE WAY FOR HARMFUL SOCIAL MOVEMENTS (2002).

86 *Id.* at 1.

87 *Id.* at 5.

88 *Id.* at 166.

89 *Id.* at 193–209.

90 *Id.* at 206–207.

91 *Id.*

92 Steven J. Heyman, FREE SPEECH AND HUMAN DIGNITY 165 (2008).

93 *Id.* at 165.

94 *Id.* at 175, explaining why political hate speech is problematic in a democratic society: "Hate speech disrespects the autonomy of others and refuses to deliberate with them. In these ways, it tends to undermine rather than to promote the formation of a genuinely common will."

95 Chris Demaske, MODERN POWER AND FREE SPEECH: CONTEMPORARY CULTURE AND ISSUES OF EQUALITY (2009).

96 *Id.* at xv.

97 For some additional examples, *see*, John C. Knechtle, *When to Regulate Hate Speech*, 110 PENN. ST. L. REV. 539 (2006) (arguing that the threshold for risk should be lowered to take into account the U.S. pluralistic environment and its record on human rights); Rory K. Little, *Hating Hate Speech: Why Current First Amendment Doctrine Does not Condemn a Careful Ban*, 45 HASTINGS CONST. L. Q. 577 (2018) (suggesting that *Virginia v. Black* offers an opening to narrowly drawn hate speech regulations); Steven H. Shiffrin, WHAT'S WRONG WITH THE FIRST AMENDMENT? (2016) (the legal tolerance of racist speech is incompatible with the commitment to equality).

98 For example, Gregory S. Gordon, *Hate Speech and Persecution: A Contextual Approach*, 46 VAND. J. TRANSNAT'L L. 303 (hate speech not directly calling for action may still qualify as persecution as a crime against humanity); Peter Molnar, *Responding to 'Hate Speech' with Art, Education and the Imminent Danger Test*, in THE CONTENT AND CONTEXT OF HATE SPEECH: RETHINKING REGULATION AND RESPONSES 183 (Michael

Hertz & Peter Molnar eds., 2012) (suggesting an approach to dealing with hate speech that does not use content-based bans); Jacob Weinrib, *What is the Purpose of Freedom of Expression*, 67 U. TORONTO FAC. L. REV. 165 (2009) (formulates a dignity-based conception of freedom of expression within the Canadian context); Caleb Yong, *Does Freedom of Speech Include Hate Speech?*, RES PUBLICA, published online July 13 (2011) (suggests that a better definition of hate speech will lead to some permissible restrictions); Katharine Gelber and Luke McNamara, *Evidencing the Harms of Hate Speech*, 22 SOC. IDENTITIES 324 (2016) and *The Effects of Civil Hate Speech Laws: Lessons from Australia*, 49 L. & SOC. 631 (2015) (addressing Australia's hate speech legislation); and Alexander Brown, HATE SPEECH LAW: A PHILOSOPHICAL EXAMINATION (2015) (offering an extensive review of laws and regulations around the world and discussing ways in which hate speech might be regulable).

 99 SPEAKING BACK: THE FREE SPEECH VERSUS HATE SPEECH DEBATE (2002); *Freedom of Political Speech, Hate Speech and the Argument from Democracy: The Transformative Contribution of Capabilities Theory*, 9 CONTEMP. POL. THEORY 304 (2010); SPEECH MATTERS: GETTING FREE SPEECH RIGHT (2011); *Speaking Back: The Likely Fate of Hate Speech Policy in the United States and Australia*, in SPEECH AND HARM: CONTROVERSIES OVER FREE SPEECH 50 (Ishani Maitra & Mary Kate McGowan eds., 2012); and Katharine Gelber and Luke McNamara, *Evidencing the Harms of Hate Speech*, 22 SOC. IDENTITIES 324 (2016) and *The Effects of Civil Hate Speech Laws: Lessons from Australia*, 49 L. & SOC'Y 631 (2015).

100 SPEAKING BACK: THE FREE SPEECH VERSUS HATE SPEECH DEBATE (2002) at 87:

> I have argued that the harms carried out in the utterance of a hate-speech-act occur because hate-speech-acts do more than simply offend people or hurt their feelings. Racist hate-speech-acts constitute discursive acts of racial discrimination against a target group, acts which reproduce and reinforce inequality of the grounds of race, and which simultaneously appeal to norms and values which legitimate such inequality.

101 *Id.* at 29.

102 *Id.* at 37:

> As a guide to policy-making, it implies more than the absence of restraint. Applied to speech policy, a positive conception of the speech liberty implies that policy ought to consider the provision of conditions to ensure participation in speaking. To conceive of speech as a positive liberty is unusual, but not impossible, and indeed a positive conception of the speech liberty is not unheard of in the areas of speech policy.

103 For a more in-depth discussion of capabilities theory, *see* Martha Nussbaum, CREATING CAPABILITIES: THE HUMAN DEVELOPMENT APPROACH (2013).

104 Gelber, SPEAKING BACK, *supra* note 100 at 44.

105 *Id.* at 135. "Victims' *counter speech* response would contradict the claims made by the hate speakers, and enable victims to overcome the silencing effects of hate speech."

106 For example, *see* Katharine Gelber, SPEECH MATTERS: GETTING FREE SPEECH RIGHT (2011) (finding that hate speech laws offer justifiable limits on free speech) and Katharine Gelber and Luke McNamara, *The Effects of Civil Hate Speech Laws: Lessons from Australia*, 49 LAW & SOC'Y REV.

631 (2015) (identifying the benefits of Australian hate speech laws over a 25-year period).

107 HATE SPEECH LAW: A PHILOSOPHICAL EXAMINATION (2015); *The "Who?" Question in the Hate Speech Debate: Part 1: Consistency, Practical, and Formal Approaches*, 29 CAN. J.L. & JURIS. 275 (2016); *The "Who?" Question in the Hate Speech Debate: Part 2: Functional and Democratic Approaches*, 30 CAN. J.L. & JURIS. 23 (2017); *What is Hate Speech? Part 1: The Myth of Hate*, 36 LAW & PHIL. 419 (2017); *What is Hate Speech? Part 2: Family Resemblances*, 36 LAW & PHIL. 561 (2017); *Averting Your Eyes in the Information Age: Online Hate Speech and the Captive Audience Doctrine*, 12 CHARLESTON L. REV. 1 (2017); *Retheorizing Actionable Injuries in Civil Lawsuits Involving Targeted Hate Speech: Hate Speech as Degradation and Humiliation*, 9 ALA. C.R. & C.L. L. REV. 1 (2018); *What is so special about online (as compared to offline) hate speech?* 18 ETHNICITIES 297 (2018); and *The Meaning of Silence in Cyberspace: The Authority Problem and Online Hate Speech*, in FREE SPEECH IN THE DIGITAL AGE (2019).

108 HATE SPEECH LAW: A PHILOSOPHICAL EXAMINATION (2015).

109 *Id.* at 3.

110 *Id.* at 106.

> My working hypothesis is that there is a positive relationship between personal development and the right to freedom of expression but that even freedom of expression may be regulated in order to uphold or safeguard real access to personal development for all.

111 *Id.* at 4.

112 Alexander Brown, *Retheorizing Actionable Injuries in Civil Lawsuits Involving Targeted Hate Speech: Hate Speech as Degradation and Humiliation*, 9 ALA. C.R. & C.L. L. REV. 1, 2 (2018). He defines hate speech in this article as: "vituperation (bitter and abusive language) or vilification (viciously disparaging or insulting language) that makes reference to the victim's race, ethnicity, nationality, citizenship status, religious, sexual orientation, gender identity, disability, or other protected characteristic, and which is directly addressed to, or targeted at, the victim, whether in face-to-face offline interactions or in online interactions."

113 *Id.* at 4. "Both of these tests are hybrid objective-subjective legal tests, meaning that a cause of action would require that degradation or humiliation have occurred both as metaphysical and as psychological states of affair."

114 For a detailed discussion of those tests, *see id.* at 25–42.

115 Other scholars are also addressing this issue of hate speech online. For a detailed discussion of that research, *see* Chapter 7.

116 *What Is So Special about Online (as Compared to Offline) Hate Speech?*, 18 ETHNICITIES 297, 298 (2018).

117 *Id.* at 321.

118 *Averting Your Eyes in the Information Age: Online Hate Speech and the Captive Audience Doctrine*, 12 CHARLESTON L. REV. 1 (2017). This doctrine gives the government the ability to restrict speech when that speech is targeting unwilling recipients who are unable to avoid the unwanted speech.

119 *Id.* at 45.

120 Jeremy Waldron, THE HARM IN HATE SPEECH (2012).

121 *Id.* at 4.

122 *Id.*

123 *Id.* at 11.

I will refer to the American debate from time to time, mostly suggesting ways in which it might be enriched by more thoughtful consideration of rival positions. But as things stand, I think it is unlikely that legislation of the kind I set out above will ever pass constitutional muster in America.

124 *Id.* at 78.
125 *Id.* at 81.
126 *Id.* at 83.
127 *Id.*
128 *Id.* at 105.
129 *Id.* at 232.
130 249 U.S. 211 (1919).
131 249 U.S. 47 (1919).
132 250 U.S. 616 (1919).
133 *Id.* at 630 (Holmes, J. dissenting).
134 David Rabban, FREE SPEECH IN ITS FORGOTTEN YEARS (1997).
135 Zechariah Chafee, FREE SPEECH IN THE UNITED STATES 31 (1941).
136 For an in-depth discussion of these cases, *see* Chapter 3, pages 41–42.
137 For more comprehensive discussions of negative and positive liberty, *see* Isaiah Berlin, FOUR ESSAYS ON LIBERTY (1969) and Michael Kammen, SPHERES OF LIBERTY: CHANGING PERCEPTIONS OF LIBERTY IN AMERICAN CULTURE (1986).
138 For additional conversations about autonomy during Phase Two, *see* Jennifer Nedelsky, *Reconceiving Autonomy: Sources, Thoughts and Possibilities*, 1 YALE J.L. & FEMINISM 7 (1989), Catharine MacKinnon, ONLY WORDS (1993); Kathryn Abrams, *From Autonomy to Agency: Feminist Perspectives on Self-Direction*, 40 WM. & MARY L. REV. 805 (1999); and Susan Williams, TRUTH, AUTONOMY AND SPEECH: FEMINIST THEORY AND THE FIRST AMENDMENT (2004).
139 R.A.V. v. City of St. Paul, Minnesota, 505 U.S. 377 (1992).

5 Social Justice, Recognition Theory, and a New Legal Response

From the review of traditional and critical perspectives, it becomes clear that the traditional approach fails to offer the flexibility needed to address the complicated realm of hate speech. In other words, the normative view offers a *fait accompli* concerning speech protection. As one scholar noted: "First Amendment discourse itself has been hegemonic – a dogmatic ideology where there is little free thought about free thought."[1] In essence, the execution of restricting hate speech in the United States requires two actions. As I outlined in the Introduction, the first step requires a fundamental shift in how we think about the role of speech in society. We must be willing to question our entrenched assumptions about why, when, and how speech is protected and to what ends. Second, once that shift has occurred, policymakers and the Courts can begin to craft legal tools that protect the speech rights of members of minority groups and the highest amount of free speech in general. In the process of developing this framework, Strossen's concern must be considered about speech restrictions being used against the disempowered groups that they propose to assist. However, the suggested hate speech restriction here is not an either/or proposition. It can be both. We can continue to have a commitment to free speech that is greater than we see in other parts of the world while also strengthening our protection of human rights. What is required to combat the proliferation of hate speech today is a legal approach that will bridge the chasm between human dignity theory and First Amendment viewpoint neutrality analysis.

In this chapter, I first explore recognition theory and explain the general concept, then discuss its pertinence to the construction of constitutionally viable hate speech restriction. I suggest that we can combine recognition theory with previous First Amendment models as a way to circumvent some of the doctrinal roadblocks existing case law and free speech discourse have created. Finally, this chapter ends with the unveiling of my suggested framework to be used when considering the constitutionality of hate speech regulations.

Recognition Theory

Traditional views of free speech in the United States have placed emphasis on a particular configuration of the autonomous individual, establishing our current narrative that claims the individual exists outside of the community. Consequently, protection of speech only protects the individual, with little to no consideration of the implications to the larger social community. Specifically, in terms of hate speech, this long-held position has proven ineffective in ensuring that all individuals have their voices heard. In fact, it has reinforced social inequalities, rendering certain groups further stigmatized, marginalized, and targeted, as shown by a multitude of social and psychological studies. Approaching hate speech through this lens of the atomistic individual will continue to produce the same results. The solution may be seen as both obvious and radical. We need a fundamental shift in the way we think about the role of free speech and its role in society. In the United States, we need to move the discussion away from the Kantian version of the autonomous individual and individual freedom to a more nuanced conception of social justice, individual dignity, and the power of communication in defining and supporting justice and dignity.

To facilitate this transformation, I suggest the use of Axel Honneth's work on recognition as a way to bridge the gap between where we are currently and the development of a free speech strategy for the global twenty-first century. Honneth is a German philosopher who combines political philosophy and moral philosophy as a way to understand power, social conflict, and social justice in contemporary culture.[2] His work incorporates (and sometimes critiques) theories from the Frankfurt school (notably Habermas and Adorno) and those theories of power related to a Foucauldian perspective.[3] Specifically, Honneth employs a new reading of Hegel to develop his core argument about the importance of recognition.[4] He defines recognition as "the reciprocal limitation of one's own egocentric desires for the benefit of the other."[5] At its core, recognition theory is an attempt to reconcile social justice within a liberal democratic framework. It asks us to consider that liberalism's reliance on autonomy is misplaced, or at least overemphasized, and that true freedom will require a different approach, one informed by recognition. Honneth explains:

> According to my interpretation, Hegel creates this link by attempting to demonstrate to contemporary proponents of liberalism that it is only by taking part in institutionalized practices of individual self-restriction that we can experience our own will as being completely free.[6]

His reliance on recognition as a key element in the understanding of ourselves suggests a system in which individual autonomy is paramount to our identity but also must be defined in relation to others. He explains:

[T]he reason I had sought to reconstruct Hegel's theory of recognition was to garner insights that would not only allow a rethinking of the concept of justice but also lead to a better account of the relationship between socialization and individuation, between social reproduction and individual identity formation.[7]

In other words, Honneth's broad interest is in developing a theory of social justice in which it is acknowledged that individuals can be whole only within the context of a larger community. According to Honneth, Hegel's line of argument is similar to Rousseau and Kant in that he is aiming to explain the principle of state order.[8] But, he differs from them in that he sees law as doing more than protecting individual freedom. Honneth points out that instead, Hegel's supposition is that "The system of law must instead create a 'realm' in which each individual's freedom can be actualized."[9] In other words, community is just as important, if not more, than the autonomy of the individual. This means that:

[I]n order to enjoy such rights, the subject must be willing to concede other subjects the same claim to the unhindered actualization of their personal freedom. For Hegel, therefore, the basis of abstract rights is an intersubjective form of recognition, which consists in mutual adherence to the demand that they each "be a person and respect others as persons."[10]

Using Hegel's philosophy as a framework, Honneth enters into an investigation of institutionalized practices in order to determine which of those practices produce or fortify reciprocal recognition.[11] He identifies three normative principles: love, judicial equality, and performance. He then applies a normative approach to illuminate the gaps between those established practices and their actual social realization. As Jonas Jakobsen explains:

The three forms of intersubjective recognition analyzed by the early Honneth are analyzed in terms of "love" (in personal relations, first and foremost in early childhood), equal respect (as a citizen with the same rights and duties as everyone else), and social esteem (as a valued contributor to a social community, such as the state in which one lives).[12]

Equal respect and social esteem seem a natural fit within the context of a recognition theory and its connection to ensuring and promoting social justice. The third intersubjective recognition discussed early on by Hegel – love – requires, I think, a bit of an explanation to clearly understand how he is using the term, and why it is important in broader social justice theory. In *The I in We: Studies in the Theory of Recognition*, Honneth explains the connection between social freedom and the concept of love:

> Recently, there have been a series of useful attempts to clarify the conception of freedom contained in this formulation. We could briefly summarize the results of these efforts as follows: as long as a subject relates, through an act of will, to an object in the world that remains foreign because the subject cannot recognize it as an extension of its own self, the subject is not yet truly free. It only finds its way to true freedom by being 'with itself' in this 'other' in such a way that is experiences the other's characteristics or particularities as something with which it can 'identify'...Hegel always identified this form of freedom with reference to love...he refers to friendship and love as the feelings in which the structure of its 'being-with-itself-in-other' can be discerned most easily.[13]

Love, then, which is a necessity for recognition, can only exist when we are able to identify with each other. Building on these three areas of recognition, Honneth argues that when essential claims for recognition occur, the state should take corrective action.[14]

Honneth criticizes the various levels of recognition in our democratic societies. He shifts the focus from the question of democracy to a question of the social conditions necessary for citizen participation in the public sphere. As one legal scholar noted:

> This demand is something very different from a demand for autonomy or freedom. Recognition requires the community to validate and to have a good opinion of each person. In this way, recognition places demands not only on the state to enforce equality and basic rights, but on members of the community to provide respect and recognition of their fellow citizens. Being left alone to pursue one's vision of the good life is not sufficient; rather the demand for recognition requires cooperation and respect between individuals within the broader community.[15]

At the crux of his argument is the idea that individual autonomy is the very reason we protect civil liberties, and yet our ability to have a fully formed autonomous identity is strongly connected to the way in which we are treated in the larger social environment. Ultimately,

> Analyzing social conflicts in terms of struggles for recognition allows us to pay attention to the way in which power (understood as self-interest and strategic action) and communication

(understood as orientation towards mutual understanding) are entangled with each other, sometimes in subtle or confusing ways.[16]

These struggles don't occur in a vacuum and as such, the legal system plays a major role in either supporting or thwarting recognition.

According to Honneth, the legal system is responsible for ensuring those civil rights that pertain to an individual's sense of self-realization.[17] This position might seem to support traditional theories about protecting speech to protect the individual. However, because Honneth's work marries the individual with society, his position steers the focus away from the negative liberty approach and requires the government to consider the effects of speech *on* civil liberties and not free speech *as* a civil liberty. He explains: "Subjects are equally in a position to determine their life-goals without external influence only to the extent to which the establishment of civil law gives them all, in principle, individual freedom to make decisions."[18] To Honneth, "[S]elf-realization is dependent on the social prerequisite of legally guaranteed autonomy."[19] But, his read on autonomy neither fits the Kantian notion of the self-realized, autonomous being untouched by social constraints, nor is it characterized by scholars who reject the concept of autonomy outright and replace it with theories of agency. Honneth explains:

> Clearly, even the alternative model of justice that I have in mind must start by acknowledging the normative idea that all members of modern societies must possess the same capacities and conditions for individual autonomy. What distinguishes this alternative conception is thus not its moral core, but its material implications. Everything turns on how we understand the social promotion of autonomy, upon whose crucial role both sides agree.[20]

Autonomy remains a key element of realizing a socially just world. The difference between typical conceptions of autonomy and Honneth's version lies in how to best achieve it. According to Honneth, the previous model relies on a distribution of goods, while his model relies on recognition. He explains:

> [M]y alternative conception understands individual autonomy not as a monological but as an intersubjective matter. Individuals achieve self-determination by learning within relations of reciprocal recognition, to view their needs, beliefs and abilities as worthy of articulation and pursuit in the public sphere.[21]

Autonomy is not innate or automatic. Material goods alone are not enough to ensure individual autonomy, nor can it be created through purely negative conceptions of liberty. The conditions for supporting autonomy must be constantly monitored and maintained which requires some level of government intervention in the form positive liberty.

In terms of freedom of speech, traditional application of the First Amendment is tied to a concept of autonomy and self-realization; however, without the additional principles enumerated by Honneth, the protection of harmful types of speech (such as hate speech) seems not only ineffective but counterproductive. Those targeted by hate speech experience not only an attack on their individual identity, but are also denied membership into the larger social community. Also, according to Honneth's reasoning, those who espouse hate speech are negatively impacted because by denying mutual recognition, they are denying themselves true social freedom.[22] He explained:

> If being free merely means acting without external restrictions or taking up a reflexive stance, then subjects can be seen as being sufficiently free even before they become involved in a social order. But if we grasp subjects as truly "free" only on the condition that their aims can be fulfilled or realized within reality itself, then we must reverse the relationship between legitimating procedures and social justice.[23]

Individual freedom, including the freedom to speak, must be situated within a larger social order for the freedom to have any real meaning, and that social order must be questioned and objectively defined for real social justice to be enforceable. The government must take a proactive approach to create a space where individuals can be "truly free."

Recognition and Previous Free Speech Arguments

From the previous discussion, it is clear that Honneth's concept of recognition theory can serve as a philosophical bedrock for why hate speech should be restricted. But what is not immediately clear is how this emphasis on human dignity can be situated in relation to our commitment to freedom of expression. It is my position that we can use some of the legal analytical tools already available to reconcile this shift from complete protection of hate speech to some restriction, when warranted, to protect and support human dignity for all. Those models of how to deal with the problem of regulating hate speech in the United States can serve as a foundation for a constitutionally sound approach to hate speech restriction. Following, I discuss two scholarly studies and one appellate court case to illustrate how the abstract theory of recognition and human dignity might bear concretely on First Amendment doctrines and, as a result, illuminate a clear path forward to a framework for case analysis that constitutionally permits some level of hate speech restriction.

Complicating Content Neutrality

As previously indicated, the concept of content neutrality is foundational in First Amendment analysis in general and has played a major role in hate speech cases specifically.[24] However, the application of this concept is questionable because it lacks, as was emphasized in Chapter 3, sufficient complexity to address many current speech issues. My 2009 book, *Modern Power and Free Speech: Contemporary Culture and Issues of Equality*, suggested a way that content neutrality could continue to be a relevant analytical tool in First Amendment cases.[25] I first explained that "Unlike areas of law where discriminatory practice is direct and obvious, the oppressive power of the First Amendment is hidden and seemingly passive."[26] I then offered that "To unmask the oppressive elements of the First Amendment, the link between power and free speech must be considered discursively, historically and relationally."[27] Put simply, speech operates in society in a way that requires legal tests concerning speech restrictions to be more complicated instead of merely asking whether or not those restrictions are content neutral. In order to add both depth and breadth to the legal conversation surrounding the restriction of hate speech, the book proposed that the Court replace the two-dimensional content neutrality standard with a three-part analytical framework. This framework asked courts to consider (1) the character, nature, and scope of the speech restriction; (2) the historical context of the cultural group involved in the speech at issue; and (3) the individual power relations occurring at the particular speech moment.[28] To illustrate how this framework might look, it was applied to the restrictions at question in *Skokie v. Illinois, R.A.V v. St. Paul,* and *Virginia v. Black.* Specifically, this framework addressed two key problems.

First, instead of abandoning the concept of content neutrality, part one of that suggested framework merely added more factors into the equation, thus allowing for a more careful consideration of the speech restrictions in question. Second, that framework would allow the Court to acknowledge that the government is not the only entity able to restrict the voice of members of socially disempowered groups. "My framework acknowledges that government censorship based on hostility or favoritism toward ideas is a genuine concern. However, this framework also acknowledges that the government is not the only oppressive power operating in U.S. society."[29] The purpose of the framework is to offer suggestions for how best to protect disempowered groups from hateful speech, while taking into account traditional First Amendment principles.

The three-pronged approach proposed a solution to the insufficient content neutrality principle by asking the Court to extend the scope of its inquisition into speech restrictions on hateful speech targeting specific historically disempowered groups. Considering the approach nearly a decade later, and viewed through the lens of recognition theory, it falls short in two areas. First, because recognition theory requires a contemplation of the government's responsibility for ensuring civil rights that pertain to a sense of self-realization, emphasis should be placed on defining what hate speech is and who is being impacted. The three-prong model suggested through my earlier work did not offer a precise definition of hate speech and also relied, perhaps too heavily, on protecting the sanctity of the concept of content neutrality. In other words, that framework did not push the boundaries far enough to adequately address the complexities of hate speech concerns today. Second, the framework has less applicability when considering Internet speech.[30] The final prong of the framework, the relational nature of the power between speakers, required a consideration of the power dynamic of the specific speech situation.[31] Implicit in these criteria is some sense of spatial proximity. As a result of the emphasis on physical location, in order for this framework to be useful in relation to Internet hate speech, it would first need to be crafted with a more direct explanation of how speech moments might still be threatening even when presented over the Internet.

Expanding the Incitement Standard

Part of the solution to the hate speech regulation puzzle might be found in a rarely discussed law review article published in the mid-1990s that addressed the true threats doctrine.[32] In his article, "Camouflaged Incitement: Freedom of Speech, Communicative Torts and the Borderland of the Brandenburg Test," David Crump argued for a more expansive understanding of true threats and incitement.[33] Specifically, he was concerned with what he termed camouflaged speech, that is speech which might seem innocuous on the surface, but through consideration of context could be viewed as threatening or inciting. This camouflaged speech in not regulable under the First Amendment standards developed in *Brandenburg* and its progeny.[34] Crump asserted that this approach to determining what qualifies as legally proscribable incitement ignores the complexity of speech and that the *Brandenburg* standard privileges protection of speech over other competing interests.[35] In other words, the current blunt instrument approach to determining incitement leaves members of disempowered groups vulnerable to veiled threats.[36]

Crump addressed the shortcomings in the *Brandenburg* test by offering a formula that could better distinguish between protected speech and unprotected "inciting" speech in cases involving more subtle types of threatening speech.[37] He built on the categorical approach recommended in *Brandenburg* by expanding the test from two parts to eight. Crump's test would ask the courts to consider the following factors when determining whether or not speech crosses the line into proscribable incitement: (1) the expressed words or symbols uttered; (2) the pattern of the utterance, including any parts that both the speaker and the audience could be expected to understand in a sense different from the ordinary; (3) the context, including the medium, the audience, and the surrounding communications; (4) the predictability and anticipated seriousness of unlawful results, and whether they actually occurred; (5) the extent of the speaker's knowledge or reckless disregard of the likelihood of violent results; (6) the availability of alternate means of expressing a similar message, without encouragement of violence; (7) the inclusion of disclaimers; and (8) whether the utterance has "serious literary, artistic, political, or scientific value."[38] Taken together, consideration of these factors would expand the current two-part incitement standard in a way that allows for a more complex approach to restricting certain threatening or inciting statements. Crump acknowledged that this type of test, like all constitutional tests, carries with it an elasticity that could lead to a variation in rulings. However, he also contended that this test, because of its more multifaceted set of criteria, is a better instrument for assessing threatening speech.[39]

Clearly, Crump's recommendation adds depth to the two-part test created in *Brandenburg*. However, this test would need work to be applicable in relation to Internet hate speech. First, because the article was published in 1994, it does not address the proliferation of social media. Second, despite Crump's explanation that all constitutional law is subjective, the reliance on this type of ad hoc balancing perhaps could leave too much room for interpretation. Finally, Crump's test was not developed to address larger scale threats connected specifically to hate speech, and so could serve to ignore or bury the importance of considering the speaker's motivation and the status of the targeted person or group. Despite these shortcomings, Crump's approach to addressing camouflaged speech adds important elements to consider in relation to possible restriction of hate speech.

Focusing on the Reasonable Listener

The final, and perhaps most compelling, place we may turn to for some guidance on how to treat hate speech is the Ninth Circuit's 2002 ruling in *Planned Parenthood v. the ACLA*, a case focused on wanted poster-style anti-abortion materials on the web.[40] The case is significant for two reasons. First, unlike the models proposed by Crump and Demaske, which don't address the Internet, *Planned Parenthood* directly focuses on Internet speech. Second, the *Planned Parenthood* ruling, while not specifically addressing hate speech concerns, offers a way for us to construct a test that would allow the courts to consider the impact of certain speech on marginalized groups because of the Ninth Circuit's application in the case of a reasonable listener test.

The Ninth Circuit stands out as a shining example of the confusion over how to best apply the intent standard.[41] Shortly after the 1969

Watts ruling, in *Roy v. the United States*, the Ninth Circuit originally adopted a "reasonable speaker" test.[42] In a later case, the Ninth Circuit would explain: "Apart from holding that Watt's crack about L.B.J was not a true threat, the Court set out no standard for determining when a statement is a true threat that is unprotected speech under the First Amendment."[43] In other words, the Supreme Court did not provide a specific test to assist lower courts in determining what would constitute as a true threat, so the Ninth Circuit developed its own.[44] As a result of this lack of direction by the U.S. Supreme Court, most circuit courts have adopted either a reasonable speaker test, in which the determination of when a "defendant may be convicted for making a threat is whether he should have reasonably foreseen that the statement he uttered would be taken as a threat by those to whom it is made,"[45] or a reasonable listener test which relies on how a listener might interpret the message. To date, the Supreme Court still has not reviewed the differing standards applied by the lower courts to determine their constitutionality.

The Ninth Circuit applied its objective test standard in multiple subsequent cases. Despite its past application, in *Planned Parenthood*, the defendant asked the court to consider applying a subjective standard in place of the reasonable speaker test that would "require evidence, albeit circumstantial or inferential in many cases, that the speaker actually intended to induce fear, intimidation or terror."[46] The majority declined this proposed standard. It also disagreed with dissent's recommendation that the proof must be offered that the speaker or someone directly under the speaker's control must intend to actually carry out the threat, and that the court must consider whether or not the speech is public or private.[47] Relying on language from *R.A.V.*, the majority rejected the subjective standard:

> Threats are outside the First Amendment to 'protect individuals from the fear of violence, from the disruption that fear engenders, and from the possibility that the threatened violence will occur.' This purpose is not served by hinging constitutionality on the speaker's subjective intent or capacity to do (or not to do) harm.[48]

Instead, the court emphasized the objective standard (the reasonable listener standard) as a better framework to draw a distinct line between true threats and speech that might merely be frightening.[49]

The objective standard test in relation to threatening speech offers a promising compromise between traditional applications of First Amendment doctrine and the concerns raised by critical legal scholars in the area of hate speech. The standard allows us to recognize that the damage caused by threatening speech is not just about the physical attack that could follow, but is about the fear itself. True threats operate, then, as a form of attack intended partly to silence the voice of those who are targeted by it. When the threats are waged against socially disempowered groups, the end result can be the silencing of an entire class of people, not just one individual. Creating legislation that would use this objective standard and tailoring that legislation to address hate speech would not be a stretch. In addition, because *Planned Parenthood* dealt specifically with online threats, the standard is already somewhat designed for more modern versions of threatening hate speech. Another limitation of using this standard to restrict Internet hate speech comes from the recent Supreme Court ruling in *Elonis v. United States.*[50] On the surface, *Elonis* seems to close the door on this type of judicial analysis by ruling that the Third Circuit had erred when it applied the reasonable person standard to Elonis' online speech. However, while the Court did take issue with the Third Circuit's approach, the majority also stressed that it was "not necessary" for them to consider any First Amendment issues in the case. The ruling in *Elonis*, then, serves more as a hindrance than a roadblock to applying the objective standard informed by the reasonable listener.

Autonomy and Social Justice: A Response to Hate Speech

If Honneth's conception of social justice is employed to frame the relationship between speech and the autonomous individual, then the power of speech must be addressed in the ways suggested by Demaske and Crump. As both of those models propose, the relationship between speech protection and individual rights for all is more complicated than traditional models acknowledge. Recognition theory forces the focus to shift from the autonomous individual to the place of those individuals within the community. This modification might seem like a major departure from traditional conceptions of free speech protection in the United States. Indeed, at first blush, it seems to be more akin to the dignity-based philosophy used in the International context, a philosophical foundation that would not be able to gain traction in U.S. courts.[51] However, given Honneth's interpretation of Hegel in the development of recognition theory, it is not as implausible as it might appear. In fact, as already noted, Honneth sees autonomy as crucial to self-identity. The key difference between Honneth's view of autonomy as expressed in recognition theory and the Kantian version adopted by traditional First Amendment advocates is a matter of how a society (and legal system) can best support autonomy. In the Kantian version, speech is protected in order to protect the individual and in doing so increases the individual's ability to be self-realized, search for his or her own individual truth, participate in democracy, and stave off tyrannical governments.[52]

When applying recognition theory to the protection of speech, individual speech is protected for those same reasons, but an individual must be defined in relation to others within the community. For example, an approach based in concerns about the health of a community rather than the rights of the individual is no less interested in fostering democracy than Bollinger, Post, or Weinstein. The difference is that for those scholars, restricting hate speech is an affront to democracy and, as Post noted, would mean "that no communication can ever be safe from legal sanction."[53] From the perspective of recognition theory, allowing hate speech to flourish without some legal intervention actually works to stifle democratic participation. This shift in perspective facilitated by recognition theory is at once subtle and transcendent, allowing for a continued privileging of freedom of speech and expression, but tempering it when that speech or expression interferes with the recognition process. On the theoretical plane, relying on recognition theory to reassess legal approaches to hate speech functions as a bridge between past treatment and future treatment. This move, however, once taken from the theoretical realm and placed into the legal system, requires a new doctrinal approach, one that will facilitate the building of that bridge.

The New Framework

This book proposes that in place of previous legal doctrines applied in hate speech cases, a new analytical framework is established that will allow courts to find certain anti-hate speech legislation to withstand First Amendment scrutiny. Specifically, this framework would be applied in two tiers. In Tier One, a court would have to consider whether the speech in question is regulable hate speech. In other words, it would address the question: is this hate speech? To answer that question, courts would apply the definition set out in Chapter 1: (1) is the speech "directed against a specified or easily identifiable individual or ...a group of individuals based on an arbitrary and normatively irrelevant feature;" (2) does the speech stigmatize those targeted by "implicitly or explicitly ascribing to it qualities widely regarded as highly undesirable;" (3) is the speech likely to cause the target group to be "viewed as an undesirable presence and a legitimate object of hostility;" and (4) are there additional factors related to history, context, and social power.[54]

Without a doubt, the most delicate issue with Tier One is that it is asking the courts to review speech based on content and/or viewpoint and to make decisions concerning hate speech restrictions based on content and/or viewpoint. The seriousness of the concerns raised should not be downplayed or ignored. Indeed, given the forceful rhetoric used in *Matal v. Tam* in defense of neutrality, any test recommending otherwise will have a high, nearly impossible bar to overcome. The criteria for review in Tier One, however, offers a tool that can be applied with laser precision, replacing the all-or-nothing sledgehammer approach currently used. The exact way in which the courts rely on the viewpoint and content neutrality principles will need to be considered with less emphasis in hate speech related cases than they are now. Clearly, diligence in combating possible government abuse of power will remain a high priority. The suggested framework takes into account that those concerns are valid and serious, but suggests that while those are valid and serious concerns, so are the effects of hate speech on targeted individuals and society as a whole. Any framework considering possible hate speech restriction must recognize that hate speech, by its very nature, is viewpoint based. The many harms enumerated in Chapters 1 and 4 expose what those specific harms are and why they are more damaging than the more generic messages restricted under fighting words or true threats doctrines.[55]

Tier Two of the framework offers a way for courts to continue to honor the commitment to free speech while still considering a viewpoint-based speech restriction. Under this tier, if speech is found in Tier One to be hate speech, then the court will look at additional factors in an attempt to assess the overall impact of that particular hate speech. These factors would include, but are not limited to, the public or private nature of the speech moment in question, the application of the reasonable listener standard as defined in *Planned Parenthood*, and a consideration of other possible mitigating factors, such as some of those outlined by Crump. That is to say, context will play an important role in determining whether or not the hate speech in question is regulable under the First Amendment, and in the particular way it is attempted to be regulated. My recommended framework, by not proscribing the exact factors, allows for the elasticity needed to allow legislators and the courts the opportunity to hone and shape its application. Relying on these additional factors in Tier Two serves multiple purposes. First, through the added rigor, it helps to ensure that merely offensive or disparaging speech will not be swept up in the restrictions. Second, it offers a way to consider the broader context and, as a result, think about the impact of hate speech in terms of those targeted, those performing the hate speech, and the community as a whole. In other words, it allows the use of Honneth's conception of recognition theory in order to address the social justice components brought into play when hate speech occurs. Finally, this tier keeps the framework still grounded in long-standing court doctrine in an effort to bridge the span between recognition theory and traditional First Amendment analysis.

Conclusion

Recognition theory offers a valuable tool for addressing hate speech restriction within the U.S. context. On the one hand, its close connection to Kant's conceptualization of the autonomous individual enables it to fit within current First Amendment doctrine. On the other hand, because it privileges the role of that autonomous individual within the larger society over the traditional notions of individual rights, it enables us to move the conversation forward in terms of hate speech regulation, allowing for an approach more in line with the needs of our globally connected world. Recognition theory breathes new life into the First Amendment while still accentuating the U.S. commitment to protecting speech in order to foster political participation, self-realization, and the search for truth.

This chapter set out to explain the specifics of how recognition theory addresses the question of hate speech restriction. Following that explanation, I reviewed several approaches to First Amendment application in an attempt to further ground recognition theory and lead to the development of a workable framework for case analysis. That two-tiered framework, which was introduced in this chapter, will be applied in the next three chapters to illustrate how it could work in allowing us some flexibility in restricting a certain level of hate speech in the United States.

Notes

1 Bart Cammaerts, *Radical Pluralism and Free Speech in Online Public Spaces*, 12 Int'l J. of Cult. Stud. 555, 559 (2009).
2 For an in-depth discussion of Honneth's theories, *see* Katia Genel and Jean-Philippe Deranty (eds.), Recognition or Disagreement: A Critical Encounter on the Politics of Freedom, Equality, and Identity (2016).
3 Honneth has been prolific over the past 20 plus years. Some of his works include: The Struggle for Recognition: The Moral Grammar of Social Conflicts (1995); with Nancy Fraser, Redistribution or Recognition: A Political-Philosophical Exchange (2004); The I in We: Studies in the Theory of Recognition (2012) and Freedom's Right: The Social Foundations of Democratic Life (2014).
4 Axel Honneth, The Struggle for Recognition: The Moral Grammar of Social Conflicts (1995).
5 Axel Honneth, The I in We: Studies in the Theory of Recognition (2012).
6 *Id.* at xiii.
7 *Id.* at 7.
8 *Id.* at 21.
9 *Id.*
10 *Id.* at 26.
11 Honneth, Struggle, *supra* note 4, at 92–130.
12 Jonas Jakobsen, *Religion and (Mis)recognition: Axel Honneth and the Danish Cartoon Controversy*, in Varieties of Liberalism: Contemporary Challenges (Jan Harald Alnes and Manuel Toscano, eds. 2014) at 25–26.
13 Honneth, The I in We, *supra* note 5, at 22.
14 Jakobsen, *supra* note 12, at 25.

> …claims to recognition made by citizens of a given polity may be justified to the extent that, without this recognition, they would be disadvantaged in their search for a good and autonomous human life. In other words, we should take the normative thrust of Honneth's theory to consist in an argument about specific forms of recognition without which human life is unlikely to be experienced as successful and free.

15 Neomi Rao, *Three Concepts of Dignity in Constitutional Law*, 86 Notre Dame L. Rev. 183, 247–248 (2013).

16 Jakobsen, *supra* note 12, at 22–23.

17 Axel Honneth, FREEDOM'S RIGHT: THE SOCIAL FOUNDATIONS OF DEMO-CRATIC LIFE 71–74 (2014) (extensively discussing Hegel's views on the inability of purely negative liberty to ensure social justice).

18 Honneth, STRUGGLE, *supra* note 4, at 177.

19 *Id.*

20 Honneth, THE I IN WE, *supra* note 5, at 46.

21 *Id.*

22 Terry Pinkard, *Review of Freedom's Right: The Social Foundation of Democratic Life*, NOTRE DAME PHIL. REV. *available at* http://ndpr.nd.edu/news/freedom-s-right-the-social-foundations-of-democratic-life/ [last accessed November 30, 2017].

23 Honneth, FREEDOM'S RIGHT, *supra* note 17.

24 For a detailed discussion, *see* Chapter 3, pages 57–60.

25 Chris Demaske, MODERN POWER AND FREE SPEECH: CONTEMPORARY CULTURE AND ISSUES OF EQUALITY 79 (2009).

26 *Id.*

27 *Id.*

28 *Id.*

29 *Id.* at 108.

30 *Id.* at 154–155. The book acknowledged the difficulties of applying this framework to Internet hate speech but did not offer a detailed explanation of how the courts might draw clear lines.

31 *Id.* at 77.

32 For an in-depth definition of true threats doctrine, *see* Chapter 3, pages 51–52.

33 David Crump, *Camouflaged Incitement: Freedom of Speech, Communicative Torts, and the Borderland of the Brandenburg Test*, 29 GA. L. REV. 1 (1994).

34 *Id.* at 5. In addition to Brandenburg, Crump offers a critique of the Court's reliance on two additional cases, *Hess v. Indiana*, 404 U.S. 105 (1973) and *Watts v. U.S.*, 394 U.S. 705 (1969).

> Such decisions as *Hess v. Indiana* and *Watts v. United States* have emphasized a literal reading of remarks creating dangers of violence or harm. By decreasing the weight given to the danger that violence may materialize, and by exercising caution in recognizing camouflaged incitement from the context, these decisions extend powerful protection to the freedom of speech.

35 *Id.* at 13.

> Of course, there also was a more ominous side to Brandenburg. The possibility remained that a person of borderline mentality attending this rally might have taken the Klan leader's words to heart and acted upon the indirect advocacy they contained. For example, this hypothetical psychopathic Klansman might have ambushed and killed a randomly selected African-American citizen for the purpose of enhancing his own reputation and exacting the 'revengeance' that his mentor had mentioned in front of the burning cross. In that case, the Supreme Court's opinion still would exonerate Mr. Brandenburg himself; in effect, it would say to the victim, 'Too bad. That's the price of freedom of speech.' This tragic possibility exists because law is not a perfect instrument of social regulation – and because of the preferred position of the First Amendment freedoms. Still, our courts should take the potential for tragedy

seriously; they should strive to make the best accommodation possible between these competing values, rather than cavalierly writing off the victims of camouflaged incitement.

36 Crump does not limit (or even focus necessarily) on hate speech. In his article, he covers speech situations including mercenaries, mob hits, and video games.

37 *Id.* at 45.

This description of the various categories into which camouflaged incitement may fit leads to the effort to formulate a test for distinguishing unprotected kinds of incitement. The task is difficult, because the question quintessentially is one of degree. In some cases, the very closeness of the question might cause us to favor speech. But the stakes are high: A slavishly literal approach would immunize coded solicitations of murder. Besides, the question is close everywhere along the continuum, and unless we are to throw up our hands entirely and immunize speech that everyone but the courts knows is incitement to crime, we must draw the line at some point – and it is sure to be drawn between close cases.

38 *Id.* at 54–69.

39 *Id.* at 53.

40 Planned Parenthood of Columbia/Willamette Inc. v. American Coalition of Life Activists, 290 f.3d at 1074, 1088 (2002).

41 For an in-depth discussion, *see* Paul Crane, *'True Threats' and the Issue of Intent*, 92 Virginia L. Rev. 1125 (2006).

42 416 F.2d 874 (9th Cir. 1969).

43 290 f.3d at 1074 (2002).

44 *Id.* at 1072. "The Supreme Court has provided benchmarks, but no definition."

45 United States v. Fulmer, 108 F.3d 1486 (1st Cir. 1997).

46 290 F.3d at 1074, 1075 (2002).

47 *Id.* at 1076.

48 *Id.*

49 *Id.*

Thus, no reasonable speaker would foresee that a patient would take the statement 'You have cancer and will die within six months,' or that a pedestrian would take a warning 'Get out the way of that bus,' as a serious expression of intent to inflict bodily harm; the harm is going to happen anyway.

50 135 S. Ct. 2001 (2015).

51 For an example of the dignity approach, *see*, Jeremy Waldron, The Harm in Hate Speech 138–140 (2012).

52 For a more detailed discussion of these aims, *see* Chapter 4, pages 67–72.

53 Robert C. Post, *Racist Speech, Democracy and the First Amendment*, 32 Wm. & Mary L. Rev. 267, 270 (1991).

54 Parts one through three of the definition come directly from Bhikhu Parekh's work, *see* Chapter 1, pages 11–12. Part four is derived from discussions by various scholars including Demaske, *supra* note 25, at 73–79, and Katharine Gelber, *Hate Speech – Definitions & Empirical Evidence*, 32 Const. Comment. 619, 626 (2017).

55 For discussion of these harms, *see* Chapter 1.

6 From R.A.V. v. St. Paul to Matal v. Tam

The Parameters of Restriction

As outlined in Chapter 3, the Supreme Court has a long and complicated relationship with how to address the issue of hate speech. In that chapter, I discussed several Court cases that touched in some way on the question of hate speech restriction. That chapter reviewed cases starting with the 1952 group libel case, *Beauharnais v. Illinois*, and ending with *Matal v. Tam*, the most recent case to address those possible limitations. The discussion of those cases in Chapter 3 was intended to highlight the various legal principles and doctrines that the Court has relied on to primarily find hate speech regulations unconstitutional in any scenario. This chapter revisits some of those Supreme Court rulings, shifting the conversation from what the Court has done in the past to what might be different if the framework suggested in Chapter 5 was applied instead. In other words, in this chapter, I review those rulings to give shape to the new framework, highlighting the parameters of what speech might or might not be regulable under its application.

Specifically, I examine four Supreme Court cases spanning a 25-year period – *R.A.V. v. St. Paul, Virginia v. Black, Snyder v. Phelps, and Matal v. Tam*. I discuss the hate speech element that exists in each of them; explain the Court's ruling and other pertinent background for the cases; and then apply the two-tiered framework developed in Chapter 5. As will become clear throughout the chapter, this alternative approach, grounded in social justice and mindful of the commitment to free speech, offers an exacting framework that is more staunchly linked to the lived experiences of those targeted by hate speech regulations.

R.A.V. v. St. Paul

In 1992, the U.S. Supreme Court would hear one of its only cases to tackle the issue of hate speech restriction.[1] The case focused on whether fighting words doctrine could be used to support the St. Paul, Minn., Bias Motivated Crime Ordinance, an ordinance that prohibited the display of a symbol "which one knows or has reason to know arouses anger, alarm, or resentment in others on the basis of race, color, creed, religion or gender." The Supreme Court in a unanimous opinion struck down the ordinance, ruling that it was facially unconstitutional because it was content-based, imposing a special prohibition on particular disfavored subjects of race, color, and creed. This case would result in wildly different rulings at the lower court levels and a unanimous, yet highly divided, Supreme Court ruling.

The trial court found in favor of R.A.V., determining that the ordinance prohibited expressive conduct which is a clear violation of the First Amendment.[2] The Minnesota Supreme Court reversed the district court decision, finding that the ordinance did not prohibit protected speech.[3] The court found the speech restricted through ordinance was fighting words and, thus, not protected. Relying on overbreadth doctrine and strict scrutiny analysis when reaching its decision, the court found that the ordinance was not overbroad – it did not restrict more speech than would be permissible within the fighting words category – and the state had met its burden of proving a compelling interest in the need to restrict the speech outlined in the ordinance.[4] In a discussion similar to the one that would later be used in *Virginia v. Black*, the Minnesota Supreme Court explained:

> There are certain symbols and regalia that in the context of history carry a clear message of racial supremacy, hatred, persecution, and degradation of certain groups. The swastika, the Klan robes, the burning cross are examples of signs – like all signs – that have no meaning on their own, but that convey a powerful message to both the user and the recipient of the sign in context.[5]

In other words, the speech subsumed under the ordinance did not violate the First Amendment because it fit into an already proscribable category – fighting words – and the state had met its burden of showing that the measure was needed to counter "hatred and violence based on racial superiority."[6]

In what First Amendment scholar W. Wat Hopkins described as "one of its most convoluted opinions involving free speech issues," the U.S. Supreme Court in 1992 reversed the Minnesota court's ruling.[7] Hopkins, along with countless other scholars, criticized the ruling in *R.A.V. v. St. Paul* for being unnecessarily complicated. As discussed at great length in Chapter 3, the majority opinion focused almost exclusively on interpreting the ordinance in light of the category of fighting words with extensive discussion of content and viewpoint neutrality, and some reference to the secondary effects doctrine.

Before turning to the application of my two-tiered framework, the issue of discriminatory harm in question in this case needs to be examined. That issue can be addressed by reviewing St. Paul's history of hate crimes, which was the driving factor behind the development of the ordinance in the first place.[8] The city was responding to concerns about escalating religious, sexist, and racist incidents that started in the late 1960s.[9] The Minnesota State Supreme Court articulated this same concern in its ruling when it wrote:

> Burning a cross in the yard of an African American family's home is deplorable conduct that the City of St. Paul may without question prohibit. The burning cross is itself an unmistakable symbol of violence and hatred based on virulent notions of racial supremacy. It is the responsibility, even the obligation, of diverse communities to confront such notions in whatever form they appear.[10]

The court did not shy away from the key reason that the ordinance existed: to ameliorate the harms associated with certain types of hatred targeted to specific groups.

In his oral argument before the Supreme Court, County Prosecutor Tom Foley emphasized this need to single out specific types of harm:

> I think the city has an absolute right and purpose to try to regulate the harm that goes onto its citizens. And certainly, this bias-motivated conduct and violence is much more harmful and has more harmful impacts to its citizens.[11]

This position was first called into question by the U.S. Supreme Court during oral arguments when its response to Foley's comment was: "That's a political judgment. I mean, you may feel strongest about race, color, creed, religion, or gender. Somebody else may feel strong as to about philosophy, about economic philosophy, about whatever."[12] In other words, the Court during oral arguments did not acknowledge or, in the very least, did not agree with the state's argument that it had a compelling interest in singling out certain harmful speech for special restriction.

This debate would continue in the Supreme Court's final ruling. Justice Scalia focused considerable attention on the content and viewpoint distinction in the ordinance, but did not address the state's position that these types of viewpoints are particularly problematic. For example, he raised this scenario:

> ...One could hold up a sign saying, for example, that all 'anti-Catholic bigots' are misbegotten; but not that all 'papists' are, for that would insult and provoke violence 'on the basis of religion.' St. Paul has no such authority to license one side of a debate to fight freestyle, while requiring the other to follow Marquis of Queensberry rules.[13]

He makes no statement to the contrary concerning the special harm that certain types of speech might cause. His reference to the speech in question being one side of the debate illustrates his lack of empathy to the state's position. He further reinforced this position when he stated:

> What makes the anger, fear, sense of dishonor, etc., produced by violation of this ordinance distinct from the anger, fear, sense of dishonor, etc., produced by other fighting words is nothing other than the fact that it is caused by a distinctive idea, conveyed by a distinctive message.[14]

In other words, the ordinance fails because it targets specific harmful speech, not because it targets speech in a broader sense; the ordinance is underinclusive as opposed to overbroad.

Justice White, on the other hand, found the ordinance content-based and did not see a problem per se with regulating fighting words based off of their message. He clarified that "a ban on all fighting words or on a subset of the fighting words category would restrict only the social evil of hate speech, without creating the danger of driving viewpoints from the marketplace."[15] To Justice White, all fighting words convey some sort of message and so restricting a subset of them is possible, even though he believed they could not constitutionally be restricted through the St. Paul ordinance.

Justice Stevens echoed those concerns about the distinctive harm of certain types of discriminatory speech. He explained:

> Conduct that creates special risks or causes special harms may be prohibited by special rules...Threatening someone because of her race or religious beliefs may cause particularly severe trauma or touch off a riot...such threats may be punished more severely than threats against someone based on, say, his support of a particular athletic team.[16]

Justice Stevens was clearly arguing that there is a significant qualitative difference between hateful speech in the general sense and hate speech that targets members of disempowered groups. Like Justice White, his issue was with the specific construction of the St. Paul ordinance, not with the possibility of the construction of a constitutionally sound anti-hate speech regulation in general.

Analyzing R.A.V.

Everything about *R.A.V.* seemed fractured, convoluted, and, at times, nearly incoherent. Multiple lower court rulings, combined with a Supreme Court opinion offering several competing legal solutions, partially highlight the fruitlessness of considering hate speech restriction under pre-existing doctrines. In particular, this case presents several areas for consideration under the framework that I am recommending here. First, the Bias Motivated Crime Ordinance itself, both in terms of the language of the ordinance and in the context and history in which it was enacted, raises interesting questions. Second, as alluded to by the points highlighted above, the Supreme Court's rationale offers a rich space for analysis in terms of its interpretation and application of the categorical approach (specifically the category of fighting words); its conflation of secondary effects analysis with analysis of speech based on category; and its ruling out of the state interest in restricting certain forms of hate speech. Perhaps the most compelling place for analysis is the Court's deliberation concerning the balance between protecting the right to free speech and the need to restrict speech that has no social value, particularly its assessment of hate speech in that equation. My framework, grounded in social justice theory, would consider different elements, ultimately reaching a different conclusion.

As outlined in Chapter 5, my recommendation is application of a two-tiered framework in cases dealing with possible hate speech restriction. Tier One establishes whether the suggested restricted material is indeed hate speech. Through a series of questions, this tier is intended to offer a more rigorous analysis than the all-or-nothing content-neutral approach. Tier Two comes into play if the suggested speech restriction is found to target hate speech. Tier Two calls for an extended consideration of additional factors before determining whether or not the hate speech in question rises to the level of regulable hate speech. This second tier gives the courts the ability to weigh the value of restricting that hate speech against the benefit of protecting it. In particular, this tier bridges the traditional conceptions of free speech protection and social justice theory's emphasis on human dignity because it asks us to weigh the two competing interests in a more balanced manner than the courts current do.

Tier One asks that the courts consider the following: (1) is the speech in question "directed against a specified or easily identifiable individual or …a group of individuals based on an arbitrary and normatively irrelevant feature;" (2) does the speech stigmatize those targeted by "implicitly or explicitly ascribing to it qualities widely regarded as highly undesirable;" (3) is the target group "viewed as an undesirable presence and a legitimate object of hostility;" and (4) are there additional factors related to history, context and social power. When taking into account the ordinance, the state's claimed interest, and the court rulings, it is apparent that the speech in question in *R.A.V v. St. Paul* is clearly hate speech – both R.A.V.'s speech and the speech subsumed in the ordinance. In answering the first question – is it "directed against a specified or easily identifiable individual group," we need look no further than the language in the ordinance, which specifically addresses speech targeting people on "the basis of race, color, creed, religion, or gender." The ordinance is directed at protecting particular groups from being targeted through speech or expressive conduct based on "arbitrary and normatively irrelevant" features. In fact, it is this specificity within the ordinance that was one of the major concerns of the Supreme Court as is evidenced by Justice Scalia when he noted that "unmodified terms make clear that the ordinance applied only to 'fighting words' that insult, or provoke violence, 'on the basis of race, color, creed, religion or gender.'"[17] Viewpoint restrictions embedded in the ordinance were found to be extremely problematic under the Court's application of fighting words doctrine. However, as is illustrate in the application of the first question in Tier One, under my suggested framework, viewpoint considerations in the case of hate speech restriction are a necessity. Hate speech by its very definition is viewpoint-based and so any regulation of it will need to be viewpoint-based as well. Justice Stevens' elaboration about conduct that "creates special risks or causes special harms" supports this need to rethink how hate speech restrictions are evaluated.

The language in the ordinance also meets the second factor for consideration – does the speech stigmatize those targeted. The ordinance singles out speech likely to stigmatize those targeted by specifically naming recognizable symbols of hatred such as the burning cross and the swastika. Those symbols are emblematic of extreme racial and religious intolerance and, as such, the restriction of them, coupled with identifying specific groups, implicitly draws attention to the connection between those group members and highly undesirable qualities. The Minnesota State Supreme Court also read the ordinance in this way, finding that the "burning cross is itself an unmistakable symbol of...racial supremacy."[18] This sentiment on the part of the Minnesota court speaks to the third question as well. Through those "unmistakable" symbols, targeted groups are "viewed as an undesirable presence and a legitimate object of hostility." This position is reinforced by both concurring opinions. Justice White raises the concern that the Court opinion is "legitimizing hate speech as a form of public discussion."[19] He points out that the burning cross expresses a "message of intimidation and racial hatred." Justice Stevens claims that targeting people based on their race can cause "particularly severe trauma."[20]

The last element to be considered in Tier One is a consideration of any other additional factors, particularly those related to history, context, and social power. In her article, *Hate Speech & Empirical Evidence,* Katharine Gelber advised that those three elements are necessary in determining the specific type of harm created through hate speech. She explained that,

> [T]he connection of hate speech with historically identifiable and systematic discrimination is key to its success in discursively enacting harm to a sufficient degree that it would imperil a target's ability to participate in the political decision making that affects them.[21]

She suggested that it this distinction that separates discriminatory hate speech from speech that merely causes offense.[22] In my previous work, I addressed a similar issue by focusing on the ways in which power operates in society, finding it to be discursive, relational and historical.[23] I asserted that

> Under the guise of free speech for everyone, the First Amendment maintains the status quo of societal power dynamics, reinforcing inequalities among certain disempowered groups...[W]hile everyone is to some degree socially constructed, members of subordinate groups are constructed primarily by those groups oppressing them.[24]

The context of the development of the St. Paul Bias Motivated Crime Ordinance is placed against the background of racial and religious intolerance in that community. The original version of the ordinance was adopted in the 1970s in reaction to a spate of attacks on synagogues and was updated twice thereafter in the 1980s, once to add gender and once to add race. While the state's argument was stronger in regard to its original version of the ordinance, on the national level, concerns about attacks based on race and gender were increasing. As such, the ordinance, when considered in regard to context, was firmly supported at both the local and national levels. In addition, the ordinance also connected to a lengthier history of targeted discrimination by focusing on particular types of symbols, including the burning cross and the swastika. Those symbols historically have been used to systematically oppress members of certain groups. In these ways, the ordinance itself meets the criteria established in the fourth section of Tier One and serves to emphasize Gelber's assessment of the difference between speech that merely offends and speech that carries with it a level of harm sufficient to impair full participation in society.

The Minnesota State Supreme Court relied on the content-neutral category of fighting words but also considered the particularly harmful effects of certain forms of fighting words. In the opinion, the court emphasized that the speech being restricted through the St. Paul ordinance was speech that, in an historical context, sent a "clear message of racial supremacy, hatred, persecution, and degradation of certain groups." This acknowledgement on the part of the court signals an understanding of the special nature of certain types of hate speech. This position was adamantly refuted, however, by the U.S. Supreme Court. Justice Scalia's response, or lack of response, to concerns about context, history, or power dynamics reinforces the concerns I raised about the First Amendment's role in perpetuating social inequalities. This lack of consideration of historical or social context first became apparent during the oral arguments before the Court when, in response to Foley's explanation of the state's need to single out certain types of hate expression for restriction, the

Court said, "That's a political judgement...somebody else may feel as to about philosophy, about economic philosophy, about whatever."[25] Justice Scalia would make a similar comparison in the opinion itself when he asked why some speech targeting certain groups should be restricted, while other speech targeting other possible groups is permitted.[26] While both Justices White and Stevens maintained the value of considering additional factors, the ruling itself did not allow history, context, or power dynamics to be considered. Despite the majority's unwillingness to embrace a more complex application of free speech principles, when applying Tier One of my framework to the *R.A.V.* case, it is clear that the speech restricted through the ordinance would be defined as regulable hate speech. However, before determining whether or not the St. Paul ordinance would be constitutional under my recommended framework, we must still consider Tier Two of the analysis.

Application of Tier Two is triggered only if the speech is identified in Tier One to be hate speech. Had the speech not met the criteria in Tier One, there would be no need to take this additional step. However, because the speech being restricted through the St. Paul ordinance is clearly regulable hate speech, then the second tier of analysis must be applied. Tier Two is important for several reasons. It adds rigor to ensure only speech that rises to the level of regulable hate speech is swept up in the wording of the restriction. Without this additional layer, the possibility exists that speech restrictions could expand into areas of speech that are merely offensive. This tier also affirms the philosophy driving the implementation of the framework. This overall framework is intended to bring a social justice component into the free speech equation. It does so by pulling from recognition theory and, as such, it needs to consider not just if a restriction is content or viewpoint based. Instead, this framework relocates the focus from the specific words themselves to a consideration of the totality of the speech moment occurring – both the intention of the speaker and impact on the target of the speech. Tier Two serves to allow the courts to engage in analysis in a way that will meet this underlying need by focusing on the impact of the speech on those targeted, on those speaking, and on society as a whole. Finally, analysis in Tier Two serves to fold that new broader focus into pre-existing doctrinal review, thus expanding our long-term commitments to free speech while exploring how best to achieve those ends by considering different variables.

As I spelled out in Chapter 5, previous studies and case law illuminate some of the more crucial questions that should be addressed in hate speech cases. Specifically, I discussed three alternative readings of First Amendment doctrine, which included my own previous scholarship complicating the application of content neutrality; a law review article focused on rethinking the test for true threats and incitement; and a court of appeals ruling applying the reasonable listener standard.

While the Court might consider additional factors when implementing Tier Two, those particular readings suggest ways to modify current doctrine that would better incorporate a social justice framework. In applying Tier Two to this case, the Court first would be required to adjust the way in which it considers content neutrality. Currently, the Court utilizes an either/or application of content neutrality – a law is either content neutral and acceptable or it is content-based and as such unacceptable in almost all circumstances. I am suggesting an alternative configuration of the content neutrality principle that would consider not just whether the law in question is content-based, but also would take into consideration the character, nature, and scope of the speech restriction. Justice Stevens made a similar recommendation in his concurrence, supporting a more complex analytical frame.[27] He suggested that the Court had always and should continue to consider scope, context, and validity when assessing content-based restrictions.[28] My own previous analysis of *R.A.V.* using the criteria I recommend here – character, nature, and scope – found the Bias Motivated Crime Ordinance to restrict only low value speech; to be both content- and viewpoint-based; and to be narrowly tailored to reach only the speech that the government had a compelling interest to restrict.[29] Applying these criteria with a social justice goal in mind, reinforces the need for clearly defining the speech to be restricted and narrowly tailoring the mechanism to encompass only that speech, while still emphasizing that in terms of hate speech, it is the very viewpoint expressed that makes the speech problematic. Attempting to address that problem with a viewpoint or content neutral law is, then, by the very nature of the problem, impossible. As a result, viewpoint neutrality should be a factor in assessing any speech regulation. However, for it to be a useful doctrine, it needs to expand to include the additional context recommended both in my earlier work and in Justice Stevens' concurrence.

While the Court in *R.A.V.* focused predominantly on application of fighting words doctrine, it could be beneficial to consider the ordinance in regard to Crump's more expansive understanding of true threats and incitement.[30] The current standard, such as was applied in *Virginia v. Black*, defines permissibly regulable threats to be "those statements where the speaker means to communicate a serious expression of intent to commit an act of unlawful violence to a particular individual or group of individuals."[31] As I outlined in Chapter 5, Crump's version adds multiple additional criteria for assessment.[32] In general, Crump's standard would require a comprehensive review of the language in question, included, but not limited to the words or symbols being used; where, when, and to whom the message is being conveyed; the predictability and anticipated seriousness of unlawful results; and the availability of alternative means to express a similar message without encouragement of violence.

In regard to the Bias Motivated Crime Ordinance, applying Crump's criteria would not offer a clear-cut answer, but it would introduce the opportunity for more robust discussion pertaining to impact, intent, and implications. For example, the ordinance singles out particular speech "including, but not limited to, a burning cross or a Nazi swastika." This type of speech historically has been used to threaten individuals and often has been followed by or used in tandem with actual physical attacks. As such, it could be argued that this type of speech is threatening, both in the meaning of the words themselves and the likelihood of ensuing actions. Crump makes clear that one of the factors which must be considered is whether there is "the availability of alternate means of expressing a similar message without, without encouragement of violence."[33] That caution about ensuring alternative means could be read in two different ways in regard to *R.A.V.* On the one hand, an argument could be made that while the ordinance does restrict certain types of messaging – the burning cross, the swastika, etc. – it does not close the door on similar messaging. One would still be free to express, say, racial superiority, but would be limited in how that message is relayed. On the other hand, one could read the ordinance's language denoting restricting of messages that "[arouse] anger, alarm and resentment" as failing to meet Crump's criteria because the phrasing does not directly speak to concerns of messages that "encourage violence." Far from this elasticity being a weakness in Crump's test, it actually illustrates that because there are often multiple ways to apply tests to facts, the more comprehensive the test, the better capable that test is of assessing the speech restriction in a holistic manner. This criterion, then, no matter which way it is read, would still need to be considered against the other seven factors in Crump's incitement test. For example, if we find the speech in question threatening because of the historical legacy of the speech, but we also find that the phrase "arouses anger, alarm and resentment" does not address possible violence, we would still need to respond to the other factors in the test. We would need to address elements including the medium, the audience (including the targeted audience, members of the group doing the targeting, and any other spectators) and the surrounding communications (what else has been happening up to and following this particular speech moment). Here, we would consider additional elements such as the previous racial incidents, R.A.V.'s membership in a skinhead organization, and the use of a burning cross on the target's property.

Finally, one additional way in which the Court could review the ordinance would be to apply the reasonable listener standard in place of the typical speaker standard. Using the reasonable listener standard, the Ninth Circuit Court of Appeals defined true threats as those made where "a reasonable person would foresee that the statement would be interpreted by those to whom the maker communicates the statement as a serious expression of an intent to harm."[34] Switching the focus from proving intent of the speaker to instead relying on the impact on the target would drastically change the Court's interpretation in *R.A.V.* For example, implied in Justice Scalia's dismissal of the state's interest in protecting members of targeted groups is the idea that the impact of language on those groups is no more or less damaging than any other negative or critical comments at large. His comparison of the regulable fighting words with the sound from a noisy truck completely ignored the difference in effect that some types of fighting words might have over others. His point was further emphasized when he specifically took issue with the ordinance's language "arouses anger, alarm or resentment in others." He noted: "Displays containing abusive invective, no matter how vicious or severe, are permissible unless they are addressed to one of the specified disfavored topics."[35] For Justice Scalia, considering the listener's reaction is a zero-sum endeavor. Either we restrict all abusive speech, no matter the topic or the target, or we restrict none except in very rare circumstances. He ignored what Justice Stevens called the "particularly severe trauma"[36] that threatening speech based on and targeted toward members of disempowered groups and goes so far as to assert that any laws considering that possible trauma would "license one side of a debate to fight freestyle, while requiring the other to follow the Marquis of Queensbury rules."[37] If the reasonable listener standard were employed, then the Court would have had to consider Justice Steven's position, while also recognizing that certain speech does not encourage debate but instead silences those it targets.

After reviewing the additional elements in Tier Two, it seems more likely that the Court would have concluded that the Bias Motivated Crime Ordinance was not facially invalid and that R.A.V.'s conviction should be upheld. It would remain to be seen if the ordinance faced problems later with inconsistent or unclear application. Of course, if a legal definition of regulable hate speech were to exist, cities such as St. Paul would be able to tailor their regulations to fit that definition.

Virginia V. Black

The next U.S. Supreme Court ruling to address, at least to some degree, the issue of hate speech regulation was the 2003 case *Virginia V. Black*.[38] As with *R.A.V.*, I discussed this case at some length in Chapter 3, reviewing at that time the way in which the Court relied on true threats doctrine in its ruling.[39] The case itself focused on a Virginia State law that made it a felony "for any person...with the intent of intimidating any person or group..., to burn...a cross on the property of another, a highway or other public place."[40] According to the statute, any cross burning "shall be considered prima facie evidence of an intent to intimidate a person or group."[41] The Court found the statute unconstitutionally content-based due to the prima facie clause. In other words, the Court found that the statute could constitutionally restrict cross burnings that were used to intimidate, but it could not assume that any time a cross was burned, it was automatically a form of intimidation. Writing for the plurality, Justice O'Connor explained: "The act of burning a cross may mean that the person is engaging in constitutionally proscribable intimidation. But that same act may mean only that the person is engaged in core political speech."[42] Cross burnings, although the majority acknowledges them a serious "symbol of hate,"[43] must be protected because they also serve for some groups, such as the Klan, as a "symbol of group solidarity."[44]

This tension between speech that intimidates those it targets and speech that facilitates bonding among in-group members was addressed by the concurring opinions. Justice Scalia agreed with the plurality that it is unconstitutional to convict a person for participating in speech that may serve as a symbol of solidarity or as part of an artistic endeavor.[45] However, he disagreed with how the plurality interpreted the meaning prima facie. To Justice Scalia, the prima facie clause in the Virginia statute was constitutionally permissible because it related specifically to conviction only. He noted:

> ...some individuals who engage in protected speech may, because of the prima-facie-evidence provision, be subject to conviction. Such convictions, assuming they are unconstitutional, could be challenged on a case-by-case basis. The plurality; however, with little in the way of explanation, leaps to the conclusion that the possibility of such convictions justifies facial invalidation of the statute.[46]

In short, he accused the majority of conflating conviction with arrest. He asserted that the statute was indeed valid and that it was only the jury instructions that were problematic.[47]

Justice Souter, joined by Justices Kennedy and Ginsburg, also raised concerns about the way in which the Virginia statute used a content-based distinction – cross burnings – to restrict speech. Justice Souter compared the Virginia statute against the one in *R.A.V.* and found that while the Virginia statute did not call out race, color, creed, religion, or gender, it was nonetheless content-based because of its emphasis on the restriction of one particular symbol. He stated:

> To be sure, that content often includes an essentially intimidating message, that the cross burner will harm the victim, most probably in a physical way, given the historical identification of burning crosses with arson, beating, and lynching. But even when the symbolic act is meant to terrify, a burning cross may carry a further, ideological message of white Protestant supremacy. The ideological message not only accompanies many threatening uses of the symbol, but is also expressed when a burning cross is not used to threaten

but merely to symbolize the supremacist ideology and the solidarity of those who espouse it.[48]

In other words, Justice Souter found the statute to be unconstitutional because the speech in question, no matter that it is often used to intimidate, must be protected because of its value in allowing white supremacists their ability to use it as a form of ideological solidarity. He saw no way to save the statute's prima facie requirement because it singles out certain ideas. He explained:

> As I see the likely significance of the evidence provision, its primary effect is to skew jury deliberations toward conviction in cases where the evidence of intent to intimidate is relatively weak and arguably consistent with a solely ideological reason for burning.[49]

This concurrence, thereby, concluded that the Virginia statute cannot be read to meet the exceptions enumerated in *R.A.V.* and that, in fact, "a content-neutral statute banning intimidation would achieve the same object without singling out particular content."[50] Again, as with the plurality and Justice Scalia's concurrence, Justice Souter's concurrence leaned in favor of protecting the perspectives of hate groups, such as the Klan, over protecting those who were targeted by that specific type of hateful message.

Justice Thomas, the sole dissenter in the ruling, asserted that the very nature of the symbolism, of what makes it a content distinction, is also what makes it constitutionally regulable conduct. He maintained:

> I believe that the majority errs in imputing an expressive component to the activity in question...A conclusion that the statute prohibiting cross burning with intent to intimidate sweeps beyond a prohibition on certain conduct into the zone of expression overlooks not only the words of the statute but also reality.[51]

He elaborated on the "reality" of cross burnings by referring back to the plurality's recitation of the history of the Klan.[52] Based on that history, he concluded that the Klan is a terrorist organization, which uses "the most brutal means" to intimidate or eliminate members of groups that it does not like.[53] Cross burnings are merely one way in which the group inflicts its terror and that message is read as a terroristic threat not only by blacks.[54] He explained: "In our culture, cross burning has almost invariably meant lawlessness and understandably instills in its victims well-grounded fear of physical violence."[55] In other words, Justice Thomas found that the statute restricted conduct, not expression, and as such, First Amendment analysis is not appropriate.[56] He postulated what the ruling would be, if indeed, the statute covered expression that might implicate the First Amendment.[57] Justice Thomas wrote:

> That the First Amendment gives way to other interests is not a remarkable proposition. What is remarkable is that, under the plurality's analysis, the determination whether an interest is sufficiently compelling depends not on the harm a regulation in question seeks to prevent, but on the area of society at which it aims.[58]

He pointedly took the plurality to task for ignoring the particularly devastating effect of cross burning on targeted groups.

Analyzing Black

The ruling in *Virginia v. Black* was more straightforward than that presented in *R.A.V. v. St. Paul*. In part, it seemed less complicated because the Court's application of First Amendment principles in *Black* was less convoluted. Mostly, though, the difference lies in the construction of the two regulations. While the ordinance in St. Paul was broadly focused and mandated a consideration of the feelings of a specifically identified group of people, the statute in Virginia was more narrowly written. As a result, the statute in *Black* swept under its provision considerably less speech and its lack of specificity of target allowed for a clear application of pre-existing, content-neutral principles. In addition, the outcome in *Black*, for the most part, allowed the anti-cross burning statute to stand as constitutional. So, it would seem on the surface that this decision fits well within the social justice framework suggested in this book. The statute in practice should protect members of disempowered groups from at least one expression of hate speech. However, application of the two-tiered framework indicates that the Court's decision to nullify the prima facie clause corrodes the social justice impact of this statute.

Tier One of the framework requires an assessment of who is being targeted and on what grounds. In this case, application of Tier One clearly indicates that the speech restricted under the statute – cross burnings "on the property of another, a highway or other public place" with the intent to intimidate – would be considered hate speech. The symbol of the burning cross being used to intimidate someone meets the first criteria. The ordinance requires an "intent to intimidate," which would necessitate the need for identification of the target or targets. The second criteria under Tier One asks if the speech in question would stigmatize those targeted by it by ascribing to them qualities widely considered undesirable. While the statute's language does not directly address this consideration, the symbol of the burning cross in the United States is so closely linked with attacks based on race, religion, and sexual orientation that the second criteria is met. This position is supported by the Court's opinion in which Justice O'Connor offered a detailed and lengthy history of cross burning. It's also supported in the concurring opinion which spoke to the symbols connection to "ideological messages of white Protestant supremacy."[59]

The third criteria – is the targeted group viewed as undesirable and a legitimate object of hostility – can be applied in the same manner as the second criteria. While the statute itself did not call out any particular categories of people, the opinion did acknowledge the relationship between cross burnings and intimidation of specific groups in U.S. society. For example, Justice O'Connor's historical references are directly focused on the use of cross burnings to intimidate based on race and religion. Justice Thomas was even more explicit on that relationship. In his dissent, he explained that cross burnings have been and continue to be one way in which a terroristic group, the Klan, inflicts terror.[60] Finally, through application of the fourth criteria in Tier One, it is easily established that the burning cross has a long and nefarious history. And, while that history implies that the burning cross must be read as an attack by anyone targeted by it, the symbol still remains more threatening to certain members of society based on what criteria one identifies as "arbitrary and normatively irrelevant" features. In sum then, the statute, both in its original form and without the prima facie clause, covers speech that would qualify as hate speech.

It is in the application of Tier Two that the Court's ruling becomes problematic, specifically in regard to the prima facie question. The social justice framework informed by recognition theory requires two things. First, it demands that we acknowledge that targeted hate speech psychologically, socially, and politically has a negative impact on systematically and historically disempowered groups. Second, it necessitates that we consider the relationship between speaker, spoken to, and society at large. Hate speech, from a recognition theory perspective, damages not only those targeted by it, but those who espouse it, and everyone who lives in the culture where these types of moments occur. From that perspective, what is most problematic about the ruling in *Black* is that by removing the prima facie clause, the Court gave support to the idea that cross burnings in and of themselves have speech value. Justice O'Connor made this clear when she wrote that while some cross burnings are done to intimidate, others occur when persons are "engaging in core political speech."[61] Justice Scalia, while writing separately to maintain the prima facie clause, agreed that not all crossing burnings should be subject to conviction because they may support group solidarity or artistic purposes.[62] Justice Souter's concurrence made clear that although cross burnings often include "essentially intimidating messages," they also contain ideological messages. Because of this possibility, he found that the prima facie clause amounted to a content-based consideration.

This reliance on the standard application of content neutrality robs the statute of its ability to offer a more socially significant solution to the complex problem of hate speech. As with the ordinance in *R.A.V.*, application of the more layered version of the content neutrality principle to the cross-burning statute in *Black* would find the character, nature, and scope of the speech restriction to be justifiable. Yes, as Justice Souter indicated, inherent in the prima facie clause is some level of content distinction. However, given the history of attacks and the social evidence of the effects of cross burnings on those targeted, the state does have a compelling interest in restricting that content and the statute is narrowly constructed, restricting only one type of particularly virulent hate speech. Further, the Court's concern about protecting the rights of hate groups, such as the Klan, also would be misguided, as those groups damage not only the immediate target but also themselves and society as a whole through the propagation of the hateful message. The slight content infringement is far outweighed by the interests being served.

One way in which the Court might have circumvented the shallow reading of the content neutrality principle would be to apply a more complex definition of true threats. Crump's suggested expansion of the test for threatening speech would incorporate several important factors into the analysis. That is to say, if the legal understanding of what constitutes intimidating speech were consistent with Crump's eight-part analysis, then the concerns about the prima facie evidence would become null and void. Whether or not the act was intimidating would need to be established by considering, among other things, the predictability and anticipated seriousness of unlawful results; the extent of the speaker's knowledge or reckless disregard of the likelihood of violent results; and whether the utterance has "serious literary, artistic, political or scientific value." By framing the analysis in this way, the Court could simultaneously send a strong message against targeted speech, while also remaining mindful about the need to protect ideological solidarity or artistic representations.

In the end, while the statute, even without the prima facie clause, will serve to protect those who are targeted by cross burners, the insistence on ignoring the increased negative impacts on members of socially and historically disempowered groups serves to further marginalize them. Namely, when a part of government, say the United States Supreme Court, focuses more on protecting the rights of hate groups than on protecting those targeted by those groups it sends, as Mari Matsuda asserted in the late 1980s, a message that the targeted groups are not valued by their government.[63]

Snyder v. Phelps

While both *R.A.V.* and *Black* were discussed in Chapter 3, *Snyder v. Phelps* was not, mainly due to the narrowness of the ruling. The case offered little in regard to the overall application of First Amendment doctrine in cases related to hate speech.[64] However, the facts in the case in *Snyder* did deal with hateful speech that both targeted particular individuals and maligned an already culturally vulnerable group of people. As such, *Snyder* serves as an interesting space to think my framework in relation to public demonstrations.

Snyder v. Phelps dealt with the picketing of U.S. soldiers' funerals by the Westboro Baptist Church, a church founded by Fred Phelps in Kansas in 1955. The Westboro congregation consists of Phelps, some of his children and grandchildren, and their spouses. The church, which the Southern Law Poverty Center has called one of the most "obnoxious and rabid hate groups in America" is known for its tagline, "God Hates Fags," and for its protests at funerals.[65] The church believes, among other things, that God hates and is punishing the United State for its tolerance of homosexuality and that part of that punishment is inflicted on the U.S. military.[66] According to the church, since 1991, members have held 65,532 demonstrations in 1,052 cities.[67] One of those "demonstrations" was held in 2006 at the funeral of Marine Lance Corporal Matthew Snyder, who was killed in the line of duty. That incident served as the background for the eventual Supreme Court ruling in 2011.

Phelps, along with six members of his congregation, travelled to Maryland where they stood on public property near Snyder's memorial service.[68] They picketed with signs that read, among other things, "Thank God for IEDs," "Thank God for Dead Soldiers," "God Hates Fags," and "You're Going to Hell."[69] The demonstration, which included the church members carrying signs, singing hymns, and reciting bible verses, was proceeded by a publicity campaign on social media. The demonstration lasted approximately 30 minutes and was peaceful. Albert Snyder, Matthew Snyder's father, subsequently filed suit against the Westboro Baptist church, alleging five state tort law claims, including intentional infliction of emotional distress.[70]

The trial court found in favor of Snyder on three of the tort claims, including the infliction of emotional distress claim, and held Westboro liable for $2.9 million in compensatory damages and $8 million in punitive damages.[71] On appeal, the Fourth Circuit found Westboro's speech protected under the First Amendment because the speech in question was "on matters of public concern, were not provably false, and were expressed solely through hyperbole."[72] The United States Supreme Court granted certiorari in March 2010.

In an 8-1 decision, the Court upheld the Fourth Circuit ruling. Chief Justice Roberts, writing for the Court, established that the case hinged on whether the speech by the Westboro Baptist Church was speech concerning public or private matters.[73] He explained:

> Speech deals with matters of public concern when it can "be fairly considered as relating to any matter of political, social, or other

concern to the community," or when it "is a subject of legitimate news interest; that is, a subject of general interest and of value and concern to the public…" The arguably "inappropriate or controversial character of a statement is irrelevant to the question whether it deals with a matter of public concern."[74]

In order to make this distinction, the Court considered the "content, form and context" of the speech.[75] The Court concluded that the speech was related to matters of public concern because

> while these messages may fall short of refined social or political commentary, the issues they highlight – the political and moral conduct of the United States and its citizens, the fate of our Nation, homosexuality in the military, and scandals involving the Catholic clergy – are matters of public import.[76]

In other words, the Court found that while the message may have been rudimentary, it still addressed issues of public importance. The majority made clear that the ruling was narrow, reaching only to the limited facts of this particular case.[77]

In his concurrence, Justice Breyer emphasized two interesting points. First, he reiterated that the Court was only focused on the picketing, not on the publicity prior to the event or the result of it.[78] Second, he noted that while he agreed with the Court that Westboro's speech constituted speech on matters of public concern, he did not agree that this was the only issue that needed to be addressed.[79] He proposed instead that the state can, consistent with past court rulings, restrict picketing even if the picketing is occurring in relation to a matter of public concern. Due to the facts in this particular case, however, Justice Breyer found that the picketing did not reach a level to require restriction.[80]

Finally, Justice Alito wrote an impassioned dissent. He began, "Our profound national commitment to free and open debate is not a license for the vicious verbal assault that occurred in this case."[81] He proposed that the court could consider the speech in question when assessing intentional infliction of emotional distress claims, and that the First Amendment does not preclude liability in such cases.[82] He saw this particular case as one of those moments.[83] Additionally, Justice Alito raised concerns about the motivation of the Westboro Church, specifically calling attention to their intention to secure publicity. He emphasized:

> The Westboro Baptist Church, however, has devised a strategy that remedies this problem. As the Court notes, church members have protested at nearly 600 military funerals. They have also picketed the funerals of police officers, firefighters, and the victims of natural disasters, accidents, and shocking crimes. And in advance of these

protests, they issue press releases to ensure that their protests will attract public attention... In this case, respondents implemented the Westboro Baptist Church's publicity-seeking strategy. Their press release stated that they were going "to picket the funeral of Lance Cpl. Matthew A. Snyder" because "God Almighty killed Lance Cpl. Snyder.[84]

Justice Alito, focused on how the Westboro Church intentionally sets out to attract the greatest amount of attention by inflicting the highest levels of pain during traumatic events. According to Justice Alito, this intention negates any claim to issues of public concern. In fact, Justice Alito understood their speech to be directly targeting Matthew Snyder and his family and as such, it crossed the line into personal attack.[85] He concluded by expressing, "In order to have a society in which public issues can be openly and vigorously debated, it is not necessary to allow the brutalization of innocent victims like the petitioner."[86]

Analyzing Snyder

Snyder v. Phelps is distinctly different from *R.A.V* and *Black*. While those cases involved the constitutionality of laws specifically designed to limit certain speech, this case was focused on whether certain speech could be actionable under the tort law for the intentional infliction of emotional distress. As I laid out above, the Court's analysis in *Snyder* hinged on whether the speech in question was "on matters of public concern." Ultimately, the Court determined that "the overall thrust and dominant theme of Westboro's demonstrations spoke to broader public issues."[87] As such, that speech was akin to political speech highly deserving of First Amendment protection. But, how might this case have been decided if the Court were to apply the framework recommended here? Would the church's speech be considered hate speech instead of speech addressing important political topics?

Answering those questions is somewhat complicated as the claim itself in this case was not directly about targeted hate speech. Albert Snyder sued for intentional infliction of emotional distress. He was not asserting that the distress was based on the targeting of his son as a member of any of the communities derided on the protestors' signs. Snyder's claim was, as Justice Alito noted in his dissent, based instead on the pain caused by having the funeral "transformed into a raucous media event."[88] Certainly, under the framework suggested here, targeted hate speech could be grounds for an infliction of emotional distress claim. But, in considering the facts in this case, the framework needs to be applied to determine whether the speech in question rises to the level of regulable hate speech. *Snyder* offers an opportunity to give shape to the framework, demonstrating the parameters of speech restriction. To this end, I examine both the speech that the Court chose to take into consideration – the public protest at the funeral – and the speech that the Court did not address – Westboro Baptist's use of television and social media.

The first criteria in Tier One asks: is the speech in question "directed against a specified or easily identifiable individual...or a group of individuals based on an arbitrary and normatively irrelevant feature." In *Snyder*, the church picketing requires further explanation in how this criterion can or should be applied. The first point relates to the language "directed against." What specially does it mean for speech to be directed against an individual or group? In *Snyder*, the picketing moment was directly focused toward Matthew Snyder and his family. The entire reason for the picketing was Snyder's funeral and the locations of the pickets were chosen to optimize reaching that audience. The speech included some pointed statements, such as "Thank God for Dead Soldiers" and "You're Going to Hell." However, there was also a broader message targeted at a group of which Snyder was not a member. The sign reading "God Hates Fags" was not in reference to Snyder, but instead was connected to a critique of the gay and lesbian community. It has already been established that the church seeks to advance hatred against gays and lesbian. In fact, that goal is the driving force behind why the group targets military funerals. Before being able to respond to the question in criteria one, there first needs to be clarity on who, for the purposes of this analysis, is the target. Is it the speech directed against Snyder and his family, the gay community, or both? As with all legal tests, there is room for interpretation (just think about the multiple readings of the fighting words doctrine in *R.A.V.*). Given the physical location of the picketers, this speech appears to be targeting Snyder and doing so in a way that is not based on "arbitrary or normatively irrelevant features" related to him specifically. This distinction is made clear by the choice of legal remedy sought and reinforced through Justice Alito's dissent in which he emphasized that the speech amounted to "the brutalization of innocent victims like the petitioner."[89] As a result, the speech does not meet the first criteria of Tier One and so is not regulable hate speech. The fact that the speech is critical and disparaging of the legal treatment of gays and lesbians does not alter this distinction. No gays or lesbians were "directly targeted" at the picketing locations, or at least none were involved in the filing of the lawsuit, and so not part of the legal question.

From this analysis, the conclusion is that Tier One doesn't apply and so there is no need to advance to Tier Two. However, as I alluded to at the beginning of this analysis of *Snyder*, I want to take a moment to consider Westboro's presence on television and social media. As already noted, Westboro Baptist Church is a hate group. The church is particularly aggressive in its messaging deriding gays and lesbians. The group's demonstrations at military funerals are closely tied to their attempts to gain maximum exposure for that messaging. For example, on its website, the group described its demonstrations as places where it can "display large, colorful signs containing Bible words and sentiments... play and sing songs that have appropriate, Bible sentiments expressed by the lyrics...[and] vocally preach."[90] A page on the website displays those "large colorful signs containing Bible words and sentiments" and a significant portion of these signs are in reference to the queer community. Examples of some of the language include: 'Christians' Caused Fag Marriage, Death Penalty 4 Fags, Dyke Sin, Fags are Beasts, Fags are Worthy of Death, God H8s Trannies, No Fags in Heaven, and Tranny Sin Dooms Nations. Additionally, many signs have a cartoon image of two men having anal sex with another message on it such as God Hates Easter, U.S.A.'s Doom, and Fag Marriage. In all, there are dozens of these "color signs containing Bible words and sentiments" espousing hatred and calling for extermination of gays, lesbians, and transgendered people.

The posters appearing on Westboro's website are reproductions of ones carried at in-person demonstrations. The demonstrations, which are held at funerals for members of the military, police officers and victims of natural disasters among others, are part of an orchestrated effort to generate as much awareness of the church's message as possible. Those demonstrations are publicized through social media, often attracting television coverage because of the outrageous nature of the picketing. The events are followed by press releases and social media accounts. That scenario played out in the *Snyder* case as well. Members of the Westboro church publicized the event ahead of time. Television crews arrived and reported on the demonstrations. Finally, following Snyder's funeral, the church reinforced its message by posting an online account.[91] The question that I wish to raise here is whether or not this extended messaging targeting the gay, lesbian and transgender community constitutes regulable hate speech? Could members of that community file a claim against the church? Could an ordinance or statute be crafted that would restrict this type of speech? Ultimately, does this speech constitute the type of speech, that from a recognition theory perspective and framed through a social justice lens, should be restricted? The first step in responding to these questions is to consider the speech in relation to Tier One. In doing so, it is easily illustrated through the description above that the speech is directed against the gay, lesbian, and transgender community; it is implicitly *and* explicitly "ascribing qualities" to that community that are "widely regarded as highly undesirable;" and it is calling for members of that community to be "viewed as an undesirable presence and a legitimate object of hostility." Finally, application of the fourth criterion in Tier One – additional factors such as history, context, and social power – would confirm that members of the gay, lesbian, and transgender community have been historically targeted and continue to be socially ostracized, politically marginalized, and culturally disenfranchised. Indeed, the speech by the Westboro Baptist Church does rise to the level of hate speech under the definition developed here. But, given that this issue wasn't the focus in *Snyder*, applying the second tier is highly speculative and requires attention to the mode of communication. Because much of the messaging in question occurs over social media, this analysis requires a more thorough review of Internet speech, a review that will occur in the next chapter. As such, I leave this question unanswered now, but will return to it again in Chapter 7.

Matal v. Tam

The final case for review in this chapter is the most recent Supreme Court ruling to address speech that could possibly fit within the category of regulable hate speech. In 2017, the Court ruled on *Matal v. Tam*, a case focusing on the government's ability to regulate disparaging speech.[92] As will be made apparent during the application of my two-tiered framework, disparaging speech does not fall into the category of regulable hate speech. This case, then, illustrates the way in which we can support restriction of some speech without limiting the ability to hold different, opposing, or even disparaging opinions of others.

When Simon Tam attempted to trademark his band name, "The Slants," his request was denied by the U.S. Trademark Office because it was found that the name would likely be disparaging toward "persons of Asian descent." Specifically, the office relied on language from the Lanham Act of 1946 that prohibits trademarks containing material that may "disparage…or bring…into contempt or disrepute any persons, living or dead, institutions, beliefs, or national symbols."[93] Tam claimed that in taking the name, the band, which was made up of all Asian musicians, was reclaiming the word.[94] In an 8-0 opinion, the Court found the Disparagement Clause to be invalid under the First Amendment because it was viewpoint based and was not narrowly tailored to serve a substantial state interest. While the decision in the case was unanimous, the opinion itself was fractured. As one commentator noted, the opinion read more like a "series of concurrences cobbled together to produce an inconclusive whole."[95] Even within the opinion itself, Justice Alito, in discussing the district court ruling, made reference to the "assortment of theories" offered up, which included the applications of government speech doctrine[96] and commercial speech doctrine.[97] In Chapter 3, I discussed *Tam*, but my focus then was more specifically on the one point of law that all the justices seemed to agree on: the application of the principle of viewpoint neutrality. I touch on that again here, but will focus on the Court's evaluation of "disparaging speech."

Justice Alito began the opinion succinctly: "We now hold that that this provision…offends a bedrock First Amendment principle: Speech may not be banned on the ground that it expresses ideas that offend."[98]

He explained the review process under the disparagement clause, which includes a two-part test administered by the Patent and Trademark Office. A PTO examiner first considers

> the likely meaning of the matter in question, taking into account not only dictionary definitions, but relationship of the matter to the other elements in the trade mark, the nature of goods or services, and the manner in which the mark is used in the marketplace in connection with the goods and services.[99]

If that meaning is found to reference identifiable persons, institutions, beliefs, or national symbols, then the examiner moves to the second part of the test. He asks "whether that meaning may be disparaging to a substantial composite, although not necessarily the majority, of the referenced groups."[100] At this point, the burden shifts to the applicant to prove that the trademark is not disparaging. Included in this process is an understanding on the part of the PTO that

> the fact that an applicant may be a member of that group or has good intentions underlying its use of a term does not obviate the fact that a substantial composite of the referenced group would find the term objectionable.[101]

In other words, the examiner weighs multiple factors. Justice Alito maintained that it was during that review that unconstitutional viewpoint decisions were being made, despite there being no mention of the restriction of specific viewpoints. He explained:

> To be sure, the clause evenhandedly prohibits disparagement of all groups. It applies equally to marks that damn Democrats and Republicans, capitalists and socialists, and those arrayed on both sides of every possible issue. It denies registration to any mark that is offensive to a substantial percentage of the members of any group. But in the sense relevant here, that is viewpoint discrimination: Giving offense is a viewpoint.[102]

In other words, "offense" within the construct of the Lanham Act is based on viewpoint restriction no matter how broadly one defines offense or the process through which the Act is carried out by the PTO. As a result, the Court concluded that the disparagement clause could not be saved even by placing it within the sphere of government speech.[103]

The Court also took into account the issue of offense when determining if the clause reached only commercial speech and so would call for application of a more relaxed level of scrutiny. While the government claimed that "trademarks are commercial," the Court found instead that "trademarks do not simply identify the source of a product or service but go on to say something more, either about the product or service or some broader issue."[104] Trademarks express ideas and even those ideas that "disparage" or "bring into contempt...or disrepute" should be protected speech. Even if the speech was purely commercial speech – a position the Court did not endorse in the ruling – the clause still would fail because it would necessitate broader restrictions on speech than the government could justify. Justice Alito elaborated on this point by outlining the government justifications for why the disparagement clause is necessary. In highlighting those reasons, he wrote:

> Echoing language in one of the opinions below, the Government asserts an interest in preventing "'underrepresented groups'" from being "'bombarded with demeaning messages in commercial advertising.'" An amicus supporting the Government refers to "encouraging racial tolerance and protecting the privacy and welfare of individuals."[105]

The Court does not address the validity of those stated government interests. Instead, the Court, in part quoting former Supreme Court Justice Oliver Wendell Holmes, maintained:

> Speech that demeans on the basis of race, ethnicity, gender, religion, age, disability, or any other similar ground is hateful; but the proudest boast of our free speech jurisprudence is that we protect the freedom to express "the thought that we hate."[106]

The concurrence, written by Justice Kennedy and joined by Justices Ginsburg, Sotomayor, and Kagan, reiterated the majority's position on the need to maintain viewpoint neutrality at all costs. The concurring justices raised concerns that the clause "might silence dissent and distort the marketplace of ideas."[107] Even more alarming, they asserted that the disparagement act could actually harm those it was intended to protect.[108] In language reminiscent of legal scholar Nadine Strossen's arguments in favor of hate speech protection, the concurring justices asserted: "A law that can be directed against speech found offensive to some portion of the public can be turned against minority and dissenting views to the detriment of all."[109]

Analyzing Tam

The government asserts that the intent of Lanham Act clause was to prevent "underrepresented groups" from being "bombarded with demeaning messages in commercial advertising" and to encourage racial tolerance.[110] These objectives mirror ones associated with the social justice commitment proposed in this book. The disparagement clause appears to endorse recognition theory's appraisal that "Being left along to pursue one's vision of the good life is not sufficient; rather the demand for recognition requires cooperation and respect between individuals within the broader community."[111] Inherent in recognition theory is the idea that the government bears some responsibility for ensuring that all members within the community have the opportunity to participate equally in a respectful space. The probability that individuals will find this space on their own or will, on their own, confer it to others without some level of government intervention is unlikely. The disparagement clause appears to offer just this type of support. What is worrisome about the clause is its lack of balance between the stated intent and the breadth of speech it could conceivably restrict. The possibility for abuse was addressed by every opinion in the case. Justice Alito succinctly stated in the majority's opinion, that even though the disparagement clause does not single out one particular message it does discriminate on any message that might cause offense. The process carried out by the PTO to determine what constitutes disparaging speech is itself problematic as well. As explained above, if in step one the proposed trademark is found to refer to identifiable persons, institutions, beliefs, or national symbols, then the examiner moves to the second part of the test. In the second part, the applicant must prove that the requested trademark is not disparaging. On its face, this process seems acceptable, but within that second step, intent can play no role in the determination. "The fact that an applicant may be a member of that group or has good intentions" is irrelevant to reaching a final determination.[112] As such, theoretically any term or symbol that was ever used to disparage would not be permitted to be trademarked no matter who is applying for the trademark or why.

Equally interesting is the ruling itself. The Court clearly is reviewing the clause in relation to the viewpoint neutrality principle. The clause is viewpoint-based, not narrowly drawn, and lacks a compelling argument from the government as to state interest. These points are clear and easily supported. However, the entire ruling is filled with heavy-handed rhetoric that conflates all speech as valuable, assumes that all opinions are open for debate, and places an either/or dichotomy on all speech restrictions. Justice Alito's opening statement that this type of restriction "offends a bedrock First Amendment principle" should have served sufficient enough dicta regarding long-standing commitments to free speech.[113] However, Justice Alito, the same justice who made an impassioned plea to punish the speech directed at Matthew Snyder and his family, invoked Oliver Wendell Holmes, when he proclaimed:

Speech that demeans on the basis of race, ethnicity, gender, religion, age, disability, or any other similar ground is hateful; but the proudest boast of our free speech jurisprudence is that we protect the freedom to express 'the thought that we hate.'[114]

For the majority, it was not enough to find the clause viewpoint-based, it needed to drive home a larger message about protection of all demeaning or hateful speech. The concurring justices were even more assertive on this point, raising the concern that *any* similar attempts at restrictions on harmful speech would be highly detrimental to members of disempowered (or typically targeted) groups. These statements both by Justice Alito and the concurring justices do not incorporate, nor do they allow for, a more refined understanding of the extent of the possible negative impacts of this type of speech or of the role that, with careful legislation, the government could play in creating a more just society.

The *Tam* case offers an opportunity to tease out the parameters of what types of speech could be restricted under the new analytical framework. As with the other cases, the first step is to review the proposed speech restriction under Tier One. The disparagement clause does not come close to meeting the definition for regulable hate speech. The clause does address speech that brings a person or group into "contempt or disrepute," but it offers no explanation for which groups or for how to determine the difference between speech that brings a person into "contempt and disrepute," which it would prohibit, and speech that merely is condescending, mocking, or ridiculing. On its face, the term disparagement simply means making unflattering statements against something or someone. While the Court's dicta may have gone beyond the essence of the clause, it is nonetheless correct that this language within the clause is problematic. From the perspective of my framework, though, it's not so much the viewpoint distinction that is the call for alarm, it is the lack of explanation as to why those viewpoints should be restricted. While the government claims to be protecting underrepresented groups and promoting racial tolerance, the clause itself does not call out which groups fall into this category, nor does it explain how restricting "disparaging" speech will meet that government interest. As a result, the disparagement clause fails Tier One.

Conclusion

The Supreme Court has not weighed in conclusively on the issue of hate speech, although it does have a nearly 30-year history of engaging with the possibility of different forms and mechanisms of restriction. In this chapter, I set out to use four of those cases to illustrate the finer points of the two-tiered framework that I developed in Chapter 5. I started with the oldest and most on-point case, *R.A.V. v. St. Paul*, and finished by discussing the latest case, *Matal v. Tam*. In terms of *R.A.V*, the ruling would have been significantly different. My framework, informed by social justice theory, would have required the court to have given more serious consideration to the state's vocalized interest in protecting members of certain disempowered groups. The long-term constitutionality of the ordinance, however, is impossible to establish because at the time of the hearing and still today, there is no legal definition for what constitutes hate speech. The application of the framework to *Virginia v. Black* created an opportunity to expose the shortcomings of true threats doctrine when assessing hate speech cases. Likewise, *Snyder v. Phelps* served as another point to consider the complexity of reconciling hate speech restriction with the First Amendment. Finally, *Tam* clarified at least one category of speech – purely offensive speech – which would still be protected. Taken together, the four cases offer a fairly comprehensive view of the boundaries of restriction under my framework.

In the next chapter, "Hate speech and the Internet: *Elonis v. U.S.*," I narrow my focus onto one of the most confusing areas of free speech law today. I first present an overview of how the courts historically have treated Internet speech regulation in general since the 1990s. I then turn my attention to controversy related to regulating Internet hate speech. What will become apparent through that review is that Internet hate speech remains one of the most difficult areas to address and yet, given the global nature of social media, one of the most important.

Notes

1 For more details about the case, *see* Chapter 3, pages 52–54.
2 In re Welfare of R.A.V., 464 N.W.2d 507 (Minn. Sup. Ct. 1991).
3 *Id.*
4 *Id.*
5 *Id.*
6 *Id.*
7 W. Wat Hopkins, *Cross Burning Revisited: What the Supreme Court Should Have Done in Virginia v. Black and Why It Didn't*, 26 HASTINGS COMM. & ENT. L.J. 269, 270 (2004).
8 For a discussion of this history, *see* Jeannine Bell, *There Are No Racists Here: The Rise of Racial Extremism When No One is a Racist*, 20 MICH. J. RACE & L. 349, 354–355 (2015) (discussing history of racial violence and R.A.V.'s admission of being a skinhead).
9 *See*, Laura Lederer, *The Prosecutor's Dilemma, An Interview with Tom Foley*, in THE PRICE WE PAY: THE CASE AGAINST RACIST SPEECH, HATE PROPAGANDA AND, PORNOGRAPHY 194, 196 (Laura Lederer and Richard Delgado, eds., 1995) (explaining that the ordinance originated in the 1970s to combat attacks on Synagogues).
10 464 N.W.2d 507, 508 (Minn. Sup. Ct. 1991).
11 Transcript of oral argument at 16, R.A.V. v. St. Paul, 505 U.S. 377 (1992) (No. 90-7675).
12 *Id.* at 21.
13 505 U.S. 377, 391–392 (1992).
14 *Id.*
15 *Id.* at 401 (White, J., concurring).
16 *Id.* at 416 (Stevens, J., concurring).
17 *Id.* at 391.
18 464 N.W.2d 507 (Minn. Sup. Ct. 1991).

19 505 U.S. 377, 402 (1992) (White, J., concurring).
20 *Id.* at 416 (Stevens, J., concurring).
21 Katharine Gelber, *Hate Speech – Definitions & Empirical Evidence*, 32 CONST. COMMENT. 619, 625 (2017).
22 *Id.* at 625–626. Gelber elaborated on this point by offering a counter-point to one raised by constitutional law scholar James Weinstein:

> It also assists in understanding the problem Weinstein raises about having a law that prevents a racist landlord from calling would-be Pakistani tenants 'cockroaches,' but does not prevent those would-be tenants from calling the (presumably Caucasian) landlord a 'cockroach.' Weinstein's steeping in the requirement under First Amendment jurisprudence to avoid viewpoint discrimination at all costs blinds him to the differential harms of these two events. Calling Pakistanis "cockroaches" is a racist term of abuse that likens a racial minority in a Western society to an animal that requires extermination. It therefore has a meaning and force that simply do not apply were the would-be tenants to call the landlord by the same epithet. Context, social power, and history matter in determining the harm that is occasioned in hate speech.

23 Chris Demaske, MODERN POWER AND FREE SPEECH: CONTEMPORARY CULTURE AND ISSUES OF EQUALITY 73 (2009).
24 *Id.* at 74.
25 Transcript of oral argument at 21, R.A.V. v. St. Paul, 505 U.S. 377 (1992) (No. 90-7675).
26 505 U.S. 377, at 391.
27 R.A.V. v. St. Paul, 505 U.S. 377, 419–431 (Stevens, J., concurring).
28 *Id.* at 429–431 (Stevens, J., concurring).
29 Demaske, *supra* note 23, at 108–109.
30 David Crump, *Camouflaged Incitement: Freedom of Speech, Communicative Torts, and the Borderland of the Brandenburg Test*, 29 GA. L. REV. 1 (1994).
31 Virginia v. Black, 538 U.S. 343, 359.
32 For an extended discussion of these criteria, *see* Chapter 5, pages 104–105.
33 Crump, *supra* note 30, at 51.
34 Planned Parenthood of the Columbia/Willamette, Inc. v. American Coalition of Life Activists, 290 F.3d 1074, 1088 (2002).
35 R.A.V. v. St. Paul, 505 U.S. 377, 391.
36 *Id.* at 416 (Stevens, J., concurring).
37 *Id.* at 391–392.
38 538 U.S. 343 (2003).
39 *See*, Chapter 3, pages 54–56.
40 Virginia v. Black, 538 U.S. 343 (2003).
41 *Id.*
42 *Id.* at 365.
43 *Id.* at 357.
44 *Id.* at 365.
45 *Id.* at 372 (Scalia, J., concurring).
46 *Id.* at 373.
47 *Id.* at 380.
48 *Id.* at 381.
49 *Id.* at 385.
50 *Id.* at 387.
51 *Id.* at 388 (Thomas, J., dissenting).

52 *Id.* at 389 (Thomas, J., dissenting).

53 *Id.* (Thomas, J., dissenting).

54 *Id.* at 391 (Thomas, J., dissenting).

But the perception that a burning cross is a threat and a precursor of worse things to come is not limited to blacks. Because the modern Klan expanded the list of its enemies beyond blacks and "radical[s]" to include Catholics, Jews, most immigrants, and labor unions, a burning cross is now widely viewed as a signal of impending terror and lawlessness. I wholeheartedly agree with the observation made by the Commonwealth of Virginia:

A white, conservative, middle-class Protestant, waking up at night to find a burning cross outside his home, will reasonably understand that someone is threatening him. His reaction is likely to be very different than if he were to find, say, a burning circle or square. In the latter case, he may call the fire department. In the former, he will probably call the police.

55 *Id.* (Thomas, J., dissenting).

56 *Id.* at 394 (Thomas, J., dissenting). "And, just as one cannot burn down someone's house to make a political point and then seek refuge in the First Amendment, those who hate cannot terrorize and intimidate to make their point."

57 *Id.* at 399 (Thomas, J., dissenting).

58 *Id.* (Thomas, J., dissenting).

59 *Id.* at 385.

60 *Id.* at 391 (Thomas, J., dissenting). For Justice Thomas, this symbol is so associated with targeting members of groups for violence that he felt it was conduct, not speech.

61 *Id.* at 365.

62 *Id.* at 373 (Scalia, J., concurring).

63 Mari Matsuda, *Public Response to Racist Speech: Considering the Victim's Story*, 87 MICHIGAN L. REV. 2320 (1989).

64 Snyder v. Phelps, 562 U.S. 443 (2011).

65 *Westboro Baptist Church*, SOUTHERN L. POVERTY CTR., *available at* https://www.splcenter.org/fighting-hate/extremist-files/group/westboro-baptist-church [last accessed January 6, 2020].

66 *Frequently Asked Questions*, WESTBORO BAPTIST CHURCH, *available at* https://www.godhatesfags.com/faq.html [last accessed January 6, 2020].

67 *Id.*

68 *Id.* The demonstrations that day also took place in front of the Maryland State House and the United States Naval Academy.

69 Snyder v. Phelps, 562 U.S. 443, 448 (2011).

70 *Id.* at 449. In addition to the church, Snyder also filed separately against Phelps and Phelps' daughters.

71 *Id.* at 450. Following several post-trial motions by Westboro, the District Court remitted the punitive damage award to $2.1 million.

72 *Id.* at 451.

73 *Id.* at 451: "Whether the First Amendment prohibits holding Westboro liable for its speech in this case turns largely on whether that speech is of public or private concern, as determined by all the circumstances of the case."

74 *Id.* at 453.

75 *Id.*

76 *Id.* at 454.
77 *Id.* at 460.
78 *Id.* at 461 (Breyer, J., concurring): That opinion restricts its analysis here to the matter raised in the petition for certiorari, namely, Westboro's picketing activity. The opinion does not examine in depth the effect of television broadcasting. Nor does it say anything about Internet postings.
79 *Id.* (Breyer, J., concurring).
80 *Id.* at 462 (Breyer, J., concurring):

> As I understand the Court's opinion, it does not hold or imply that the State is always powerless to provide private individuals with necessary protection. Rather, the Court has reviewed the underlying facts in detail, as will sometimes prove necessary where First Amendment values and state-protected (say, privacy-related) interests seriously conflict. That review makes clear that Westboro's means of communicating its views consisted of picketing in a place where picketing was lawful and in compliance with all police directions.

81 *Id.* at 463 (Alito, J., dissenting).
82 *Id.* at 465 (Alito, J., dissenting).
83 *Id.* at 465–466 (Alito, J., dissenting): "When grave injury is intentionally inflicted by means of an attack like the one at issue here, the First Amendment should not interfere with recovery."
84 *Id.* at 466–467 (Alito, J., dissenting).
85 *Id.* at 470 (Alito, J., dissenting):

> In light of this evidence, it is abundantly clear that respondents, going far beyond commentary on matters of public concern, specifically attacked Matthew Snyder because (1) he was a Catholic and (2) he was a member of the United States military. Both Matthew and petitioner were private figures, and this attack was not speech on a matter of public concern. While commentary on the Catholic Church or the United States military constitutes speech on matters of public concern, speech regarding Matthew Snyder's purely private conduct does not.

86 *Id.* at 475 (Alito, J., dissenting).
87 *Id.* at 454.
88 *Id.* (Alito, J., dissenting).
89 *Id.* at 475 (Alito, J., dissenting).
90 Westboro Baptist Church, *available at* godhatesfags.com [last accessed February 23, 2020].
91 Snyder v. Phelps, 562 U.S. 443, 469–470 (2011). In his dissent, Justice Alito took the Court to task for not considering this posting (referred to in the case as "the epic") when ruling on the question of intentional infliction of emotional distress. In a footnote, he wrote: The Court refuses to consider the epic because it was not discussed in Snyder's petition for certiorari. The epic, however, is not a distinct claim but a piece of evidence that the jury considered in imposing liability for the claims now before this Court. The protest and the epic are parts of a single course of conduct that the jury found to constitute intentional infliction of emotional distress. The Court's strange insistence that the epic "is not properly before us," means that the Court has not actually made "an independent examination of the whole record." And the Court's refusal to consider the epic contrasts sharply with its willingness to take notice of Westboro's protest activities at other times and locations.

92 Matal v. Tam, 137 S.Ct. 1744 (2017).

93 *Id.*

94 *Id.* at 1754: "Simon Tam...chose this moniker in order to 'reclaim' and 'take ownership' of stereotypes about people of Asian ethnicity. The group 'draws inspiration for its lyrics from childhood slurs and mocking nursery rhymes' and has given its albums names such as 'The Yellow Album' and Slanted Eyes, Slanted Hearts.'"

95 Mark Conrad, *Matal v. Tam — A Victory for the Slants, A Touchdown for the Redskins, But an Ambiguous Journey for the First Amendment and Trademark Law*, 36 CARDOZA ARTS & ENT. L.J. 83 (2018).

96 Pleasant Grove City v. Summum, 555U.S. 460, 467 (2009): "The Free Speech Clause restricts government regulation of private speech; it does not regulate government speech."

97 The Court has determined that commercial speech warrants less First Amendment protection than many other forms of speech. Commercial speech doctrine is used to determine the appropriate level of protection.

98 Matal v. Tam, 137 S.Ct. 1744, 1751 (2017).

99 *Id.* at 1753.

100 *Id.*

101 *Id.* at 1753–1754.

102 *Id.* at 1763.

103 *Id.* "For this reason, the disparagement clause cannot be saved by analyzing it as a type of government program in which some content- and speaker-based restrictions are permitted."

104 *Id.*

105 *Id.*

106 *Id.*

107 *Id.* at 1771 (Kennedy, J., concurring).

108 *Id.* at 1773 (Kennedy, J., concurring).

109 *Id.* (Kennedy, J., concurring).

110 *Id.* at 1764.

111 Neomi Rao, *Three Concepts of Dignity in Constitutional Law*, 86 NOTRE DAME L. REV. 183, 248 (2013). For an extended discussion, *see* Chapter 5, pages 89–90.

112 Matal v. Tam, 137 S.Ct. 1744, 1754 (2017).

113 Matal v. Tam, 137 S.Ct. 1744, 1751 (2017).

114 *Id.* at 1764 (Holmes, J., dissenting).

7   Hate Speech and the Internet

Elonis v. United States

In comparison to the international community, the United States is significantly more lenient regarding hate speech on the Internet. As a result of this permissive position, the United States is increasingly becoming a virtual safe haven for hate groups.[1] The Internet has been called the "fastest growing communication medium for hate groups."[2] For example, a 2004 rhetorical analysis of Ku Klux Klan websites illustrated how white supremacist groups rely on anti-Semitic discourse to engage in community building.[3] More recently, others have echoed these concerns about the role of the web in spreading white supremacist ideology and in serving as a hub for the organizing of hate actions against various marginalized groups.[4] In addition to the use of their own websites, extremist hate groups are also embracing social media tools. As one scholar noted, "As online platforms like Twitter and Facebook become increasingly important for the dissemination of breaking news, extremist leaders are recognizing the power of subverting mainstream coverage in the service of their own agendas."[5] This proliferation of web-based hate sites can have real-life consequences in the physical world.

The Internet generates speech concerns not present in earlier forms of mass communication. For example, the Internet often makes it difficult to determine who the user (speaker) is, challenges application of legal concepts such as true threats, and raises questions about jurisdiction. As a result, the contentious question of how to balance free speech protection with hate speech restriction invokes an even higher level of antagonism when the Internet is brought into the equation. Despite the seeming urgency to address the issue, the U.S. Supreme Court has ruled on relatively few cases dealing with speech on the Internet and has not dealt at all with hate speech-related cases.

The Court has yet to hear any cases directly pertaining to Internet hate speech. However, understanding the reasoning that lawmakers and the courts have applied in other Internet speech cases can shed light on the problems and possibilities of restricting hate speech in that medium. In this chapter, I begin by reviewing the early history of Internet from the late 1990s and early 2000s. I then outline the legal struggle over net neutrality. Finally, I explore some the current legal challenges of Internet speech, which include increasing concerns about content restriction. From that overview, I identify key issues that could impact successful application of hate speech regulations on the Internet. While hate speech regulations in the United States already must overcome many legal challenges, the Internet itself adds another layer of complexity in considering constitutionally acceptable ways to implement those types of restrictions. I highlight why, despite those challenges, the Internet, specifically social media, makes hate speech legislation there even more necessary than in other parts of society. Finally, I apply my two-tiered framework to the U.S. Supreme Court ruling in *Elonis v. United States*, a 2015 case concerning threatening language on the Internet.

History of the Cases

The Internet was first used as a commercial venture in the early 1990s and has since become a pervasive force in society.[6] In 1995, less than 1 percent of the world population had an Internet connection. As of January 2020, that number is approximately 59 percent.[7] In 2016, according to the U.S. Census Bureau, 77 percent of all households had a desktop or laptop, 76.5 percent had a handheld computer (such as a smartphone), nearly 78 percent had a tablet or other portable wireless computer, and near 82 percent had an Internet subscription.[8] Of those surveyed, nearly 90 percent had more than one computer in their home and only 10 percent reported having no computer device at all.[9] Overall, 62 percent of American households reached the status of "high connectivity," meaning the household had a laptop or desktop computer, a smartphone, a tablet, and a broadband Internet connection.[10] Seventy-six percent of households had at least one smartphone.[11]

According to the Pew Research Center, nine out of 10 adults in the U.S. are Internet users.[12] Perhaps even more astounding are the number of people participating on social media sites. As of February 2019, the Pew Center estimates this number to account for 72 percent of adults in the United States.[13]

The 1990s – Pornography and the Internet

The Supreme Court would hear its first Internet speech case in 1997. In *Reno v. the ACLU*, the Court reviewed the Communications Decency Act, examining whether the indecency provision and the patently offensive provision in the CDA were unconstitutional under the First Amendment.[14] The most significant issue tackled by the Court in this case was the question of determining what type of medium the Internet should be treated as. Medium type historically has been used to determine the level of scrutiny applied to government regulations of speech. For example, broadcast regulations have a significantly lower level of scrutiny applied to them than do regulations of printed material. In *Reno*, the Court determined that the Internet was more akin to print media than broadcast and, as a result, applied strict scrutiny and found that the CDA was not narrowly tailored and that the government had failed to supply a compelling state interest for restricting that speech.

The ruling in *Reno* would set the stage for Internet speech cases for the next 20 years. For much of the first decade following *Reno*, the Supreme Court focused its attention on cases pertaining to Internet pornography mostly in reaction to an onslaught of congressional acts intended to protect children from sexual images and content on the Internet.[15] Immediately following *Reno*, Congress fashioned multiple federal laws attempting to sidestep constitutionality concerns raised in the ruling. The first of these legislative attempts was the Child On-Line Protection Act (COPA) in 1998. COPA prohibited "commercial websites from knowingly transmitting to minors (under the age of 17) material that is harmful to minors."[16] Proponents of the law felt that it sufficiently corrected the overbreadth and vagueness issues in the CDA. They contended that unlike the CDA, COPA only applied to commercial speech, not all speech, and so had adequately narrowed the scope of restriction. They also expressed that the phrase "harmful to minors" served to correct the vagueness problem.[17] COPA led to a series of rulings, including three U.S. Supreme Court decisions.[18] The case was resolved in June of 2004, when the Supreme Court issued its final ruling in *Ashcroft v. ACLU II*.[19] The Court ruled 5 to 4 that COPA failed the strict scrutiny analysis by not offering the least restrictive means available.[20]

In addition to COPA, the Court also struck down the Children's Internet Protection Act (CIPA) in 2000[21] and the Child Pornography Prevention Act (CPPA) in 2002.[22] CIPA, enacted as part of the Consolidated Appropriations Act, required libraries in the LSTA and E-rate (government programs that give funding to libraries) to demonstrate that they were using certain filtering software. The American Library Association (ALA), along with groups representing libraries, patrons, web publishers and others, filed suit claiming that CIPA was unconstitutional under the First Amendment because it would limit adults from accessing protected speech.[23] In a plurality opinion, Chief Justice Rehnquist used reasoning grounded in government speech doctrine and found that CIPA, because it did not require all libraries to have filtering software, only those libraries that accept government funding, did not constitute an unconstitutional prior restraint. In 2002, the U.S. Supreme Court continued its review of Internet pornography restrictions, this time focusing on the Child Pornography Prevention Act (CPPA), which made it illegal to publish pornography with content that "is or appears to be a minor engaged in sexual conduct."[24] Because of the language "appears to be," it would sweep under its restrictive purview even computer-generated images that did not involve actual children in the production of the pornography or pornography employing legal-aged adults who looked like children. In *Ashcroft v. Free Speech Coalition*, the U.S. Supreme Court found that the CPPA violated the First Amendment because the "images do not involve, let alone harm, any children in the production process."[25] In short, the First Amendment has served as a barrier for those laws aimed at protecting children with few exceptions, such as Congress' most recent legislation on the topic, the PROTECT ACT.[26] This act made it illegal to transfer, offer to transfer or attempt to receive materials that contain either "an obscene visual depiction of a minor engaging in sexually explicit conduct or a visual depiction of an actual minor engaging in sexually explicit conduct."[27]

The 2000s – Net Neutrality Battles

Since the early 2000s, and picking up speed in the 2010s, the question over the need for neutral rules on the Internet has been highly contested. Columbia University law professor Tim Wu coined the term "net neutrality" in 2003 to describe the idea that all Internet traffic should be treated similarly without Internet service providers discriminating based on user, content, or platform.[28] Broadly speaking, there are two sides to the debate. Those in support of net neutrality are concerned about issues such as equality of access for Internet users, freedom of expression without corporate oversight, the ability for larger corporations to squeeze out smaller companies or block small startup companies, and possible higher costs for service providers and/or users. Those opposed to net neutrality believe that the market will correct itself, with the primary argument being that government interference will stifle innovation and limit further development of the Internet and Internet-related technologies. Since 2016, net neutrality rules have been in place in European law with EU directives establishing that ISPs "should treat all traffic equally, without discrimination, restriction or interference, independently of its sender or receiver, content, application or service, or terminal equipment."[29] In the United States, the legal battle has been less one of established rules and more like a yoyo with the rules seemingly changing on political whim.

The first attempt by the Federal Communication Commission to regulate net neutrality came in 2005 when it adopted a policy statement outlining four principles intended "to encourage broadband deployment and preserve and promote the open and interconnected nature of public Internet."[30] The policy statement, which does not carry the authority or force of a regulation, focused heavily on the right of consumers to, among other things, access content, run applications and services of their choice, and connect their choice of legal devices.[31] The FCC's authority to control the Internet in this way would be tested several times. In 2007, in response to a suit filed by several Comcast high-speed Internet subscribers, an appeals court ruled that "the Commission has failed to tie its assertion of ancillary authority over Comcast's Internet service to any 'statutorily mandated responsibility.'"[32] In response, the FCC fashioned another attempt at enforcing net neutrality. Relying on Section 706 of the Telecommunications Act of 1996,[33] the 2010 order focused on three principles – transparency, no blocking, and antidiscrimination – in an attempt "to preserve the Internet as an open platform for innovation, investment, job creation, economic growth, competition, and free expression."[34] The FCC again would find themselves before the Court of Appeals in D.C., this time in a case brought Verizon.[35] Verizon claimed that the FCC, "lacked affirmative statutory authority to promulgate the rules, that its decision to impose the rules was arbitrary and capricious, and that the rules contravene statutory provisions prohibiting the Commission from treating broadband providers as common carriers."[36] The district court agreed with Verizon, holding that the 2010 order violated the Telecommunications Act.

In 2015, the FCC would again focus on the need to regulate the Internet in order "to protect the Open Internet and ensure that Americans reap the economic, social, and civic benefits of an Open Internet today and into the future."[37] The 2015 order placed several (more severe) limitations on broadband providers, which kicked off a firestorm of complaints.[38] In 2016, the D.C. Court of Appeals, in a 2-1 vote, upheld the order.[39] The victory was short lived, however. In 2018, the FCC, under control of a different political party, passed the Restoring Internet Freedom Order.[40] This new order claims to provide "a framework for protecting an open Internet while paving the way for better, faster and cheaper Internet access for consumers" and that it "replaces unnecessary, heavy-handed regulations that were developed way back in 1934 with strong consumer protections, increased transparency, and common-sense rules that will promote investment and broadband deployment."[41] This latest FCC order has already resulted in a district court ruling and calls from approximately 30 state legislators and four members of Congress to enact some form of net neutrality provisions.[42]

In addition to the stream of district court cases related to the multiple FCC Internet orders, a 2019 U.S. Supreme Court ruling in a non-Internet case, *Manhattan Community Access Corp. v. Halleck*, could have an impact on the future of net neutrality as well.[43] In a 5-4 decision, the Court found that private operators of public access stations should not be considered state actors and so are not held liable under the state action doctrine.[44] As Justice Kavanagh explained,

> ...[W]hen a private entity provides a forum for speech, the private entity is not ordinarily constrained by the First Amendment because the private entity is not a state actor. The private entity may thus exercise editorial discretion over the speech and speakers in the forum.[45]

In other words, attempts to apply state action doctrine to public access stations failed.[46] The implications for Internet service providers seems obvious. Those providers occupy a similar space to the private operations of broadcast stations and, as a result, likely would be treated the same. While, the Court in *Halleck* did not directly address the implications for the Internet, the possibility is being played at the lower court level. For example, Prager University, a non-profit right-wing political organization, filed a lawsuit against Google claiming a First Amendment violation after YouTube (which is owned by Google) placed nearly 40 of its videos on "restricted mode."[47] In its suit, Prager claimed that YouTube placed its videos on restricted mode "based on [Defendants'] animus towards [Plaintiff's] political identity and viewpoint."[48]

In February 2020, the Ninth Circuit Court of Appeals rejected Prager's claim, finding Google not to be controlled by state action doctrine.[49]

New Concerns: Government Operated Sites

While the status of who controls the Internet continues to hang in the balance, First Amendment concerns increasingly are being raised concerning the current practice of government actors removing, limiting, or banning from their social media sites speech and/or speakers with whom they disagree.[50] There is little consensus yet from the courts on how to handle these cases. One excellent example of this are three cases filed by the same person, two of them heard by the same judge.[51] The cases were all initiated in Eastern Virginia by Brian Davison, a citizen who filed suits against three political figures he believed were unconstitutionally restricting him from engaging on their social media pages. Two of the cases, the ones heard by the same judge, applied public forum analysis and subsequently addressed the question of viewpoint neutrality. While Judge Cacheris applied similar tests, his rulings were not the same. In one case, he determined that Davison's speech was constitutionally restricted because it "did not comport with the purpose of the forum."[52] In the second case, Judge Cacheris ruled that the County School Board Chair violated Davison's First Amendment rights by blocking from her Facebook page his allegations of corruption.[53] In that case, Judge Cacheris found first that the Facebook page was indeed maintained as a government page and second, that the speech restriction in question was viewpoint-based because it was restricted due to dislike of the message.[54] Judge Cacheris cautioned:

> All of this isn't to say that public officials are forbidden to moderate comments on their social media websites, or that it will always violate the First Amendment to ban or block commenters from such websites. Indeed, a degree of moderation is necessary to preserve social media websites as useful forums for the exchange of ideas.[55]

This statement speaks both to the newness of this First Amendment concern and to the importance of thinking carefully about how this type of social media speech should be assessed. The third of Davison's cases, *Davison v. Rose*, was dismissed after the judge concluded that individual county officials are entitled to qualified immunity, exactly opposite of the position taken by Judge Cacheris is his rulings.[56]

The most recent and most highly visible case involving possible impermissible government speech restriction on social media involves President Trump's Twitter account. In 2018, the U.S. District Court of Southern New York ruled on a complaint filed by the Knight First Amendment Institute of Columbia University.[57] The Institute claimed that President Trump, along, with his White House Director of Social Media Donald Scavino, violated the First Amendment rights of several people when they blocked them from Trump's Twitter account @realDonaldTrump.[58] Judge Naomi Reice Buchwald issued a declaratory judgment against Trump and Scavino finding that they had engaged in viewpoint discrimination. Judge Buchwald first sought to address the question of whether the Twitter account was operated by the government because that would make it subject to First Amendment public forum analysis. She reviewed the ways in which the president and Scavino used the site to broadcast information related to Trumps' role as president and so concluded that the site was indeed open to public forum analysis.[59] As such, any speech restriction on it would need to be viewpoint neutral. Judge Buchwald determined that the speakers were blocked because of their criticism of the president, making the blocking viewpoint-based and unconstitutional.[60]

The Second Circuit Court of Appeals agreed that the president had unconstitutionally infringed on the plaintiffs' First Amendment rights.[61] In its ruling, the appeals court clarified the scope of its finding:

> The salient issues in this case arise from the decision of the President to use a relatively new type of social media platform to conduct official business and to interact with the public....the First Amendment does not permit a public official who utilizes a social media account for all manner of official purposes to exclude persons from an otherwise-open online dialogue because they expressed views with which the official disagrees.[62]

The Second Circuit's position is clear that social media sites operated as part of the official government duties are subject to First Amendment application. However, until the Supreme Court hears one of these cases focused on government actors and their social media pages, it is likely that the rulings will continue to be at odds, relying on different analytical tools and reaching different outcomes.

The Supreme Court in 2017 did weigh in on the parameters of free speech protection on the Internet, offering again the almost absolutist protection of speech that it established in *Reno* 20 years earlier.[63] At issue in *Packingham v. North Carolina* was a law that made it a felony for a registered sex offender "to access a commercial social networking Web site where the sex offender knows that the site permits minor children to become members or to create or maintain personal Web pages."[64] In a unanimous opinion, the Court concluded that the law violated the First Amendment because it was not narrowly tailored. In other words, the North Carolina law would have restricted access to virtually all online spaces. While the opinion was unanimous, the justices disagreed on just how expansive First Amendment protections should be in relation to Internet speech. Writing for the majority, Justice Kennedy called the Internet "the modern public square," equating it with traditional public forums such as streets or parks where speech has historically been granted the highest protection.[65] Relying on language from *Reno*, he explained that today cyberspace is one of "the most important places for the exchange of views."[66] Justice Alito, joined by Chief Justice Roberts and Justice Thomas, took the majority to task for its "undisciplined dicta."[67] Specifically, Justice Alito warned of the comparison made between the cyberworld and the physical world. He stated, "The Court should be more attentive to the implications of its rhetoric for, contrary to the Court's suggestion, there are important differences between cyberspace and the physical world."[68] Given that this case is so recent, it remains to be seen what, if any, implications this ruling will have for future speech restrictions on the Internet.[69] However, the concurring justices raised concerns that this could stifle states' abilities to construct laws to protect against dangerous sex offenders.

Restricting Internet Hate Speech

Trying to address hate speech on the Internet carries it with it layers of complications, making it one of the most difficult areas to apply my framework. These complications are due almost exclusively to the way in which the Supreme Court and the FCC have framed Internet speech issues. The foundation of these concerns can be traced back to the Court's Internet speech case, *Reno v. ACLU*. That case lacked a nuanced understanding of how the Internet operates and set the stage for later cases to reproduce that same lack of finesse.[70] Specifically, because the Court in *Reno* conflated the Internet with print media, it misread how the Internet functions in society. The Court squandered the opportunity to address the Internet as a distinctly different medium. As a result, the Court continues to apply ill-fitting doctrines, such as public forum and true threats, to the Internet, despite those doctrines not being developed for that medium. In its most recent Internet decision in *Packingham*, the Court continued this trend, this time going so far as to equate the physical world with the online world. As one scholar noted, the majority reasoning in *Packingham* is "crucially incomplete" because it fails to address questions related to the unique public/private nature of social media.[71] As a result, the Court ended up supporting a contradictory position. If the Internet is truly "a modern public park," then the government should be able to set guidelines for speech restriction. However, to date that has not been the approach taken by the Court. Instead, the Courts have considered the Internet to be a private space in which corporate owners hold a First Amendment right to dictate content. That reading, of course, means that corporate owners will control what speech is or is not allowed on the Internet. Social media companies and Internet service providers have become the "new governors" of online speech, emboldened with the ability to set, sway and direct political debate, police content for indecency, and define what constitutes regulable hate speech.[72] While similar concerns were lobbied in the past against mainstream broadcast media, the level of apprehension deepens in relation to the Internet, particularly regarding social media, because the actions of the directors or "governors" of the content are hidden from social media users. In other words, Internet platforms are not necessarily the best stewards of democratic participation as, by nature, they are driven by profit, not by public fiat. By giving them this role, the Court has in effect given corporations free reign in "developing a de facto free speech jurisprudence."[73]

In terms of hate speech, as I touched on in Chapter 2, those social media companies are attempting to restrict hate speech.[74] Unfortunately, those restrictions are often not transparent and are spurred by financial concerns, not necessarily social or democratic ones. In addition, because those social media companies operate in the global community, they are beholden to the laws in those countries, most of which restrict some level of hate speech. As a result, those companies create blanket policies at the direction of those other countries, and the United States is swept into their regulations. In other words, our speech is being restricted, just without any clear input from our government.

Overall, this issue of Internet hate speech is particularly significant today as new studies are indicating a close correlation between hate speech on social media sites and physical actions. In one of the most far-reaching studies, researchers studied anti-refugee rhetoric on the Facebook page for the far-right "Alternative for Germany," a group with nearly 420,000 followers.[75] The researchers looked at users on the page and their location and then compared that with the more than 3,300 anti-refugee attacks during a specific time period. The researchers also reviewed, during that same time period, Germany-wide Facebook outages that occurred due to programming or server problems. They found that "anti-refugee hate crimes disproportionately increase in areas with higher Facebook usage during periods of high anti-refugee salience."[76] The correlation was even greater in areas where there was higher engagement with Facebook via likes and comments.[77] When re-searchers factored in Facebook outages, they discovered a reduction in hate crimes, particularly in areas with many user of the AFG page.[78] From this, they concluded that "social media has not only become a fertile soil for the spread of hateful ideas but also motivates real-life action"[79] Other studies conducted in the past two years have similar findings. One scholar, after reviewing hate sites in North America over a decade, determined that "hate speech does inspire crime."[80] In another study, a team of researchers in London concluded that in the digital age, hate crime should be understood as a process, not a discrete event.[81]

As indicated previously, many scholars and jurists are already con-sidering ways to meet this challenge. Some are recommending a more cautious approach that would utilize already developed doctrines, such as the state action doctrine, to offer some minimal opportunity for reg-ulation. Others are proposing more radical solutions, ones that call for a complete overhaul of how we think about First Amendment protections. It is out of the purview of this book to develop a comprehensive argu-ment for how the First Amendment can or should apply to social media outlets. Instead, my goal here is to illustrate how the framework devel-oped in Chapter 5 might offer some relief from the abundance of hate speech on the Internet. To that end, I will look at two Supreme Court cases, *Elonis v. U.S.* and *Snyder v. Phelps.*

Elonis v. U.S.

Elonis v. U.S is the most recent Supreme Court case to touch on, albeit tangentially, the issue of hate speech on the Internet.[82] The case held promise to clarify several murky areas of First Amendment law includ-ing appropriate intent standard in true threats cases, Internet threats, and threatening material in creative works. Had the Court addressed those concerns, *Elonis* also would have provided direction on what to do, or what could be done, to combat increasing levels of hate speech on social media. However, the Court chose not to address any of those areas directly. The majority failed to attend to the question of whether a subjective or an objective test should be applied in true threats cases. It discounted Elonis' claim that his posts were rap lyrics and so bypassed the question of threats as art. Perhaps most interesting, the Court did not devote any attention to the uniqueness of the medium. My frame-work offers an opportunity to better assess the role of speech in society and the power of the Internet to disseminate that speech. In addition, applying the framework to *Elonis* further illustrates the inherent prob-lems in using true threats doctrine to judge the constitutionality of hate speech restrictions. Finally, application of the framework suggests a path forward that could resolve the lack of clarity in place following the rul-ings in *Black* and *Elonis.*

At issue in *Elonis* was whether Anthony Elonis' Facebook posts targeting his ex-wife and an FBI agent (among others) constituted threats under 18 U. S. C. §875(c), a 1939 statute making it illegal in interstate commerce to transmit "any communication containing any threat ... to injure the person of another."[83] Those posts included one in which he recommended that his son should "dress up as matricide for Halloween" with his wife's "head on a stick."[84] In a second instance, after his wife had secured a Protection From Abuse Order, he posted, "Fold up your PFA and put it in your pocket. Is it thick enough to stop a bullet."[85] After reading the posts, his wife felt "extremely afraid for [her] life."[86] Elonis was ultimately indicted on five counts of threats.[87] The Third Circuit Court of Appeals asked if the true threats exception required a finding that the speaker "subjectively intended his statements to be understood as threats."[88] In other words, at issue was what standard should be applied to make this determination.

The Third Circuit applied the objective standard, a standard that relies on the listener to determine the level of threat. The court applied that standard despite Elonis' claim that the standard, following the ruling in *Virginia v. Black,* had to be a subjective intent standard.[89] Instead, Judge Scirica advised that limiting the definition of true threats to only those statements where the speaker subjectively intended to threaten would fail to protect individuals from "the fear of violence" and the "disruption that fear engenders," because it would protect speech that a reasonable speaker would understand to be threatening.[90] According to Judge Scirica, to understand true threats only through the mindset of the speaker would completely nullify true threats doctrine. It is the threat itself being restricted under true threats doctrine, not the physical outcome of the threat. Once the threat becomes action, then that becomes a separate crime, such as assault or murder. The Third Circuit upheld Elonis' conviction. On appeal, prosecutors argued that his conviction for making threats on Facebook should stand, while he claimed he was just "venting" about his personal problems and did not actually mean to threaten his ex-wife and an FBI agent.[91]

In an 8-1 opinion,[92] the Court overturned the appellate court ruling, finding that the lower court had applied the wrong standard when determining whether the comments posted by Elonis qualified as legally proscribable threats. While the Third Circuit Court of Appeals applied a reasonable person standard, the Supreme Court instead relied on a question of whether or not Elonis actually intended to carry out the acts in his threats.[93] Writing for the majority, Chief Justice Roberts first explained the intent of the law:

> This statute requires that a communication be transmitted and that the communication contain a threat. It does not specify that the defendant must have any mental state with respect to these elements.

In particular, it does not indicate whether the defendant must intend that his communication contain a threat.[94]

What the majority focused on was the question of mental state. It did not address Elonis' mental state, per se, but instead raised the question of the role of mental state in application of the true threats standard. In its analysis, the Court found that "neither Elonis nor the Government has identified any indication of a particular mental state requirement in the text of Section 875(c)."[95] While the Court saw mental state as having some bearing, it was particularly leery of applying the reasonable listener standard in this type of criminal case. Chief Justice Roberts pointed out:

> Elonis's conviction, however, was premised solely on how his posts would be understood by a reasonable person. Such a "reasonable person" standard is a familiar feature of civil liability in tort law, but is inconsistent with "the conventional requirement for criminal conduct—*awareness* of some wrongdoing"...and we "have long been reluctant to infer that a negligence standard was intended in criminal statutes."[96]

As a result, the majority did not consider the true threats standard developed in First Amendment jurisprudence. Instead, it focused solely on the application of the reasonable person standard in a criminal case. As Chief Justice Roberts wrote: "Given our disposition, it is not necessary to consider any First Amendment issues."[97] The majority took this position despite the fact that Elonis' lawyers had raised the argument, focusing on his First Amendment right to publish his opinions on Facebook.

In his concurrence, Justice Alito criticized the majority for not responding to the First Amendment implications.[98] He offered instead that the First Amendment should be invoked. If it were considered, then Elonis' position would be rejected. He explained: "True threats inflict great harm and have little if any social value...It is true that a communication containing a threat may include other statements that have value and are entitled to protection. But that does not justify constitutional protection for the threat itself."[99] Justice Alito squarely placed the *Elonis* case within the confines of the First Amendment. He additional critiqued the majority's reliance on the speaker's mental state. He proposed:

> But whether or not the person making a threat intends to cause harm, the damage is the same. And the fact that making a threat may have a therapeutic or cathartic effect for the speaker is not sufficient to justify constitutional protection. Some people may experience a therapeutic or cathartic benefit only if they know that their words will cause harm or only if they actually plan to carry out the threat, but surely the First Amendment does not protect them.[100]

In other words, according to Justice Alito, relying only on what a person notes as his mental state does not change the impact of the message.

Justice Thomas, in his dissent, asserted that the court of appeals had "properly applied the general intent standard" and, as a result, "the communications transmitted by Elonis were 'true threats' unprotected by the First Amendment."[101] He felt that the majority in its error would cause further confusion at the lower court levels. In addition, he critiqued the rational that intent-to-threaten is a necessary component for punishing the speech. He explained:

> [T]here is nothing absurd about punishing an individual who, with knowledge of the words he uses and their ordinary meaning in context, makes a threat. For instance, a high school student who sends a letter to his principal stating that he will massacre his classmates with a machinegun, even if he intended the letter as a joke, cannot fairly be described as engaging in innocent conduct.[102]

In short, Justice Thomas agreed that intent is important but found the majority's approach to determining intent to be misguided. Intent should be determined by the intent of making the statements, not the intent of carrying out the actions.

Analyzing *Elonis* and *Snyder*

While *Elonis* offered the Court an opportunity to create a substantive ruling on threatening speech on the web, its decision not to focus on the First Amendment implications resulted in no clear direction from the highest court on what to do with harmful speech on the Internet. Considering Elonis through the framework developed in Chapter 5 indicates the need for a different mechanism to address threatening or hateful speech on the Internet and illuminates a path toward that end.

Tier One asks the Court first to determine if the speech in question is hate speech. To make this determination, Tier One asks four questions. First, is the speech in question "directed against a specified or easily identifiable individual or ...a group of individuals based on an arbitrary and normatively irrelevant feature?" The answer to this question in regard to *Elonis* is both yes and maybe. Yes, clearly Elonis targeted his comments to "specified and easily identifiable" individuals. There is no dispute that his comments were aimed at his wife and the FBI agent. What is less certain is whether his posts targeted those individuals "based on an arbitrary or normatively irrelevant feature." The comments he made did not specifically include mention of any normatively irrelevant features based on gender. Instead, he directed the hostile comments at individuals with whom he had personal contact. However, if the various comments are considered as a whole, then we might see a pattern emerging that could be read as meeting the type of speech being referenced in this first question in Tier One. The only people that Elonis directly targets via his Facebook posts are women. Even when he had an opportunity to verbally threaten both FBI agents who showed up at his home, he only directed his venomous comments at the female agent.

The second and third questions in Tier One are: does the speech stigmatize those targeted by "implicitly or explicitly ascribing to it qualities widely regarded as highly undesirable;" and is the target group "viewed as an undesirable presence and a legitimate object of hostility?" Looking at these additional questions makes Elonis' speech seem even less likely to be defined as hate speech. Yes, he does "implicitly or explicitly" ascribe qualities to the women he is targeting that might be regarded as undesirable. He accuses his wife of having sex with random men and he refers to the FBI agent as "Little Agent Lady." However, while these comments might be "widely regarded as undesirable," they would likely not be found to rise to the level of "highly" undesirable. And, while Elonis' comments certainly are intended to project his hostility toward those particular women, the comments themselves do not indicate an attack on all women. The additional elements in part four of Tier One – history, context, and social power – certainly apply to hate speech based on the category of gender. However, in this scenario, again, the comments Elonis makes clearly are enveloped in history and social power. Still, it is the individual relations between Elonis and those women, not women in general.

As a whole, it would be far too speculative to assess Elonis' speech as regulable hate speech as defined through my framework. In fact, this case serves a reminder of the need to be mindful to not be overzealous. This framework is designed to ensure that merely obnoxious speech or speech that is threatening to individuals, but not based on group membership, should not be restricted under the guise of hate speech. Speech can't just *possibly* meet the criteria in Tier One; it must *clearly* meet it without any reservation. The Elonis case serves to illustrate that while there is elasticity in the application of my framework, there are also hard parameters that will allow for the protection of the speech – even detestable and obnoxious speech – if that speech does not fall into the category of hate speech. In addition, despite the fact that Elonis's speech does not rise to the level of regulable hate speech, this case, along with *Snyder v. Phelps*, offers an opportunity to address the issue of Internet hate speech.

In Chapter 6 during my analysis of *Snyder*, I indicated that I would return to that case in Chapter 7. In *Snyder*, the ruling only addressed the demonstrations that the Westboro Baptist Church held at the funeral of Matthew Snyder. However, the opinion introduced that the church maintained a social media publicity campaign connected to the in-person demonstrations. Through social media, the Westboro Baptist

Church amplified its anti-gay message, promoting its upcoming demonstrations and its permanent website, both of which also emphasized hatred against the gay, lesbian and transgender communities.[103] I applied Tier One of the framework to that speech and found it to fit within my definition of hate speech. I did not apply Tier Two in Chapter 6 because I felt it made more sense to discuss it in relation to the question of the restriction of Internet speech.

Tier Two of the framework is essential in determining whether or not hate speech can be restricted without overly encroaching on freedom of speech. In other words, Tier Two facilitates a balance between the competing interests of protecting free speech and fostering human dignity. In this tier, the Courts can consider additional factors that including, but not limited to, questions concerning content or viewpoint neutrality, the level of threat, and the impact on the listener. Applying Tier Two to either *Elonis* or *Snyder* is tricky. In the case of *Snyder,* the Court did not devote attention to the social media speech and, in the case of *Elonis*, the speech in question did not rise to the level of hate speech through Tier One analysis. However, some discussion of how Tier Two might be applied can illustrate its usefulness in cases dealing with Internet hate speech and offer some perspective on how legal approaches could be fashioned. As I outlined in Chapter 5, courts may consider multiple additional elements when applying Tier Two. I specifically considered three models that can assist the courts in implementing an alternative analysis that allows for consideration of hate speech restriction. The first model I discussed was my own previous test designed to add context to the content neutrality principle by expanding the either/or approach into a three-part test. Neither *Elonis* or *Snyder* deal with laws or ordinances restricting hate speech and so that content neutrality test cannot be applied here. However, were an ordinance to be fashioned attempting to restrict the types of hate speech in question in say, *Snyder,* then it would be important to consider that content restriction using the more complex test.

Specifically, in relation to the speech in question in these two cases, Tier Two analysis would focus on application of the true threats standard. In *Snyder,* the Court considered only that speech which occurred at the funeral demonstrations and so its focus stayed predominantly on infliction of emotional distress, a type of speech related to true threats but significantly different. However, my point of focus is not the physical demonstrations, but instead the Westboro Baptist Church's orchestrated social media campaign designed to propagate hatred against members of a culturally vulnerable group. That language, which included statements such as "Fags are Beasts," "Fags are Worthy of Death," and "Tranny Sin Dooms Nations," is more akin to a threat, than mere infliction of emotional distress. In *Elonis*, even though the majority ultimately did not address the question of true threats doctrine, the entirety of the case concerned the prospect of threatening speech. In other words, the concept of true threats is heavily embedded in the scenarios in both of these cases.

The first place to start with Tier Two analysis, then, would be to look to Crump's version of the incitement standard. As I outlined in Chapter 5, this approach developed by Crump offers one way to consider additional context in cases dealing with hate speech regulation. Crump expanded the incitement test from two parts to eight parts. His revised test would require the Court to consider, among other things, context, including the medium, the audience and the surrounding communications; the predictability and anticipated seriousness of unlawful results (and whether they actually occurred); the inclusion of disclaimers; and whether the utterance has "serious literary, artistic, political or scientific value."[104] In terms of considering the context, both *Elonis* and *Snyder's* speech was on social media. As previously noted in this chapter, recent studies are indicating a difference in the way in which we interact with speech on-line versus in-person, and those studies are showing a strong correlation between on-line hate speech and real-life hate-motivated actions. In terms of audience, Elonis' speech was posted on his own social media page. He did not directly reach out to the people he was targeting with his speech, but his Facebook page was public. On the other hand, members of the Westboro Baptist Church successfully utilized their combination of social media and in-person demonstrations to attract mainstream media attention, thus exponentially increasing the size of their audience and the possible impact their message.

In both cases, the speech fed into an overall message of hate. Also, in both cases, no direct violence occurred, as far as we know, from the messaging. However, that is a different question than predictability and anticipated seriousness of unlawful events. In his article, Crump outlined the complexity involved in answering these questions. He explained that while some speech may "operate with a lesser degree of certainty in the identification of the individuals who will act upon them," there is the possibility that the speech could "create a high degree of likelihood that some listeners will act, with varying degrees of seriousness."[105] In other words, it may be difficult to predict with certainty that an individual or individuals will react violently, but the possibility must be considered. He cautioned, though, that juries and jurists need to be careful not to "overemphasize the predictability of violence by some individuals, no matter how seriously we may regard that consequence."[106]

What does this mean for the social media posts by Elonis and the Westboro Baptist Church? While Elonis claimed artistic license for his speech, the language found in his posts, such as asking if the restraining order could stop a bullet, might indicate a predictor of his own violent intentions. Given the general history of violence predicated against women who have filed restraining orders, it would not be a stretch to infer likely and serious action. Would that one statement by Elonis be sufficient to warrant the same level of concern if he had in his "rap lyrics" made mention of targeting all women who filed restraining orders? While a jury might certainly still reach the same conclusion, this speech might fall more squarely into Crump's concern about overemphasizing predictability. One phrase, no matter how distasteful, said only once and done so in the cloak of art does not seem a high predicator of violence, even though, we can't predict with certainty that no individual violence would occur. *Snyder* offers a significantly different situation. There is not just one instance of a threat of violence, but a long-term, extensive, and highly organized attempt at dispersing hate speech targeting members of the gay, lesbian and transgender communities. This rhetoric is intentionally broadcast across multiple mediums, and directly calls for acts of violence – including the death of – members of those groups. Taken together – the content of the message, the use of various platforms, and the orchestrated effort involved in the dissemination of those messages across those platforms – the church's speech clearly could be read to contain a high level of predictability of violence against members of those targeted communities.

Two other parts of Crump's test warrant discussion. The criteria dealing with disclaimers is relevant as both Elonis and the Westboro Baptist Church offered them in regard to their speech. Elonis repeatedly stated on his Facebook page that he was simply expressing his First Amendment rights.[107] In a similar vein, Westboro Baptist Church made note in several places on its website that it "neither condone[s] nor advocate[s] human hatred."[108] Under Crump's test, the appearance of disclaimers should be taken into consideration, but should not be taken necessarily at face value. In other words, while Elonis and Westboro might write disclaimers, those disclaimers have to be weighed against the rest of the message. Finally, from Crump's test is the question of the social or political value of the speech. Crump considers this to be "one of the most significant criteria in determining whether prohibited incitement is present."[109] Despite the concerns of the possible harmful effects of certain speech, we must be vigilant in protecting the rights of people to express themselves and to hold and express political opinions. This vigilance is required not only under traditional notions of freedom of speech, but also through the social justice framework that I am recommending. Recognition theory with its emphasis on human dignity and self-realization demands this vigilance as well. As Honneth explained, "The system of law must create a 'realm' in which each individual's freedom can be actualized."[110] The recommendation is not the privileging on one person's speech over another, but instead is to balance more keenly the competing interests so to protect the most amount of individual speech. Both Elonis and Westboro Baptist Church claim that their speech is either artistically motivated (Elonis) or religious/political speech (Westboro). Again, as with the disclaimer factor, Crump explained the importance of a thorough reading of the situation to assess the value of the speech. He wrote:

> But although it is important, even this factor should not be considered in a vacuum. A crime boss who speaks in iambic pentameter while ordering an underworld rubout, for example, still is a party to a homicide, and "serious artistic value" in the language does not legitimize his solicitation of murder.[111]

In other words, consideration of this factor stipulates a complex balancing between the stated purpose of the speech, the presumed purpose of the speech, and the importance of protecting that speech weighed against its possible and/or likely harmful impact.

Before completing the application of Tier Two, these cases also call for a discussion of the intent standard. The question of how to measure intent was at the crux of the *Elonis* case. The Third Circuit Court of Appeals opted to apply the objective standard in which the determination of threat is based on what a reasonable listener would construe as threatening.[112] As Judge Scirica explained, applying a subjective standard would "fail to protect individuals from 'the fear of violence' and the 'disruption that fear engenders.'"[113] As a result of that reasoning, the Third Circuit upheld Elonis's conviction. However, the U.S. Supreme Court elected to forgo making a firm determination on which standard should be applied, thus leaving the question open for further confusion at the lower court level. While the majority sidestepped the question, Justice Alito's concurrence touched on the heart of why the objective standard is the more logical choice for the assessment of true threats. He noted that whether or not a person *intends* to cause harm with threatening language is in some ways irrelevant as the "damage is the same" regardless.[114]

In his dissent, Justice Thomas took a similar position, as illustrated through his example of the high school student who threatens to kill his classmates; even if he thinks it is a joke, the conduct of making that type of statement is far from innocent.[115] This line of reasoning presented by both justices fits well within my social justice framework. If we extend the conversation to include hate speech as defined through Tier One of my framework, then we could envision legislation that understands hate speech in terms of its impact on its targets, not as a First Amendment right to target those groups. Several lower courts, such as the Third Circuit, already apply the objective standard in true threats cases. And, while it is a missed opportunity on the part of the Supreme Court to finally resolve this debate, the *Elonis* case leaves it still an open question. Had the objective standard been applied in *Elonis*, without any doubt, his conviction would have been upheld. In relation to Westboro Baptist Church and its social media campaign against the gay, lesbian and transgender communities, without a clear regulable category of hate speech, the objective standard as it exists currently would have little impact except in the most extreme and individually targeted incidents. However, with the addition of the regulable category of hate speech suggested here, the objective, reasonable listener standard offers a way to balance the expression of distasteful opinions against hate speech. Even more significant is the possible impact of application of the standard in Internet hate speech cases, where there is a less direct threat, but no less threatening effect than in-person.

Analyzing the social media speech of Elonis and the Westboro Baptist Church through the lens of social justice and recognition theory commands a more complicated review of the relationship between the speaker and the audience, as well as a rethinking of how social-mediated speech on the Internet carries threat in different, but just as impactful, means as in-person speech. Given that Elonis' speech targeted specifically individuals, his speech would not rise to the level of hate speech through Tier One. So, application of Tier Two simply showed what that case might have looked like if his speech had crossed the line into regulable hate speech. The discussion of Westboro Baptist Church and its anti-gay social media campaign is much more illuminating. Under the framework suggested here, much of the church's speech would fall into the category of regulable hate speech. The church, of course, could continue to preach that homosexuality is a sin, but the extreme language suggesting violence and death would not be protected under the First Amendment.

Conclusion

The Internet is a game-changer in terms of how we think about freedom of speech. However, despite efforts throughout the rest of the world accounting for the differences in how social media impacts people, the United States has remained steadfast in its hands-off approach. Starting in the 1990s and continuing today, the U.S. Supreme Court has consistently maintained this approach. As a result, it has yet to address the special characteristics of the Internet, leaving lower courts to struggle with a variety of speech-related issues. In terms of hate speech specifically, the Internet through social media usage has become a particularly problematic area. This problem is not just an anecdotal one. Large, empirical studies are beginning to demonstrate the correlation between hate speech and actions. Any speech restrictions will need to apply to the Internet as well if they are to have real impact in today's culture saturated in and driven by social media. In this chapter, I applied my framework for hate speech restriction to two cases – *Elonis v. U.S.* and *Snyder v. Phelps*. Through that analysis, I illustrated the shortcomings of current free speech doctrine in relation to Internet speech. I also offered a path forward that could better account for the individual and social harms caused by hate speech on the Internet.

In the next chapter, *Campus Speech: Hate Speech versus Free Speech*, I again apply my framework to another contentious contemporary battleground over hate speech restriction. This final chapter allows yet one more opportunity to consider how shifting the way we define and restrict hate speech could have important implications for various arenas in U.S. society.

Notes

1 Jessica S. Henry, *Beyond Free Speech: Novel Approaches to Hate on the Internet in the United States*, 18 INFO. & COMM. TECH L. 235, 236 (2009).

2 Christopher Brown, *WWW.HATE.COM: White Supremacist Discourse on the Internet and the Construction of Whiteness Ideology*, 20 HOW. J. OF COMM. 189, 192 (2009).

3 Denise M. Bostdorff, *The Internet Rhetoric of the Ku Klux Klan: A Case Study in Website Community Building Run Amok*, 55 COMM. STUD. 340 (2004).

4 For example, *see* Michael Wines and Stephanie Saul, *Supremacists Extend Reach With the Web*, NEW YORK TIMES, July 6, 2015, *available at* https://www.nytimes.com/2015/07/06/us/white-supremacists-extend-their-reach-through-websites.html [last accessed March 1, 2020] and Mark Potok, *The Number of Hate and Antigovernment 'Patriot' Groups Grew Last Year, and Terrorist Attacks and Radical Plots Proliferated*, INTELLIGENCE REPORT, February 17, 2016, *available at* https://www.splcenter.org/fighting-hate/intelligence-report/2016/year-hate-and-extremism [last accessed July 4, 2016].

5 *See* Keegan Hankes, *How the Extremist Right Hijacked 'Star Wars,' Taylor Swift and the Mizzou Student Protests to Promote Racism*, HATEWATCH, January 5, 2016, *available at* https://www.splcenter.org/hatewatch/2016/01/05/how-extremist-right-hijacked-'star-wars'-taylor-swift-and-mizzou-student-protests-promote [last accessed July 4, 2016].

6 For discussions of the beginning of personal use of the Internet/World Wide Web *see*, *Commercialization of the Internet*, 37 COMM. OF THE AMC 1994, *available at* http://som.csudh.edu/fac/lpress/comm.htm [last accessed March 1, 2020] (explaining that while there were a handful of commercial activities on the web in the 1980s, the business potential didn't take off until the early 1990s). For additional statistical historical user information *see*, Don Heider and Dustin Harp, *New Hope or Old Power: Democracy, Pornography and the Internet*, 13 HOW. J. COMM. 285, 286 (2002); Martha McCarthy, *The Continuing Saga of Internet Censorship: The Child On-Line Protection Act*, 2005 BYU EDUC. & L.J. 83, 84; D.J. Gunkel and A.H. Gunkel, *Virtual Geographies: The New Worlds of Cyberspace*, 14 CRIT. STUD. MASS COMM. 123 (1997); and SUSAN J. DRUCKER AND GARY GUMPERT, REAL LAW @ VIRTUAL SPACE: REGULATION IN CYBERSPACE (2005).

7 *Global digital population January 2020*, STATISTA, *available at* https://www.statista.com/statistics/617136/digital-population-worldwide/ [last accessed February 8, 2020].

8 *Computer and Internet Use in the United States: 2015*, U.S. CENSUS BUREAU, *available at* https://www.census.gov/library/publications/2017/acs/acs-37.html [last accessed March 1, 2020].

9 *Id.*

10 *Id.* According to the census report, High connectivity ranged from 80 percent of households with an income of $150,000 or more, to 21 percent of households with an income under $25,000.

11 *Id.*

> Smartphone use has become common among younger households (headed by people under age 45), households headed by Blacks or Hispanics, and households with low incomes (under $25,000) where smartphones were more prevalent than traditional laptop and desktop computers. Households headed by Hispanics were more likely to have a smartphone than households headed by non-Hispanic Whites.

12 *Internet/Broadband Fact Sheet*, Pew Res. Ctr, *available at* https://www. pewresearch.org/internet/fact-sheet/internet-broadband/ [last accessed February 8, 2020].

13 *Id.*

14 521 U.S. 844 (1997). This case dealt with language from the Telecommunications Act of 1996 (Pub. LA. No. 104-104, 110 Stat. 56 (1996)). The Act was comprised of seven Titles, six of which were the result of extensive committee hearings. One of those Titles, the Communication Decency Act (CDA), had two provisions written with the purpose of protecting minors from "indecent" and "patently offensive" communications on the Internet. The CDA prohibited the knowing transmission of indecent content to anyone under the age of 18. The prohibited material was sexually explicit but not legally defined as obscene.

15 Brian G. Slocum, *Virtual Child Pornography: Does it Mean the End of the Child Pornography Exception to the First Amendment*, 14 ALB. L.J. Sci. & Tech. 637, 639 (2004) ("From its inception, child pornography law has attempted to reconcile two powerful interests: the First Amendment and the prevention of sexual exploitation of children.").

16 47 USCS § 231.

17 47 USCS § 231 (e)(6).

18 The path of litigation started in a Pennsylvania District in 1996 (929 F. Supp. 824) shortly after the passage of the Communication Decency Act. The Supreme Court heard the case in 1997, ruling that the CDA was unconstitutional (521 U.S. 844). Congress rewrote the CDA, leading to multiple cases reviewing the Child Pornography On-Line Protection Act.

19 542 U.S. 656 (2004).

20 *Id.* at 666–670.

21 47 CFR § 54.520.

22 18 USCS § 2252A.

23 Am. Library Ass'n v. United States, 201 F. Supp. 2d 401 (E.D. Pa., 2002).

24 18 USCS § 2252A.

25 535 U.S. 234, 241 (2002).

26 553 U.S. 285 (2008).

27 *Id.* This act made it illegal to transfer, offer to transfer or attempt to receive materials that contain either "an obscene visual depiction of a minor engaging in sexually explicit conduct or a visual depiction of an actual minor engaging in sexually explicit conduct." In 2008, the Court ruled to uphold the PRO-TECT Act in *U.S. v. Williams*, disagreeing with the Eleventh Circuit Court of Appeals decision that the act was unconstitutionally vague and overbroad.

28 Tim Wu, *Network Neutrality, Broadband Discrimination*, 2 J. Tele-comm. & High Tech. L. 141, 145 (2003): "So what is attractive about a

neutral network – that is, an internet that does not favor one application (say, the world wide web), over others (say, email)? Who cares if the Internet is better for some things than others?"

29 *Regulation (EU) 2015/2120 of the European Parliament*, EUR-LEX, *available at* https://eur-lex.europa.eu/legal content/EN/TXT/?uri=uriserv: OJ.L_.2015.310.01.0001.01.ENG&toc=OJ:L:2015:310:TOC[lastaccessed February 9, 2020].

30 *FCC Adopts Policy Statement*, FCC NEWS, *available at* file:///Users/cd2/ Downloads/DOC-260435A1.pdf [last accessed February 9, 2020].

31 *FCC Policy Statement, Adopted, August 5, 2005*, FCC, *available at* file:/// Users/cd2/Downloads/FCC-05-151A1.pdf [last accessed February 9, 2020]. Additionally, the policy statement stated that "consumers are entitled to competition among network providers, application and service providers, and content providers."

32 Comcast Corp. v. FCC, 600 F.3d 642, 661 (2010). For a more detailed discussion, *see* Macklin K. Everly, *Net Neutrality and "The Department of the Internet": Creating Problems Through Solutions*, 42 DAYTON L. REV. 55, 65–66 (2017).

33 47 U.S.C. § 1302(a) (1996):

> The commission…shall encourage the deployment on a reasonable and timely basis of advanced telecommunications capability to all Americans… by utilizing, in a manner consistent with the public interest, convenience, and necessity, price cap regulation, regulatory forbearance, measures that promote competition in local telecommunications market, or other regulating methods that remove barriers to infrastructure investment.

34 *Federal Communication Commission order, FCC 10-201, Adopted on Dec. 21, 2010*, FCC, *available at* file:///Users/cd2/Downloads/FCC-10-201A1_Rcd%20(1).pdf [last accessed February 9, 2020].

35 740 F.3d 623 (D.C. Cir. 2014)

36 *Id.* at 634.

37 *FCC Releases Open Internet Order*, FCC NEWS, *available at* https://www. fcc.gov/document/fcc-releases-open-internet-order [last accessed February 9, 2020].

38 Everly, *supra* note 32, at 67–70.

39 359 F.3d 554 (2016).

40 *Restoring Internet Freedom*, FCC NEWS, *available at* https://www.fcc.gov/ restoring-internet-freedom [last accessed March 2, 2020].

41 *Id.*

42 Caitlin Chin, *In the Net Neutrality Debate, What Might Follow Mozilla v. FCC*, BROOKINGS, October 7, 2019, *available at* https://www.brookings. edu/blog/techtank/2019/10/07/in-the-net-neutrality-debate-what-might-follow-mozilla-v-fcc/ [last accessed March 2, 2020].

43 139 S.Ct. 1921, 1926 (2019).

44 139 S.Ct. 1921, 1926 (2019).

> To draw the line between governmental and private, this Court applies what is known as the state-action doctrine. Under that doctrine, as relevant here, a private entity may be considered a state actor when it exercises a function 'traditionally exclusively reserved to the State.'

45 *Id.* at 1930.

46 For examples of scholars discussing state action doctrine and the Internet, *see* Matthew P. Hooker, *Censorship, Free Speech & Facebook:*

Applying the First Amendment to Social Media Platforms via the Public Function Exception, 15 WASH. J.L. TECH. & ARTS 36 (2019) (finding state action doctrine applied to the Internet to be an "unstable approach"); Colby M. Everett, *Free Speech on Privately-Owned For a: A Discussion on Speech Freedoms and Policy for Social Media*, 28 KAN. J.L. & PUB. POL'Y 113 (2018) (calling for congressional action to protect end-users due to challenges of applying state action doctrine); and Jonathan Peters, *The 'Sovereigns of Cyberspace' and State Action: The First Amendment's Application – or Lack Thereof – to Third-Party Platforms*, 32 BERKELEY TECH. L.J. 991, 1007–1008 (2017) (recommending the development of a "state action theory suitable for the digital world").

47 Jacob Gershman, *Conservative Group Argues First Amendment Should Apply to YouTube* (August 27, 2019), THE WALL STREET JOURNAL, *available at* https://www.wsj.com/articles/conservative-group-argues-first-amendment-should-apply-to-youtube-11566937988 [last accessed February 10, 2020].

48 Prager University v. Google, No. 17-CV-06064-LHK (D. Calif. March 26, 2018).

49 Prager University v. Google, No. 5:17-cv-06064-LHK (3rd Cir. February 26, 2020).

50 For a more detailed discussion, *see* Kathleen McGarvey Hidy, *Social Media Use and Viewpoint Discrimination: A First Amendment Judicial Tightrope Walk with Rights and Risks Hanging in the Balance*, 102 MARQ. L. REV. 1045 (2019).

51 Davison v. Plowman, 247 F. Sup. 3d 767 (E.D. Va. 2017), aff'd 715 F. App'x 298 (4th Cir. 2018); Davison v. Loudoun County Board of Supervisors, 267 F. Supp. 3d 702 (E.D. Va. 2017); and Davison v. Rose, No. 1:16cv0540 (AJT/IDD), 2017 U.S. Dist. LEXIS 120176 (E.D. Va. 2017).

52 Davison v. Plowman, 247 F. Sup. 3d 767, 777 (E.D. Va. 2017).

53 Davison v. Loudoun County Board of Supervisors, 267 F. Supp. 3d 702.

54 *Id*. at 718–719.

55 *Id*. at 719 (citing Packingham v. North Carolina, 137 S.Ct. 1730, 1736 (2017).

56 Davison v. Rose, No. 1:16cv0540 (AJT/IDD), 2017 U.S. Dist. LEXIS 120176 (E.D. Va. 2017).

57 302 F. Supp. 3d 541, 554 (2018): "The Knight First Amendment Institute at Columbia University is a 501(c)(3) organization that works to defend and strengthen the freedoms of speech and the press in the digital age through strategic litigation, research, and public education."

58 302 F. Supp. 3d 541 (2018).

59 *Id*. at 552–553:

> ...President Trump uses @realDonaldTrump, often multiple times a day, to announce, describe, and defend his policies; to promote his Administration's legislative agenda; to announce official decisions; to engage with foreign political leaders; to publicize state visits; to challenge media organizations whose coverage of his Administration he believes to be unfair; and for other statements, including on occasion statements unrelated to official government business. President Trump sometimes uses the account to announce matters related to official government business before those matters are announced to the public through other official channels.

60 *Id*. at 575. Judge Buchwald noted: "The record establishes that '[s]hortly after the Individual Plaintiffs posted the tweets ... in which they criticized

the President or his policies, the President blocked each of the Individual Plaintiffs,' and defendants do 'not contest Plaintiffs' allegation that the Individual Plaintiffs were blocked from the President's Twitter account because the Individual Plaintiffs posted tweets that criticized the President or his policies.' The continued exclusion of the individual plaintiffs based on viewpoint is, therefore, impermissible under the First Amendment."

61 928 F.3d 226 (2019).

62 *Id.* at 230.

63 Packingham v. North Carolina, 137 S.Ct. 1730 (2017).

64 *Id.*

65 *Id.* at 1737.

66 *Id.* at 1735.

67 *Id.* at 1738.

68 *Id.* at 1743.

69 As of October 2019, the ruling in *Packingham* was cited in 112 lower court cases, followed in 24 cases, distinguished from the fact patterns in 49 cases, and mentioned in 24 cases.

70 For critiques of *Reno, see* Stephen J. Shapiro, *One and the Same: How Internet Non-Regulation Undermines the Rationales Used to Support Broadcast Regulation Fall*, 8 MEDIA L. & POL'Y 1 (1999) (arguing that the Internet should be regulated like broadcast media); Debra M. Keiser, *Regulating the Internet: A Critique of Reno v. ACLU*, 62 ALBANY L. REV. 769 (1998) (claiming the Court misclassified the medium of the Internet); and Louis John Seminski, Jr., *Tinkering with Student Free Speech: The Internet and the Need for a New Standard*, 33 RUTGERS L.J. 165 (2001) (critiquing the Court for not giving a more extensive review of the way in which Internet operates).

71 Reporter Note. *The Supreme Court 2016 Term. Leading Case: Constitutional Law: First Amendment – Freedom of Speech – Public Forum Doctrine – Packingham v. North Carolina*, 131 HARVARD L. REV. 233 (2017).

72 Kate Klonick, *The New Governors: The People, Rules, and Processes Governing On-line Speech*, 131 HARVARD L. REV. 1603 (2018).

73 Peters, *supra* note 46, at 1007–1008.

74 For this discussion, *see* Chapter 2, pages 30–32.

75 Karsten Müller and Carlo Schwartz, *Fanning the Flames of Hate: Social Media and Hate Crime*, SSRN *Electronic Journal*, 1–37. doi: 10.2139/ssrn.3082972 (2019).

76 *Id.* at 3.

77 *Id.* at 5.

78 *Id.* at 4.

79 *Id.* at 42.

80 Raphael Cohen-Almagor, *Taking North American White Supremacist Groups Seriously: The Scope and Challenge of Hate Speech on the Internet*, 7 INT'L J. FOR CRIME, JUSTICE, AND SOC. DEMOCRACY 39 (2018).

81 Matthew L. Williams, et al., *Hate in the Machine: Anti-black and Anti-muslim Social Media Posts as Predictors of Offline Racially and Religiously Aggravated Crime*, 60 BRIT J. CRIMINOL. 93 (2019).

82 Elonis v. U.S, 135 S.Ct. 2001 (2015).

83 *Id.*

84 Brief for Petitioner, 2013 U.S. Briefs 983 (2014).

85 *Id.*

86 *Id.*

87 *Id.*

88 United States v. Elonis, 730 F.3d 321, 329 (3rd Cir. 2013).
89 *Id*. The court would elaborate on the lower confusion over the Virginia v. Black intent standard by highlighting multiple conflicting rulings, at pages 331–332.
90 *Id*. at 329–330 (citing R.A.V. v. St. Paul, 505 U.S. 377 (1992).
91 Elonis posted statements on multiple occasions to his Facebook page that appeared to threaten his ex-wife, previous co-workers and an FBI agent. These postings included, among other things, violent song lyrics. Elonis claimed that he was an aspiring artist and that his postings constituted a form of artistic expression.
92 While this was an 8-1 opinion, it should be noted that Justice Alito concurred in part but also dissented in part. Justice Thomas wrote a dissenting opinion.
93 Elonis v. U.S. 135 S.Ct. 2001, at 2012.

> In light of the foregoing, Elonis' conviction cannot stand. The jury was instructed that the Government need prove only that a reasonable person would regard Elonis' communications as threats, and that was error. Federal criminal liability generally does not turn solely on the results of an act without considering the defendant's mental state. That understanding 'took deep and early root in American soil' and Congress left it intact here: Under Section 875(c), wrongdoing must be conscious to be criminal.

94 *Id*. at 2008.
95 *Id*. at 2008–2009.
96 *Id*. at 2011.
97 *Id*. at 2012.
98 *Id*. at 2016.
99 *Id*. at 2016.
100 *Id*.
101 *Id*. at 2018.
102 *Id*. at 2023.
103 For a detailed discussion of the social media campaign, *see* Chapter 6, pages 132–134.
104 For a detailed discussion of the test, *see* Chapter 5, pages 104–105.
105 David Crump, *Camouflaged Incitement: Freedom of Speech, Communicative Tors, and the Borderland of the Brandenburg Test*, 29 Ga. L. Rev. 1, 57 (1994).
106 *Id*. at 57–58.
107 Brief for Petitioner, 2013 U.S. Briefs 983 (2014). In one instance, he actually included a photograph from a Westboro Baptist Church along with his disclaimer.
108 *Frequently Asked Questions*, Westboro Baptist Church, *available at* https://www.godhatesfags.com/faq.html [last accessed March 2, 2020].
109 Crump, *supra* note 105, at 66.
110 Axel Honneth, The I in We: Studies in the Theory of Recognition, 21 (2012).
111 *Id*. at 68.
112 For a more detailed discussion of the objective/subjective standards, *see* Chapter 5, pages 105–107.
113 United States v. Elonis, 730 F.3d 321, 330 (3rd Cir. 2013).
114 Elonis v. U.S, 135 S.Ct. 2001, 2016 (2015).
115 *Id*. at 2023.

8 Campus Speech

Hate Speech versus Free Speech

In a letter to the Senate Judiciary Committee, the Anti-Defamation League ADL reported that the first half of 2017 included "a spike in anti-Semitic/hateful incidents on campus."[1] In that same letter, the ADL warned that "white supremacists are engaged in unprecedented outreach efforts on American college campuses."[2] During the 2017–2018 school year, it reported a 77 percent rise in white supremacist propaganda on U.S. college campuses.[3] In tandem with the increase in hate speech was a reported increase in hate crimes. For example, the *Chronicle of Higher Education* reported an increase from 970 hate crimes reported in 2015 to 1,250 the following year.[4] While some of those criminal situations, such as the riots in Charlottesville, received national attention, most garnered little or no media attention.

Hate speech on college campuses and the tension over protecting speech versus protecting a safe learning environment has been an issue to one degree or another ever since universities began enrolling a diverse student population. In the 1960s, it took the form of the National Guard being called in to enable James Meredith to attend classes at the University of Mississippi. By the 1980s, many universities were actively attempting to curb discriminatory incidents through campus speech codes. Today, the concerns and solutions take many different forms. Campuses now contend with a gambit of infractions from micro-aggressions to hateful social media posts by students or faculty to coordinated campaigns of hate by external groups. Schools have responded in a multitude of ways, including faculty reprimands, student expulsions, creation of free speech zones and/or safe spaces, the introduction of trigger warnings, and disinviting or refusing to allow the invitation of inflammatory speakers.

While all of these situations are worthy of analysis, in this chapter, my focus is on addressing only one question – what to do with external speakers who come to campus spewing hate speech? This chapter begins with a brief overview of the history of the hate speech debate on college campuses. That discussion is followed by a review of recent incidents and the scholarly response to them. Next, I address the legal landscape, focusing on current legal doctrines, as well as new solutions by universities and government officials. Finally, through application of the framework developed in Chapter 5, I suggest a way in which we might better balance the competing interests.

History of Hate Speech Restrictions on Campus

The question of whether or to what degree to restrict hate speech on college campuses is not new due, in most part, to the unique nature of the university environment, which calls for both the expression of ideas and the protection of diverse learners. Alexander Tsesis explained: "Those who administer the effectiveness of young adults' educational experiences must walk a tightrope of providing their charges with the means to discuss controversial issues while preventing debate from deteriorating into harassment."[5] The history of this tension is typically traced to the late 1980s and early 1990s. At that time, critical race theorists such as Richard Delgado, Charles Lawrence, and Mari Matsuda were proposing that freedom of speech on campuses without attention to the disproportionate subordinating impacts of that speech on members of disempowered groups was counter to the promise of higher education.[6] Those scholars offered solutions attempting to balance the protection free speech with the restriction of racial discrimination. For example, Lawrence suggested that racial insults on college campuses could be treated similarly to fighting words.[7] He argued that universities, in their role of providing an equal education, should be required to maintain a safe learning environment.[8] During that time, more than 350 universities across the United States passed campus speech codes offering the type of support that Lawrence was calling for.[9] Many of those codes were challenged in court and, across the board, were found to be unconstitutional under the First Amendment, most often because of issues with vagueness and overbreadth.[10] Two cases in particular – one involving the University of Michigan and the other the University of Wisconsin – generated attention within the legal community.

In *Doe v. the University of Michigan,* a student brought a case questioning the constitutionality of the campus' Policy on Discrimination and Discriminatory Harassment of Students in the University Environment.[11] The policy placed penalties on individuals who stigmatized or victimized "individuals or groups on the basis of race, ethnicity, religion, sex, sexual orientation, creed, national origin, ancestry, age, marital status, handicap or Vietnam-era veteran status."[12] The university developed the policy following escalating racism and racial harassment, which included distribution of a flier calling for "open season" on black students, racist jokes on the campus radio station, and display of a KKK uniform in a dormitory window.[13] The district court found the policy to be overbroad and vague, noting that "it was simply impossible to discern any limitation on its scope or any conceptual distinction between protected and unprotected conduct."[14] The court concluded that while it was "sympathetic to the University's obligation to ensure equal educational opportunities for all of its students," that goal could not be met "at the expense of free speech."[15]

Two years later, a district court in Wisconsin reviewed another campus speech code and again would rule it an unconstitutional violation of freedom of speech.[16] The situation at the University of Wisconsin was similar to that of the University of Michigan. The campus was experiencing escalating incidents of discriminatory harassment, including the erection of a large caricature of a black Fiji Islander at a frat party and the holding of "slave auction" at another fraternity event.[17] In response, the Board of Regents adopted a plan intended to "increase minority representation, multi-cultural understanding and greater diversity throughout the University of Wisconsin System's campuses."[18] The board utilized a working group, which included Delgado and other members of the law school faculty, to assist in developing a plan that would withstand First Amendment scrutiny.[19] The rule developed by UW considered it an actionable offense to, among other things, make racist or discriminatory comments, demean people based on "race, sex, religion, color, creed, disability, sexual orientation, national origin, ancestry or age of the individual or individuals," or to create "intimidating, hostile or demeaning environment for education."[20] The policy specifically covered comments and behavior directed at specific individuals or groups of individuals. Derogatory opinions based on race, gender, ethnicity, etc., made as part of class discussion would not be actionable. In other words, the university believed that by constructing the rules in this manner, the speech impacted would be considered as part of the regulable category of fighting words. The court disagreed. Finding that the language in the ordinance would lead to an overbroad application, it explained:

> The problems of bigotry and discrimination sought to be addressed here are real and truly corrosive of the educational environment. But freedom of speech is almost absolute in our land and the only restriction the fighting words doctrine can abide is that based on the fear of violent reaction. Content-based prohibitions such as that in the UW Rule, however well intended, simply cannot survive the screening which our Constitution demands.[21]

The rulings in these two cases ensured that anti-discrimination codes at universities across the country would be revoked. Universities would attempt to develop more narrowly tailored rules, but many of those would be found unconstitutional as well.[22] However, as Richard Delgado and Jean Stefancic noted in 2017,

> Still, over 200 universities have such rules on the books, in clear defiance of judicial precedent, thereby evincing their concern that the

campus climate be as civil as possible, or at least devoid of the worst forms of racial or sexual harassment and invective.[23]

These various approaches are being tested now, too, as incidents of hate and discrimination are on the rise on campuses across the country.

On-Campus Speakers: Current Incidents

While those instances cover a variety of circumstances, one area that has captured the interest of scholars, the media, and the general public is the current contentious relationship between universities and invited speakers. At the heart of this tension is the same issue that drove the campus speech codes in the 1980s. What is perhaps new in today's environment is the number of speakers seeking access to the college campus with the sole intention of maligning students and faculty based on their group affiliations. These instances have occurred so frequently in the last few years, that they can't all be addressed here in detail.[24] However, it is worthwhile to review some of the more prominent incidents.

Some of the most publicized of these battles are the ones involving Milo Yiannopoulos, former editor at the ultraconservative Breitbart News. Yiannopoulos, who considers himself a "conservative gay man" and who is a known associate of neo-Nazi and white supremacist Richard Spencer, began to have his speaking engagements at colleges cancelled or not approved during 2016.[25] Most publicized of those incidents was one at the University of Washington in January of 2017 in which a 34-year-old man was shot while protesting the event on campus. Less than two weeks later, with tensions on the rise, riots broke out at the University of California, Berkeley, in the face of an impending speaking engagement by Yiannopoulos.[26] Berkeley was ultimately forced to cancel the event after clashes broke out between far-left and far-right protestors. The rioters cost the university approximately $10,000 in property damage.[27]

Despite the violence and damage in February, by September Yiannopoulos was again scheduled to speak at Berkeley, this time as part of Free Speech Week, a week-long event with many right-wing speakers invited by a conservative student group. Controversy ensued again with the mayor of Berkeley requesting that the university cancel its event and the conservative student group claiming that the university "had been hostile and placed bureaucratic obstacles in their way."[28] The student group, citing concerns that they could not ensure speaker safety, revoked its invitation; however, Yiannopoulos did show up. He spent approximately 15 minutes saying a few words, singing the national anthem, and signing autographs before leaving.[29] University spokesperson Dan Mogulaf described it as "probably the most expensive photo opp in the university's history."[30] Yiannopoulos continues to push for speaking engagements on college campuses. Meanwhile, he was also banned from Twitter in 2016 for violating their policy that restricts inciting or engaging in targeted abuse or harassment against other users. In March of 2019, he was barred from entering Australia after he made hateful comments targeting Muslims following the Christchurch massacre.[31]

While Yiannopoulos might be attracting the bigger headlines, he is far from the only invited speaker testing the limits of university officials to maintain a safe learning environment. He also has not generated the most violence on campus. The aforementioned white nationalist Richard Spencer was at the center of the Charlottesville riot that left one person dead. While those riots did not occur during an invited speaking engagement at the University of Virginia, they did set off a chain reaction of universities banning or disinviting Spencer, who had been an integral part of the Charlottesville episode. It was Spencer who led the torch-bearing group of white nationalists through the campus.[32] Immediately following those events, the University of Florida denied Spencer's request to speak on campus, citing concerns over violence. After a lawsuit was threatened, the university allowed Spencer to speak there, claiming that it had not intended the ban to be permanent.[33] Several other universities would attempt to keep Spencer from speaking on campus, including Texas A&M, University of Cincinnati, Pennsylvania State University, Louisiana State University, Michigan State University, Auburn University, and University of North Carolina. Many of those speaking engagements were permitted following lawsuits or threats of lawsuits.[34]

Other recent and continual controversial speakers embroiled in high profile battles with university administrators and students include Charles Murray, Ben Shapiro, and Anne Coulter.[35] In all of these cases, when the universities deny or disinvite these inflammatory speakers, the administrators are accused of coddling students, promoting political correctness, and riding roughshod over sacred First Amendment ideals.

Scholar Responses

A legal scholar recently wrote:

> The debate over how colleges and universities should respond to contentious guest speakers on campus is not a new one. A quick look back to the early 1990s, among other times, shows commentators squaring off much as they do today about the tensions between protecting free expression and ensuring meaningful equality.[36]

This sentiment has been echoed by many scholars today. Indeed, in some ways, the argument is the same. However, I would postulate that there are key differences. First, the speech restrictions in the 1980s and early 1990s were instituted primarily by administrators trying to curb student-on-student harassment and verbal abuse. Today, the administration seems more concerned about protecting free speech, and it is, instead, students who are driving the call for enforcement of a safe learning environment for all. In the past the need to enact speech codes was compelled for the most part by actions perpetrated by members of the campus community. Today, that threat is still there, but the broader issues are those concerning external speakers and intentional agitators.

For the most part, the scholarly response has remained the same. In one corner are those who believe that equality on campus may require restricting discriminating or hateful speech. For example, long-term hate speech restriction proponent Richard Delgado continues to write on the subject of hate speech on college campuses. In a 2018 article, he expounded on the most common arguments lobbied against hate speech regulation with an emphasis on those related to university campuses, ultimately assessing that we must find a way to strike a balance between equal protection and free speech.[37] Delgado would privilege the balance in favor of protecting students, given today's current antagonistic social climate.[38]

In the other corner are those who believe that free speech trumps the concerns raised by Delgado and others. Just as they did in the 1980s, they label the alternate position as "political correctness."[39] Much of the arguments favoring speech over restriction on campuses mirror the responses to hate speech restriction in general. For example, Erwin Chemerinsky seemed to encapsulate much of the current scholarship when he invoked the axiom of more speech as a solution. He stated:

> I think that Justice Brandies got it exactly right when he said, the best remedy for the speech we don't like is 'more speech not enforced silence.' When I say this I know that more speech cannot cure the pain of hateful speech. But more speech in the context of a college or university can proclaim the principles of the community that we aspire to live by.[40]

In an article written the same year, Joseph Russomanno quoted another Supreme Court Justice in his defense of allowing hate speakers on campus: "This is at the core of Justice Oliver Wendell Holmes' opinion that the Constitution calls for the principle of free thought – 'Not free thought for those who are with us but freedom for the thought we hate.'"[41] Still others seem to be approaching the issue from a middle ground perspective, highlighting that there may be legal options for restrictions even within current First Amendment readings.[42]

The Legal Landscape

As already discussed at length throughout this book, the First Amendment does not allow content or viewpoint restrictions except in very limited circumstances such as incitement, fighting words, obscenity, and libel. Previously discussed cases, such as *R.A.V., Black, and Tam*, apply to hate speech on college campuses as well. However, speech at the university level invokes additional case law and legislation. Following is a brief review of key principals and court cases that have helped shape the legal discussion surrounding hate speech on college campuses. I will keep this conversation focused on those legal principles and cases that have a bearing on the question of what to do with inflammatory and hateful invited speakers.

In terms of Supreme Court cases, there are two additional areas that haven't been addressed yet previously in this book. First are the cases dealing with speech on public school campuses in general. In terms of speech rights at the university level, several Supreme Court cases offer insight into the legal treatments of speech in those environments. Starting in the 1950s in one of the earlier academic freedom cases, the Court began to build the foundation for protecting speech on college campuses. In *Sweezy v. New Hampshire*, a case involving faculty speech, the Court took notice of the important role of higher education in a democracy.[43] Chief Justice Earl Warren wrote,

> The essentiality of freedom in the community of American universities is almost self-evident. No one should underestimate the vital role in a democracy that is played by those who guide and train our youth. To impose any straightjacket upon the intellectual leaders in our colleges and universities would imperil the future of our Nation.[44]

To place restrictions on speech in this environment would be an especially egregious offense. This sentiment would be not only reproduced but expanded on 10 years later in *Keyishian v. Board of Regents*.[45] In language frequently cited in defense of academic freedom, Justice Brennan stated:

> Our nation is deeply committed to safeguarding academic freedom, which is of transcendent value to all of us and not merely to the teachers concerned. That freedom is therefore a special concern of the First Amendment, which does not tolerate laws that cast a pall of orthodoxy over the classroom.[46]

Keyishian's designation of the freedom in the academic setting as "a special concern of the First Amendment" has been used protect scholarly inquiry, student protests, autonomy in the classroom, and invited speakers spewing hatred.

Perhaps the most on-point case related to the invited speaker question is the 1972 *Healy v. James*.[47] *Healy* concerned the actions of administrators at Central Connecticut State College who did not allow students to organize a local chapter of Students For a Democratic Society, a national organization affiliated with the far-left. The college president said that the group and its values were "antithetical to the school's policies."[48] In an 8-0 vote, the Supreme Court ruled in favor of the students, finding that the university had overstepped its bounds and unconstitutionally infringed on the First Amendment rights of the students. While this case was more about freedom of association, the crux of the administration's position had to do with maintaining order, one of the key issues also raised concerning invited speakers today. Justice Powell began the opinion by applying the seminal high school speech case *Tinker v. Des Moines*, which just a few years earlier had established that the First Amendment applies to the public school setting.[49] Extending the *Tinker* ruling to the college environment, he wrote: "And, where state-operated educational institutions are involved, this Court has long recognized 'the need for affirming the comprehensive authority of the States and of school officials, consistent with fundamental constitutional safeguards, to prescribe and control conduct in the schools.'"[50] Schools can exercise authority to promote a safe and functional learning environment. However, that need cannot override First Amendment protections. In fact, as Justice Powell explained: "The college classroom with its surrounding environs is peculiarly the 'marketplace of ideas,' and we break no new constitutional ground in reaffirming this Nation's dedication to safeguarding academic freedom."[51] In balancing these two competing interests in *Healy*, the Court found that the administration failed to show proof of possible disruption.[52] The Court concluded by reaffirming its position that despite the "risk to the maintenance of civility and an ordered society," freedom of speech and association are worth the cost.[53] A year later in another university speech case, the Court would emphasize that "*Healy* makes it clear that the mere dissemination of ideas – no matter how offensive to good taste – on a state university campus may not be shut off in the name alone of 'conventions of decency.'"[54]

Despite those early Supreme Court rulings, in the 1980s, universities began to develop policies aimed at restricting certain types of hateful or harassing speech. I have already addressed two of the key rulings stemming from those policies – *Doe v. Michigan and UWM v. Wisconsin*.[55] Cases would continue through the early 2000.[56] In the past decade and continuing today, lower courts are still being asked to consider the constitutionality of university policies designed to limit hateful speech and promote a safe and welcoming learning environment. Those cases review a myriad of campus-related speech issues including free speech zones, faculty speech, admissions requirements, student social media use, and discrimination and harassment policies. Recently, several lawsuits have focused specifically on campus speakers.[57] For example, the University of Washington chapter of the College Republicans sought legal action in 2017 after the university attempted to charge the group a $17,000 security fee to allow them to bring controversial Patriot Prayer speaker Joey Gibson.[58] Patriot Prayer gatherings typically attract white supremacists and have sometimes ended in violence. The fee charged by the university was intended to cover additional expenses in holding the event, particularly costs associated with security. A district court in Seattle blocked the fee, which it determined was "neither reasonable nor viewpoint neutral."[59] UW agreed to pay $122,500 to settle the lawsuit.[60] Other suits have been filed related to Shapiro's presence on campuses. In autumn of 2017, Auburn University was required to allow Shapiro to speak after it had cancelled a contractual agreement with him.[61] In February of 2019, the district court found that the University of Minnesota policy on space use was not facially overbroad or viewpoint-driven on its face.[62] While all of these cases involved plaintiffs accusing the universities of viewpoint-based discrimination, none of the policies in question were directly addressing hate speech.

In addition to the plethora of court cases, legislative action is also being taken. In June of 2019, Texas became the 17th state to pass some type of legislation aimed at encouraging free speech on college campuses.[63] Many of those bills are based in total or in part on the Campus Free Speech Act, a model state legislation produced in 2017 by the conservative think tank the Goldwater Institute.[64] According to the Institute, this model creates "an official university policy that strongly affirms the importance of free expression, nullifying any existing restrictive speech codes in the process."[65] Some of those bills carry with them harsh penalties, such as expulsion, for students who are seen to use tactics to silence speakers – the so-named Heckler's veto.[66] In addition to these state-by state efforts, in March 2019 President Trump signed an executive order requiring that colleges and universities "promote free inquiry" on their campuses or they lose federal funding.[67]

The Supreme Court has yet to evaluate any cases of external speakers on college campuses. However, as I've supported in this chapter, the lower courts have had several opportunities to review recently. Unfortunately, many of those cases were settled prior to final rulings. For that reason, I am going to offer analysis of a slightly older, but on-point lower court case, *Gilles v. Davis*. This case illustrates that the issue is a not new, but instead is a chronic concern just recently receiving attention due to politically motivated actors such as Yiannopoulos and Shapiro. This case also reveals the problems that universities face when trying to protect students against hateful and discriminatory speech without the ability to legally address the actual problem – hate speech – head-on.

Gilles v. Davis

The 2005 Third Circuit Court of Appeals case, *Gilles v. Davis*, provides an excellent example to demonstrate the implications of this new approach.[68] In October 2001, James Gilles, a self-proclaimed "campus evangelist" appearing on college campuses across the country since 1982, set up in an open space on the Indiana University of Pennsylvania campus. He then began preaching loudly that the student body was full of "fornicators," "whores," "drunken little devils," "drunkards," and "drugs, sex, booze, and rock and roll freaks."[69]

Much of his preaching targeted hostility toward members of the gay and lesbian communities. For example, he cautioned the students to "watch out [because] the homosexuals are after you on this campus" and proclaimed that "there is nothing lower than a lesbian."[70] The district court estimated that approximately 75–100 students were present. Several of those in attendance engaged with Gilles. One woman in the crowd stated that she was a Christian lesbian, which drew disparaging taunts from Gilles (including asking her "Are you a bestiality lover") and led to someone calling campus security.[71]

Ultimately, Gilles was arrested for disorderly conduct and other charges. He filed a suit against campus police, asserting that they had violated his First Amendment rights. The Third Circuit disagreed. Writing for the court, Chief Judge Anthony Joseph Scirica first addressed the question of whether Gilles' speech amounted to fighting words. The court found that the derogatory words aimed at the general crowd were not fighting words,[72] while the words that targeted the woman "were abusive, akin to a racial slur" and reached the threshold of fighting words.[73] Gilles also claimed that the university's permit registration process violated his First Amendment rights, but the court found that he lacked standing because he had not filed for a permit.[74] The dissenting opinion in the case argued that Gilles' speech did not rise to the level of fighting words and that "the officers violated longstanding, fundamental principles of First Amendment law."[75] According to the dissent, the opinion found no showing of intent to provoke violence; the audience listening to Gilles was "some distance away" and so physically not in the immediate area to have a violent display.[76] In fact, the dissent found Gilles' speech to be exactly the type of speech "desirable" in a democracy and that the finding of fighting words was derived almost entirely from the "offensive" nature of his words.[77]

Several issues raised in the case speak directly to the concerns that the approach suggested in this book are attempting to address. First, the court's differentiation between speech targeted toward the group (which it found to be acceptable) and speech targeted toward an individual (which it found not to be protected) seems a red herring distinction with little to no justification offered as to why one speech moment is fundamentally more or less harmful than the other. Why is the same speech targeted at a specific individual more likely to lead to a breach of peace and violence than the same or similar comments targeted at a group of people? Framing the facts in the case through a different lens could not only attend to the issue raised in this particular case but could also offer guidance that is lacking in the overall doctrine in general. Instead of framing this analysis through the category of fighting words, the court could conceive of this speech moment as hate speech (using the definition recommended in this article) and could consider the harms of that hate speech through the social justice perspective offered by recognition theory. Shifting the analysis in this way would allow the court's review to be more grounded in the actual effects of hate speech and likely would lead to a more nuanced review of the incident and, in this particular case, a different result.

Tier One raises four questions to assess whether the speech rises to the level of hate speech. The first question asks, is the speech "directed against a specified or easily identifiable individual or...group of individuals based on an arbitrary and normatively irrelevant feature?" In Gilles' case, the answer is clearly yes. He addressed his statements to students at-large, the gay community in general, and to one lesbian student specifically. The language that he used included accusing all students of being "drunkards," "whores," and "fornicators." Also, the sentiments directed at the gay and lesbian community were based on "arbitrary and normatively irrelevant features." The broader comments regarding college students in general cover a wide and nonhomogeneous group and so would not be considered hate speech. The speech directly targeting members of the gay lesbian community, however, falls squarely within the parameters of the first question in Tier One. Gilles targeted a group of individuals based on their sexual orientation, while also singling out one student in a similar fashion.

Question two considers whether the speech stigmatizes those targeted by "implicitly or explicitly ascribing to it qualities widely regarded as highly undesirable." Gilles' speech is reminiscent of the anti-gay messaging propagated by the Westboro Baptist Church. In Chapter 6, I explained how those statements met this question in Tier One. The same holds true for Gilles' speech. His statements, including "watch out [because] the homosexuals are after you on this campus," "there is nothing lower than a lesbian," and "do you lay down with dogs," clearly are meant to demean gays and lesbians. In the best-case scenario, such language paints a picture of them as less worthy than others ("there is nothing lower than a lesbian") and in the worst case as disgusting and predatory ("watch out...homosexuals are after you" and "do you lay down with dogs").[78]

That speech also fits within the parameters of the third question: is the targeted group "viewed as an undesirable presence and a legitimate object of hostility?" First, Gilles' attempts to portray gays and lesbians as dangerous by saying "watch out [because] the homosexuals are after you on this campus." He doesn't elaborate on what he means by that statement, but any implication in any interpretation would be a negative one.

His comments directed at the lesbian student even more aggressively suggest that her presence as a lesbian is so immoral (he compares her lifestyle to bestiality) that the only way one could view her would be "as an undesirable presence and a legitimate object of hostility."[79] Finally, Tier One addresses factors such as history, context and social power. Again, as with Westboro Baptist's online speech targeting gays and lesbians, so is the case with Gilles' speech on campus. Both Westboro and Gilles are targeting a particular subgroup – members of the gay, lesbian, and transgendered communities. Those communities have historically been targeted and, as evidenced by these incidences, they continue to be socially ostracized, with their very existence being equated with filth and sin. In addition to a lack of social standing, members of those communities continue to have their legal rights questioned.

In short, Gilles' speech on the college campus meets the definition of hate speech through Tier One. Applying the factors in Tier One shows no real distinction between the speech targeted toward a group and the speech targeted toward an individual. The court would likely find both types of speech to be problematic if it assessed the characteristics of the language being used, the context in which it occurred and the history of those negative attributes in relation to those targeted – both the group and the individual. Also, applying Tier Two would not only demand a consideration of the negative impact not only on those directly targeted, but on the others in the audience, as well as the speaker himself because, as previously noted, those who espouse hate speech are negatively impacted because by denying mutual recognition, they are denying themselves true social freedom.

As previously outlined, application of Tier Two is prompted if the speech in question is identified as hate speech under Tier One. Application of this tier invokes an in-depth examination of the factors surrounding the speech incident. By considering those additional elements, the courts can both continue to safeguard the greatest amount of speech while also acknowledging shortcomings in First Amendment doctrine and its treatment of hate speech restrictions. The ruling in this case relied heavily on the concept of fighting words, a standard that is problematic for two main reasons: it nearly always is discounted in Supreme Court cases and it ignores what is most troubling about hate speech. As already discussed, the Court in *R.A.V. v. St. Paul* found that the category of fighting words could not be used to defend hate speech restrictions because that would require having a viewpoint distinction attached to the fighting words. Despite Justice Stevens' assessment in the dissent in *R.A.V.* that at least some content-based distinctions could be considered, the Court has not yet adopted that approach and, as a result, use of fighting words requires the courts to explicitly disregard the exact nature of the speech. Restricting hate speech requires just the opposite. The content of the speech, combined with the viewpoint of the speaker, is paramount in determining whether a particular speech event constitutes hate speech as defined in Tier One. The power in that moment and the possible harmful effects of the speech are directly related to the viewpoint that is being espoused and the group being targeted. In addition, this case illustrates the lack of consistency in how the courts assess speech in relation to the fighting words category.

Here, the court ruled that the words Gilles aimed at the individual woman "were abusive, akin to a racial slur" and reached the threshold of fighting words. The dissent, on the other hand, claimed that the court found the speech to fall into the fighting words category based solely on the offensive nature of the speech. The lack of consistency in how the courts assess speech is not unique to this case. However, this type of subjective disagreement seeping into speech cases is often used to argue against hate speech restriction. In other words, according to that position, hate speech restrictions cannot be considered because the courts would not be able to sufficiently define what constitutes hate speech. This difficulty in distinguishing protected from non-protected speech is already occurring as evidenced here. Perhaps this argument shouldn't be used to say no to hate speech restrictions, but instead could be used to consider how a well-defined category of regulable hate speech such as the one recommended in this book might address not only the social problems caused by rampant hate speech today but also more general concerns about the doctrine.

Related to the discussion of the fighting words category is the reliance on viewpoint neutrality. Both the majority and the dissent in Gilles referenced the importance of viewpoint neutrality in determining whether the speech at the rally was protected. Both relied on fighting words and breach of peace concerns to assess the speech. However, as I have already established hate speech by its very definition is not viewpoint neutral and its impact on individuals and society as a whole also is not neutral. The dissent claimed the type of speech that occurred because of Gilles' presence on campus was exactly the type of speech the First Amendment is intended to protect, speech that is most desirable in a democratic system. However, that same speech viewed through recognition theory serves exactly the opposite purpose. Hate speech, such as that espoused by Gilles, attacks both the individual liberty of those targeted and denies them membership in the larger community, thus greatly impairing their ability to be active in the democratic conversation or to be considered as valued, respected members in that arena.

This case also illustrates problems associated with current application of the true threats standard and whether the objective or subjective standard should be applied. Much of the discussion by the court and the dissent hinged on whether the speech by Gilles rose to the level of incitement to violence. Chief Judge Scirica found the speech directed to the general audience as "not likely to incite an immediate breach of the peace."[80] He based part of this ruling on Gilles' observed behavior, noting that the behavior "varied between hostile and jaunty, and sometimes exuded an air of theatrical exaggeration."[81] His words and demeanor "lacked bite."[82] The dissent found "no indication, and certainly no showing, that Gilles acted with the intention of provoking violence."[83] It emphasized that the crowd engaging with Gilles was "some distance away from him."[84] While context should be considered in hate speech-related cases, in *Gilles* the reliance on speaker intent further illustrates the already identified confusion among the courts about whether a subjective or objective standard should apply. In other words, is it the intention of the speaker that matters or is it the assessment of the audience? Should hate speech be defined by the intent of the speaker or by the impact of the speech on the targets of that speech? Based on the framework recommended in this article, the reasonable listener standard is the one that offers the best option for combating hate speech. The framework recommended in this book includes a consideration of the intent of the speaker and of the way in which the listener or listeners might interpret that.

Finally, and more broadly, the language in this case raises questions about the conventional wisdom of valuing virtually all speech as contributing to political discourse. The dissent makes an impassioned speech about how Gilles was actually promoting democracy through his comments because some "students responded to him by engaging in argument regarding important issues of religious and sexual tolerance and personal privacy."[85] However, this position fails to acknowledge the silencing effect that such speech might have on others in the audience and the ability of hate speech to vilify members of targeted groups. It also does not take into consideration the special nature of a college campus. University administration has an obligation to protect students from discrimination and to offer a safe learning environment for all students, no matter their gender, race, or sexual orientation. Switching how we privilege the balance between these two competing interests would impact the ability of hateful speakers to use the campus environment to spread hatred, intimidate students, or simply promote their own political careers or social popularity. Applying the two-tiered framework suggested circumvents this past unprovable debate and requires the court to recognize the actual factors at play when a possible hate speech moment occurs on the college campus.

Conclusion

Tensions on college campuses between freedom of speech and protection against discrimination is not new. For decades, university officials, legal scholars, and the court system have established, appraised, and (typically) dismissed attempts to restrict some level of hate speech within the University setting. Today, campuses are seeing an increase in the volume of external speakers wishing to use the campus as their own personal soapbox for expressions of hatred against social and politically marginalized groups. These actions continue to be defended. Many First Amendment scholars contend that universities must remain a space for "unfettered intellectual inquiry" and "the discovery and dissemination of basic knowledge."[86] However, that position assumes that hate speech has some relationship to knowledge production and that it is designed to encourage intellectual debate.

Framing this speech instead through the lens of human dignity and social justice offers a significantly different view and calls for a new response, one in which hate speech such as that espoused by Gilles, Shapiro, Yiannopoulos and others is revealed to be detrimental to the free flow of ideas, antithetical to the basic mission of a university, and damaging to the overall campus learning environment.

Notes

1 Letter from Elissa Buxbaum, Michelle Deutchman, and Oren Segal, leaders in the Anti-Defamation League, to Charles Grassley, chair of the Senate Judiciary Committee and Diane Feinstein, ranking member of the Senate Judiciary Committee (June 20, 2017), *available at* https://www.adl.org/sites/default/ files/documents/ADL%20Statement%20to%20Senate%20Judiciary%20 Regarding%20Campus%20Free%20Speech%206%2020%202017.pdf [last accessed March 26, 2020].

2 *Id.* The letter noted:

> Throughout the 2016–2017 school year, students, faculty, and staff on 110 American college campuses were confronted by 159 separate incidents of racist fliers and stickers, as well as numerous on-campus appearances by white supremacists and several rounds of anti-Semitic, targeted racist faxes, and emails.

3 Jake Sheridan, *Incidents on Campus Part of National Trend, Says Southern Poverty Law Center* (November 25, 2018), THE CHRONICLE, *available at* https://www.dukechronicle.com/article/2018/11/hate-on-campus-part-of-national-trend-says-southern-poverty-law-center [last accessed March 23, 2020].

4 *Toolkit on Campus Hate and Bias: Strategies to Create More Inclusive Campuses* (February 2019), THE LEAD FUND, *available at* https://www.aaaed. org/images/aaaed/LEAD_Fund/LEAD-FUND-Toolkit.pdf [last accessed March 23, 2020].

5 Alexander Tsesis, *Campus Speech and Harassment*, 101 MINN. L. REV. 1863 (2017).

6 For a more detailed review of these critical race theorists, *see* Chapter 4, pages 83–86.

7 Charles Lawrence, *If he Hollers, Let him Go: Regulating Racist Speech on Campus*, 1990 DUKE L. J. 431 (1990).

8 *Id.* at 456. "A black, Latino, Asian or Native American student should not have to risk being the target of racially assaulting speech every time she chooses to walk across campus."

9 Erwin Chemerinsky, *Tobriner Memorial Lecture: Free Speech on Campus*, 69 HASTINGS L.J. 1339, 1347 (2018).

10 *Id.* For more history, also *see*, Richard Delgado and Jean Stefancic, *Retheorizing Actions for Targeted Hate Speech: A Comment on Professor Brown*, 9 ALA. C.R. & C.L. REV. 169 (2018).

11 721 F.Supp. 852 (E.D. Mich. 1989).

12 *Id.* at 853.

13 *Id* at 854.

14 *Id.* at 868.

15 *Id.* at 868.

16 UWM v. Regents, University of Wisconsin, 774 F. Supp. 1163 (E.D. Wis. 1991).

17 *Id.* at 1165.

18 *Id.* at 1164.

19 *Id.* at 1165. "The professors agreed that the proposed rule would likely withstand attack on First Amendment grounds if it included a requirement that the speaker intended to make the educational environment hostile for the individual being addressed."

20 *Id.*

21 *Id.* at 1181.

22 For an extended discussion, *see* Richard Delgado and Jean Stefancic, *Four Ironies of Campus Climate*, 10 MINN. L. REV. 1919 (2017).

23 *Id.* at 1922.

24 For discussion of these encounters between universities and external speakers, *see* Eric T. Kasper, *Public Universities and the First Amendment: Controversial Speakers, Protests, and Free Speech Policies*, 47 CAP. U.L. REV. 529 (2019); Stephen Feldman, *Broken Platforms, Broken Communities? Free Speech on Campus*, 27 WM. & MARY BILL OF RTS. J. 949 (2019); Elisabeth E. Constantino, *Free Speech, Public Safety & Controversial Speakers: Balancing Universities' Dual Roles After Charlottesville*, 92 ST. JOHN'S L. REV. 637 (2018); and Catherine Ross, *Campus Discourse and Democracy: Free Speech Principles Provide Sound Guidance Even After the Tumult of 2017*, 20 U. PA. J. CONST. L. 788 (2018).

25 Most of those cancellations occurred as a result of threats to individuals, concerns of incitement to violence, or excessive cost for maintaining safety. For a list of some of those cancellations and the reasons for them, *see* Kasia Kovacs, *Inflammatory and Turned Away*, INSIDE HIGHER ED, October 21, 2016, *available at* https://www.insidehighered.com/news/2016/10/21/several-universities-cancel-appearances-conservative-writer-milo-yiannopoulos [last accessed March 14, 2020].

26 For a review of these events, *see* Ross, *supra* note 24, at 803–804; Constantino, *supra* note 24, at 645–647; and Lindsay M. Eichenger, *How Free is Free Speech in our Nation's Colleges and Universities*, 28 WIDENER COMMW. L. REV. 191, 205–206 (2019).

27 Lindsay M. Eichenger, *How Free is Free Speech in our Nation's Colleges and Universities*, 28 WIDENER COMMW. L. REV. 191, 205 (2019).

28 Ross, *supra* note 24, at 803.

29 Jay Barmann, *Milo Yiannopoulos Spent 15 Minutes at UC Berkeley, Cost Them $800,000* (September 25, 2017), SFIST.COM, *available at* https://sfist.com/2017/09/25/milo_spent_15_minutes_at_uc_berkele/ [last accessed March 14, 2020].

30 *Id.*

31 Dan Cancian, *Milo Yiannopoulos Barred from Entering Australia: 'Australian Tours for the World's Hate Speakers Must Stop,' says MP* (March 16, 2019), NEWSWEEK, *available at* https://www.newsweek.com/

milo-yiannopoulos-australia-ban-christchurch-attacks-1365449 [last accessed March 14, 2020].

32 For more details, *see* Ross, *supra* note 24, at 805.

33 Anemona Hartocollis, *University of Florida Braces for Richard Spencer.* NEW YORK TIMES, October 17, 2017, *available at* https://www.nytimes.com/2017/10/17/us/florida-richard-spencer.html [last accessed March 24, 2020].

34 For examples of those lawsuits, *see* Susan Svrluga, *Michigan State Agrees to Let Richard Spencer Give a Speech on Campus* (January 18, 2018), WASHINGTON POST, *available at* https://www.washingtonpost.com/news/grade-point/wp/2018/01/18/michigan-state-agrees-to-let-richard-spencer-give-a-speech-on-campus/ [last accessed March 16, 2020]; Jacob Fisher, *Richard Spencer Supporter Drops Lawsuit; Suspends Plans to Visit UC* (April 25, 2018), THE NEWS RECORD, *available at* https://www.newsrecord.org/news/richard-spencer-supporter-drops-lawsuit-suspends-plans-to-visit-uc/article_ab500468-48dd-11e8-9ccf-2ff2e2dba041.html [last accessed March 24, 2020]; *Auburn University Pays $29,000 to Settle Richard Spencer Related Lawsuit* (May 15, 2017), ASSOCIATED PRESS, *available at* https://www.al.com/news/2017/05/auburn_pays_29000_to_settle_ri.html [last accessed March 24, 2020].

35 Kenneth Lasson, *The Decline of Free Speech on the Postmodern Campus: The Troubling Evolution of the Heckler's Veto*, 37 QUINNIPIAC L. REV. 1 (2018) (discussing Murray, Shapiro, and Coulter); Joseph Russomanno, *Tribalism on Campus: Factors, Igen and the Threat to Free Speech*, 24 COMM. L. & POL'Y 539 (2019) (discussing Shapiro); Eichenger, *supra* note 26 (discussing Shapiro and Coulter) Chemerinsky, *supra* note 9 (discussing Shapiro and Coulter); Feldman, *supra* note 24, at 950–951 (discussing Murray).

36 Suzanne B. Goldberg, *Free Expression on Campus: Mitigating the Costs of Contentious Speakers*, 41 HARV. J.L. & PUB. POL'Y 163 (2018).

37 Richard Delgado, *Legal Realism and the Controversy over Campus Speech Codes*, 69 CASE W. RES. 275 (2018). For other recent works in this area, see with Jean Stefancic, *Retheorizing Actions for Targeted Hate Speech: A comment on Professor Brown*, 9 ALA. C.R. & C.L. L. REV. 169, 178–179 (2018) and MUST WE DEFEND NAZIS: WHY THE FIRST AMENDMENT SHOULD NOT PROTECT HATE SPEECH AND WHITE SUPREMACY 23–39 (2018).

38 *Id.* at 298.

> It is time to remind everyone – indeed, each other – of the need to proceed with equality and equal personhood in mind. This would include protection for struggling groups encountering a tide of hate speech in institutions, such as college campuses.

39 For example, *see*, Heidi Kitrosser, *Free Speech, High Education, and the PC Narrative*, 101 MINN. L. REV. 1987 (2017) (elaborating on the discursive use of 'political correctness' in the campus speech debate); Teri R. Day and Danielle Weatherby, *Speech Narcissism*, 70 FLA. L. REV. 839 (2018) ("[T]he use of political correctness measures on college campuses has had the unintended consequence of chilling speech."); Joe Dryden, *Protecting Diverse Thought in the Free Marketplace of Ideas: Conservatism and Free Speech in Higher Education*, 23 Tex. Rev. L. & Pol. 229 (2018) ("As a result of the rising tide of political orthodoxy, the free marketplace of ideas has become more of an echo chamber, and the free-speech rights of conservatives are under attack.").

40 Chemerinsky, *supra* note 9, at 1353.

41 Joseph Russomanno, *Speech on Campus: How American's Crisis in Confidence is Eroding Free Speech Values*, 45 HASTINGS CONST. L.Q. 273, 277 (2018).

42 Constantino, *supra* note 24, at 660 (proposing that universities need "guidelines and autonomy, in order to empower institutions to protect student safety, without engaging in censorship") Goldberg, *supra* note 36, at 171–172 ("Still, colleges and universities are entitled to substantial discretion in determining how to fulfill their educational mission.").

43 354 U.S. 234 (1957).

44 *Id.* at 250.

45 385 U.S. 589 (1967).

46 *Id.* at 603.

47 408 U.S. 169 (1972).

48 *Id.*

49 *Id.* at 180 (citing Tinker v. Des Moines, 393 U.S. 503, at 506 (1969)).

50 *Id.* (quoting Tinker v. Des Moines, 393 U.S. 503, at 507 (1969)).

51 *Id.* at 180–181 (citing *Keyishian v. Board of Regents*, 385 U.S. 589, 603 (1967)); *Sweezy v. New Hampshire*, 354 U.S. 234, 249–250 (1957) (plurality opinion of Mr. Chief Justice Warren), 262 (Frankfurter, J., concurring in result).

52 *Id.* at 190–191: Dean Judd's remark reaffirms, in accord with the full record, that there was no substantial evidence that these particular individuals acting together would constitute a disruptive force on campus. Therefore, insofar as nonrecognition flowed from such fears, it constituted little more than the sort of "undifferentiated fear or apprehension of disturbance [which] is not enough to overcome the right to freedom of expression." (citing Tinker v. Des Moines, 393 U.S. 503, at 508 (1969)).

53 *Id.* at 194:

> Indeed, this latitude often has resulted, on the campus and elsewhere, in the infringement of the rights of others. Though we deplore the tendency of some to abuse the very constitutional privileges they invoke, and although the infringement of rights of others certainly should not be tolerated, we reaffirm this Court's dedication to the principles of the Bill of Rights upon which our vigorous and free society is founded.

54 Papish v. Board of Curators of the University of Missouri, 410 U.S. 667, 670 (1973).

55 Other cases from that time period include: Dambrot v. Central Michigan University, 839 F. Supp. 477 (E.D. Mich. 1993) (found the university's discriminatory harassment policy to be unconstitutional); Iota Xi Chapter of Sigma Chi Fraternity v. George Mason University, 773 F. Supp. 792, 794 (E.D. Va. 1991) (ruled that a skit a in which a fraternity member dressed in black face was "consistent with GMU's educational mission in conveying ideas and promoting the free flow and expression of those ideas)."

56 For example *see*, Bair v. Shippensburg University, 280 F.Supp.2d 357, 369 (M.D. Pa. 2003) (found the university's speech code to be unconstitutional because "regulations that prohibit speech on the basis of listener reaction alone are unconstitutional both in the public high school and university settings"); Roberts v. Haragan, 346 F. Supp. 2d 853, 872 (N.D. Tex. 2004) (found the speech policy to be overbroad because "no matter how offensive" the speech included within the policy is still protected by the First Amendment); and College Republicans at San Francisco State University v. Reed, 523 F. Supp. 2d 1005 (N.D. Calif. 2007) (issued injunction due to likelihood that the school's civility requirement would chill speech).

57 For cases involving free speech zones, *see* Bloedorn v. Grube, 631 F.3d 1218 (11th Cir. 2011); Smith v. Tarrant County College District, 694 F.Supp.2d 610 (N. D. Tex. 2010); University of Cincinnati Young Americans for Liberty v. Williams 1:12-cv-00155-TSB (S.D. Ohio 2012); College Republicans of SIEU v. Dunn (settled out of court) (2018): and Turning Point U.S.A. at Arkansas State University v. Rhodes (pending). For faculty speech cases, *see* Churchill v. University of Colorado at Boulder, 293 P.3d16 (61. App. 2010) aff'd 285 P.3d 986 (Colo. 2012); Josephon v. Bendapudi (3:19-cv-00230) (W.D. Kentucky 2019); and Jorjani v. New Jersey Institute of Technology Docket No. 18-CV-11693 (ongoing). Other suits include: Keefe v. Adams, 840 F.3d 523 (8th Cir. 2016) (student threats via social media); John Doe #1 et al. v. Syracuse University No. 5:2018cv00496 – Document 24 (N.D.N.Y 2018) (pending now) (racist post by fraternity); Jergins v. Williams (2015) (settled) (campus speech policy); Young Americans for Liberty at Kellogg Community College v. Kellogg Community College (settled) (2018) (campus speech policy); Abbot v. Pastides 900 F.3d 160 (4th Cir. 2018) (campus harassment policy).

58 The fee was part of the university's Security Fee Policy. Gibson's appearance would come on the heels of the January visit that year by Yiannopoulos which had turned violent.

59 College Republicans of the University of Washington v. Cauce, NO. C18-189-MJP (W.D. Wash. February 9, 2018), at page 5.

60 Incidentally, in April 2018, the College Republican National Committee revoked the UW chapter for conduct unbecoming. That questionable behavior included an "affirmative-action bake sale," where the group based prices on buyers' race and gender. For additional details, *see* Katherine Mangan, U. *Washington College Republicans' Recognition is Yanked Over 'Hurtful and Inappropriate Conduct* (November 1, 2019), THE CHRONICLE OF HIGHER EDUCATION, *available at* https://www.chronicle.com/article/U-of-Washington-College/247475 [last accessed March 21, 2020].

61 Padgett v. Auburn University, Case No. 3:17-CV-231-WKW. (M.D. Ala 2017).

62 Young America's Foundation v. Kaler, 370 F.Supp.3d 967 (D. Minn. 2019).

63 For additional discussion of these acts, *see* Constantino, *supra* note 24, at 648–651 (addressing the "explosion of legislation seeking to protect free speech") and Kasper, *supra* note 24, at 531–533 (reviewing state laws and campus rules based on the Campus Free Speech Act).

64 *Campus Free Speech Act*, GOLDWATER INSTITUTE, *available at* https://goldwaterinstitute.org/wp-content/uploads/2019/04/Campus-Free-Speech_Model-Legislation_Web.pdf [last accessed March 21, 2020].

65 *Restoring Free Speech on Campus*, GOLDWATER INSTITUTE, *available at* https://goldwaterinstitute.org/campus-free-speech/ [last accessed March 21, 2020].

66 The Heckler's Veto, a term original coined by Constitutional Law Scholar Harry Kalven, describes a situation where the government allows a listener or group of listeners to silence a speaker. In other words, fear of a negative reaction from an audience or the allowing of an audience to drown out a speaker is not permitted under the First Amendment. Many of the campus speech laws being designed today are attempting to address this issue. In Wisconsin, for example, proposed bill; AB444 would enforce severe punishments on students who disrupt campus speakers. For a more in-depth discussion of the proposed Wisconsin bill, *see* Yvonn Kim, *Wisconsin Lawmakers Continue Heated Debate on Campus Free Speech Bill*, THE CAP TIMES, December 13, 2019, *available at* https://madison.com/ct/news/local/education/university/wisconsin-lawmakers-continue-

heated-debate-on-campus-free-speech-bill/article_3e4194cc-509b-53e3-8acb-0301ab17793c.html [last accessed March 21, 2020].

67 *Executive Order on Improving Free Inquiry, Transparency, and Account-ability at Colleges and Universities, DCPD-201900165 - Executive Order 13864*, 84 Fed. Reg. 11401, March 21, 2019, *available at* https://www.federalregister.gov/documents/2019/03/26/2019-05934/improving-free-inquiry-transparency-and-accountability-at-colleges-and-universities [last accessed March 26, 2020]. *Section Three reads:* Sec. 3. Improving Free Inquiry on Campus. 1(a)To advance the policy described in subsection 2(a) of this order, the heads of covered agencies shall, in coordination with the Director of the Office of Management and Budget, take appropriate steps, in a manner consistent with applicable law, including the First Amendment, to ensure institutions that receive Federal research or education grants promote free inquiry, including through compliance with all applicable Federal laws, regulations, and policies.

68 427 F.3d 197 (3d Cir. 2005).

69 *Id.* at 201.

70 *Id.* at 202.

71 *Id.* at 202

> Gilles took a pejorative tone, taunting, 'oh, my, you ma'am are most con-fused. She thinks she's a Christian lesbo. She's a lesbian for Jesus.' Gilles asked the woman, 'Do you lay down with dogs? Are you a bestiality lover? … Can you be a bestiality lover and a Christian also?'.

72 *Id.* at 205 ("This type of language, when not personally directed at a partic-ular member of the audience, is not likely to incite an immediate breach of the peace.")

73 *Id.* at 206.

74 *Id.* at 208. Under a First Amendment exception to the traditional standing rules, litigants "are permitted to challenge a statute not because their own rights of free expression are violated, but because of a judicial prediction or assumption that the statute's very existence may cause others not before the court to refrain from constitutionally protected speech or expression." Broadrick v. Oklahoma, 413 U.S. 601, 612 (1973). The court found this exception to be inapplicable to Gilles because the campus policy does not unduly restrict First Amendment freedoms, it merely allows the university to regulate the time, place and manner.

75 *Id.* at 212 (Fuentes, J., dissenting).

76 *Id.* 213 (Fuentes, J., dissenting).

77 *Id.* at 213–214 (Fuentes, J., dissenting) ("Indeed, in this case, Gilles pro-voked exactly the response desirable in a democracy: students responded to him by engaging in argument regarding important issues of religious and sexual tolerance and personal privacy.")

78 *Id.* at 201.

79 *Id.* at 202.

80 *Id.* at 205.

81 *Id.*

82 *Id.*

83 *Id.* at 213 (Fuentes, J., dissenting).

84 *Id.* at 213 (Fuentes, J., dissenting).

85 Id. at 213 (Fuentes, J., dissenting).

86 Ross, *supra* note 24, at 793.

Conclusion

On Friday, March 6, 2020, I received notification from the University of Washington that due to concerns about the coronavirus, all classes for the remainder of the quarter would be moved online. By March 23, Washington State Governor Jay Inslee had issued a stay-at-home order; the numbers of sick and dying were continuing to rise in the Seattle-Tacoma area; and the virus was taking hold in other parts of the country. During this time, I was in the process of completing this manuscript. I wondered what the pandemic might mean in terms of hatred in our country. Would we step up, unite, and become a kinder, more unified nation? Or, would we continue down the same hateful path that we had been on for quite some time? I got an answer rather quickly: hate doesn't take a break during a pandemic. Not only were hate groups continuing their standard operating procedures, but much like a virus mutates to adapt to its environment, so too do the actions of those wanting to spread hateful messages.

While long-established forms of disseminating hate continued, new forms were added. In diverse neighborhood stores, people intentionally coughed on foods in an attempt to infect members of certain groups. Zoombombing, an unwanted and disruptive intrusion into a video conference call, encouraged the spread of hatred into scheduled Zoom meetings, many of which were being held by universities or government agencies. By the end of March, the FBI warned of increases in hate speech and hate crime incidents. Physical and verbal attacks continued against groups such as African Americans, Muslims, LGBTQ, immigrants, and Jewish people, but Asians and Asian Americans were now being aggressively targeted on a large-scale level as well. Hate speech was not only surviving the pandemic; it was thriving.

In the introduction, I noted that this book contained two main objectives: (1) to address the question: What can be done to curb the proliferation of hate speech and hate acts in the United States? and (2) to shift the discourse around free speech protection away from promoting individual autonomy and toward promoting social justice. My response to the first objective was at once both simple and complicated. The simple answer is that we can hinder the spread of hate by restricting some level of speech. The question of how to restrict that speech while still maintaining the commitment to freedom of speech and expression, which is so valuable in our society, is more complex. Other scholars have come before me with recommendations and no doubt others will come after me. My goal with this book was to offer a new way to think about framing the discussion and with that, an alternative analytical framework that could be applied when considering the regulation of hate speech.

To accomplish that goal, I argued that we must de-emphasize the autonomous individual in our analysis, increasing instead our emphasis on the promotion of positive liberty. I have set out a path to do so by presenting a definition of hate speech and then using that definition as one tier of a two-tier framework that could be applied when considering the constitutionality of laws designed to restrict hate speech. That framework was developed taking into account traditional free speech values, legal tests, and doctrines employed in First Amendment cases, and social justice theory. I started with the premise that the overall reason for speech protection is to promote and foster a free and democratic society, and only within such a society can one reach any level of self-fulfillment or self-realization. Using Honneth's recognition theory as a guide, I suggested that the emphasis should instead include a more complex and contemporary assessment of social justice, individual dignity, and the role of communication in defining and supporting those goals. Through recognition theory, individual autonomy is best supported when the government promotes some level of positive liberty. In the case of hate speech, that promotion would take the shape of hate speech legislation.

The two-tiered framework asked first if the speech in question was indeed hate speech. Tier One is calling for the permissible restriction of speech based on both content and viewpoint. As I noted throughout, if the speech in Tier One was identified as hate speech, then application of Tier Two of the framework was triggered. Tier Two requires the courts to further evaluate the hate speech restriction by employing pre-existing tests and doctrines, and to do so in a manner that extends our long-term commitment to free speech, while also recognizing the limitations of current interpretations of those tests and doctrines. To illustrate how this new framework might impact the way the courts treat hate speech restrictions, I applied it to multiple scenarios. Specifically, in Chapter 6, I highlighted four U.S. Supreme Court cases that touched in some way on the area of hate speech. Although none of them are hate speech cases per se – there wasn't and still isn't a legal category of hate speech – review of those cases served to illustrate the parameters of speech that would be regulable under my framework. In Chapters 7 and 8, I turned my attention to two areas where hate speech is currently rampant – the Internet and college campuses. Application of the framework in those two environments demonstrated the need for some level of hate speech restriction and set forth a way to fulfill that need.

Unlike most First Amendment scholarship, which separates the United States from the rest of the world, my work joins a new group of scholars who are placing free speech discussions within a global context. The United States is not bound by what happens in other parts of the world; however, given the global nature of the Internet and the overall connectedness of communication systems today, what happens around the world impacts us. As a result, while this book is predominantly engaging with hate speech restriction in the United States, I sought to infuse a more global perspective into it. Not only did I designate an entire chapter to reviewing international approaches to hate speech restriction, but I also wove those ideas throughout the book. Indeed, the international conception of dignity propels the foundation of my framework and informs my thinking on the restriction of hate speech. Still, much more work needs to be done in this area, with considerably more attention paid to balancing free speech protection with the promotion of individual human dignity.

Free speech activist Ursula Owen stated: "Hate speech, free speech absolutists say, is the painful price we must pay for safeguarding free expression above all other rights. But how high is the price and who exactly is paying it?"[1] She would answer her own question with yet another: "Is there a moment where the quantitative consequences of hate speech change qualitatively the argument about how we must deal with it?"[2] I maintain that given the increasing number of hate crimes both in the United States and abroad, that moment is now. The intrusiveness of social media in private and public spaces adds a level of intensity to the debates about the restriction of hate speech in those particular media. In addition, the global nature of speech through the Internet demands that the international community cannot be ignored.

This book illustrates not only the urgency of addressing the problem of hate speech, but also the difficulties in constructing a response that will fit current conceptions of the First Amendment. The solution proposed in this book will undoubtedly face an uphill battle due both to the entrenchment of legal scholars in their resistance to restricting hate speech, and the Court's unwillingness to find virtually any viewpoint-based speech restriction acceptable.[3] In moving forward, the dangers of hate speech must be acknowledged, and then legislation will need to be carefully tailored to pass constitutional scrutiny. This means that the courts will need to rethink the emphasis they place on carte blanche protection of speech, instead applying a more refined analysis that balances free speech protection against the societal harm that hate speech causes. This approach should be informed by the focus on human dignity and social justice that serves as a foundation for many international laws and regulations. While it may seem that the First Amendment makes this path impassable, the two-tiered framework for analysis introduced here suggests that room exists for the courts to adjust the pre-existing doctrines and develop a space for protecting both freedom of speech and the intrinsic right to be recognized.

Notes

1 Ursula Owen, *The Long View: How High Is the Price of Hate Speech, Asks Ursula Owen, and Who Pays?*, 41 INDEX ON CENSORSHIP 203 (2012).
2 *Id.* at 205.
3 For discussions of the Roberts Court's view on freedom of speech, *see* Clay Calvert, *Beyond Headlines & Holdings: Exploring Some Less Obvious Ramifications of the Supreme Court's 2017 Free-Speech Rulings*, 26 WM & MARY BILL OF RTS. J. 899 (2018); Minch Minchin, *A Doctrine at Risk: Content Neutrality in a Post-Reed Landscape*, 22 COMM. L. & POL'Y 123 (2017).

Index

Note: Page numbers followed by "n" denote endnotes.